DATF

THE REVOLUTION IN

INTERNATIONAL RELATIONS

By the Same Author

FOOD SUPPLY AND RAW MATERIALS IN JAPAN
(University of Chicago Press, 1930)

POPULATION THEORIES AND THEIR APPLICATION,
WITH SPECIAL REFERENCE TO JAPAN
(Food Research Institute and P. S. King, 1934)

ECONOMIC ASPECTS OF MEDICAL CARE
(in collaboration with P. A. Dodd)
(Cresset Press, 1938)

THE INDUSTRIAL DEVELOPMENT OF JAPAN AND MANCHUKUO, 1930–40
(in collaboration with E. B. Schumpeter, G. C. Allen
and M. S. Gordon)
(Macmillan & Co. Ltd., 1940)

STUDIES IN WAR ECONOMICS
(Editor)
(International Labour Office, 1941)

ECONOMIC PLANNING FOR THE PEACE
(Princeton and Oxford University Press, 1953)

THE
REVOLUTION
IN
INTERNATIONAL
RELATIONS

A Study in the
Changing Nature and
Balance of Power

E. F. PENROSE

FRANK CASS & CO. LTD.
1965

First published in 1965 by
Frank Cass & Co. Ltd.
10, Woburn Walk, London, W.C.1

Printed in Great Britain by
Thomas Nelson (Printers) Ltd, London and Edinburgh

To
PERRAN
and
TREVEAR
and
IN MEMORIAM
TREVAN

PREFACE

THIS study is addressed to a wider public than the professional student of international relations. It began as an attempt to write an introduction to the subject for the educated general reader, adapted to an age in which international relations have become the most important of all fields of human activity, and a matter of life and death for the entire human race.

But as I wrote I found myself, sometimes consciously, sometimes, as seen in retrospect, unconsciously, addressing particular audiences within the general public which I have known during years of residence in four continents. In writing, for example, on colonisation I was acutely conscious of the attitudes of large numbers of Asian students whom I have taught in the Far East and Middle East. In writing on decolonisation I was aware all the time of those British onlookers who have been tempted into saying, " I told you so ", of some of the early results of decolonisation. In writing on the idea of balance of power and on the role of " ideology "—or, as I prefer to call it, political doctrines—in international affairs, I was drawn into a more detailed exposition than I might otherwise have made, by the attitudes which I encountered in periods of residence in the United States.

It by no means follows, however, that what is said with one particular audience in mind is of little concern to others. Although the educated Asian or African reader will not need to be given reasons why decolonisation was necessary, he will do well to consider carefully what foundation there may have been for the fears and misgivings of those who thought it premature when it came. And western readers, few of whom have had or sought the opportunity to live among the emerging peoples, may benefit from an analysis of the viewpoint of the latter on what to them is or has been foreign rule or domination. In international studies we should strive, not only to see ourselves as others see us, but also to see others as they see themselves. Again, the underlying differences in the attitudes in Europe and the United States respectively towards the role of doctrines, especially that of communism, in international relations are not yet fully appreciated and it is necessary to address both audiences.

In such a wide sweep as this study attempts it seemed best, therefore, to err by including more than is necessary for some readers rather than less than is necessary for others, especially in view of the continuing growth of specialisation within the general field of international relations. Many professional students and writers in the western countries, for example, concentrate mainly on great power relations and have little or no experience of Asia, Africa, and Latin America, while in some of the Asian and African countries the whole intellectual environment restricts the international outlook of writers and students.

Finally I have avoided jargon and special vocabulary in the effort to write for the educated public in general. If, in the end, some points are expounded in more detail than the professional student needs in his specialised branch of study, that seems a small price to pay for keeping open to the educated public a field of study and discourse of infinite importance to Everyman.

Subject to the customary assurance that no individual or institution to whom acknowledgements are made is in any way responsible for the shortcomings of, or the views expressed in, this study, I am indebted to the following : Professor Kenneth Robinson, Director of the Institute of Commonwealth Studies, for a close criticism of the first draft and suggestions for reorganising it which enabled me to overcome the most difficult problems of structure which are inescapeable in so wide-ranging a study ; Dr Peter Lyon, lecturer in International Relations in the London School of Economics, for a searching critique of a late draft which enabled me to correct a number of errors and modify or clarify the exposition at important points ; Professor Harold Beales, Professor Emeritus of the University of London, for criticisms which led to a revised and extended exposition of the role of communism in international affairs, and for his unflagging interest in the progress of the study ; to Professor Richard W. van Alstyne, of the University of Southern California, with whom I had valuable discussions when this study was in its infancy ; and to my wife, Professor Edith Penrose, with whom a long-standing reciprocal trade agreement in the scrutiny and criticism of draft manuscripts enabled me to obtain help promptly when it was needed and removes the occasion for the customary domestic apologies for silent hours.

This study has been written in intervals between periods of residence abroad, and it is impossible to enumerate all those with whom I have had profitable discussions in a number of countries, especially on regional affairs, which have influenced these pages. My debt to the studies of others is only inadequately represented in footnote references covering only a small proportion of the works, particularly the French works, from which I have benefited. And, on contemporary affairs, the great French journal, Le *Monde*, with its ancillary, *Le Monde Diplomatique*, is indispensable to a world outlook on international relations, and the quarterly journal *Orient* (Paris) to the study of the Middle East. Finally, my thanks are due to the staffs of the libraries of the Royal Institute of International Affairs, Chatham House, the London School of Economics and Political Science, and the School of Oriental and African Studies of the Univesity of London, and of the London Library, St James's Square.

October 1964   E. F. PENROSE
London

CONTENTS

PART ONE

CHAPTER I

The doctrinal split between the Super-Powers—The idea of balance of power not a doctrine nor a panacea but an essential accompaniment of the principle of nationality and of the independence of states— Doctrines criss-crossing balance of power in both world wars— Division of world into " communist " and " free " worlds illusory— Korean War and balance of power—Clashes in interests among communist states—Failure of communism to displace nationalism— Communist world a world of independent states—Attempts to adjust doctrines to balance of power—Difficulties of adjusting Marxist doctrines to a world of independent communist states.

CHAPTER II

Wide variations in the non-communist world—Failure of communism in Western countries—Economic and political differences between communist and non-communist worlds—Internal obstacles to spread of communism and seizure of power by communist parties in non-communist countries—Doctrinal anti-communism and its effects on Western policies—Disastrous effects of the doctrine of non-recognition—Influence of political doctrines and balance of power in south-eastern Asia—Motives of British and French aggression in the Middle East and U.S. aggression in Latin America—Differences among Western Allies—Dangers to Atlantic Alliance from pathological forms of anti-communism in the U.S.—Post-war readjustment of balance of power hindered by doctrinal excesses.

CHAPTER III

A necessary digression on the role of morality in international affairs, with special reference to imperialism and colonialism—The " Machiavellian " view—Chain of responsibilities from statesmen to the

PART THREE

CHAPTER VIII

NATIONALISM, SELF-GOVERNMENT, AND POLITICAL FREEDOM

CHAPTER IX

THE INTEGRATION AND DISINTEGRATION OF STATES .

CHAPTER X

PART FOUR

CHAPTER XI

CHAPTER XII

tion of criticisms of principle of " one state, one vote "—Interpretations of the idea of the equality of states by international lawyers
and by Mr. Hammarskjold—Defence of equality of votes—No
alternative to " international personalities " as the unit of representation in international organisations—Growth in power of emerging
countries consisting mainly in other forms of power than armaments
—Their frequent failures to use it to advance the rule of law and
press for disarmament—Setbacks through intra-regional imperialism.

CHAPTER XIII

Imbalance in Atlantic Alliance after Second World War, aggravated
by development of, and monopolies in, nuclear weapons—Hegemony
of a single power unacceptable in either communist or non-communist
world—Weakness of Europe in immediate post-war years leading
to dependence on U.S. in face of real or supposed danger from enhanced
Russian power—Rapid reconstruction of Europe to a position of
greater strength than ever—Difficulties of psychological adjustment
in U.S. and U.K.—Commonwealth of unique importance as bridge
between Britain, the " Dominions ", and leading parts of *le tiers
monde,* but not a substitute for or alternative to union with Europe—
Misconceptions on supposed " special relationship " of U.K. to U.S.
—Valid elements underlying President de Gaulle's outlook—Necessity of independent united Europe—The President's error of tactics
in excluding Britain from Common Market—Fallacious doctrine of
unilateral nuclear disarmament and of European concentration on
" conventional " weapons and reliance wholly on U.S. nuclear
weapons—The cases for and against British neutralism—Desirability
of Anglo-French pooling of nuclear weapons and research.

CHAPTER XIV

Conditions now appropriate for unification in stages of Britain and
countries of Common Market into a single multi-national state—
Individual liberties and representative government assured in such
a union, in contrast to some unions proposed among the emerging
countries—Pooling of U.K. and French weapons as nucleus for development of independent European defence contributing to Atlantic
alliance—Misleading use of term " Third Force "—Necessity for
frank acceptance in U.S. and U.K. of genuine and not merely verbal
equality of strong, integrated Europe with U.S.—Europe not less
but more trustworthy than the super-powers with respec tto nuclear
weapons—Dangers from U.S. public opinion in respect to China
and parts of Latin America—Serious political difficties in respect
to economic aid disbursed by the great powers lnto the emerging
countries.

CHAPTER XV

World-wide struggle for group freedom from alien rule—Group freedom not necessarily coincident with individual freedom— Mutual respect for independence of states indispensable to international peace —Nation-state and multi-national states where toleration exists still the best *milieu* for development of individual freedom—But nationalism alone not enough to create an international community —Vital role of the international organisations—Opportunities in them to mobilise the forms of power other than armed power—These forms increasingly important during deadlock in atomic weapons— Grave dangers persisting from present size and distribution of armed power—General disarmament still the foremost need—Uselessness of unilateral disarmament or renunciation of nuclear arms—Britain a part of Europe and its most important special relationship that with France—Necessity of European outlook with respect to defence and international policy—International peace only possible through spread of the rule of law, which cannot develop in world divided into two opposing camps or in international organisations not universal in membership—Necessity of a developing moral sense in international relations, rejecting doctrinal fanaticisms and self-righteous crusading attitudes.

INTRODUCTION

I. That international relations are the most important aspect of human relations in our time ; that their scope has expanded in many directions since the Second World War ; and that on their future course the survival of the human race depends, is hardly open to dispute. There are now over a hundred independent states in the world, and international affairs cover a great variety of political, economic, technical, and social matters. The number of people engaged in international activities, and the knowledge and experience required of them, have grown correspondingly. A higher order of ability is needed in statesmen, and greater understanding on the part of the public, than ever before, though they are not always—perhaps not often—forthcoming.

If the conduct of international affairs could be separated from the conduct of domestic affairs, and the formation of international policies from that of domestic policies, the difficulties and dangers would be greatly reduced. But in practice this is impossible, either in democracies or under authoritarian régimes. The politicians in many countries continue to treat international issues as if they were secondary to domestic issues, and tend to choose those policies abroad that are most likely to maintain them in office at home, even when they are aware that the results may be disturbing to international harmony. Opposition parties likewise tend to oppose government policies on international issues, not so much on the intrinsic merits of the latter as on a desire to discredit and replace their rivals who are in power. Authoritarian rulers continue from time to time to engage in adventures abroad in order to divert attention from troubles at home. Thus the student of international relations cannot afford to limit his field to the direct relations, official and unofficial, among the peoples of different countries. Yet it would be a formidable undertaking to examine the relations between the internal and external policies in over a hundred countries !

II. It is not only the scope and complexity of international relations at any particular time, but also the frequent, uneven, and sometimes rapid changes that take place from time to time, which create difficulties for the statesman, the public, and the student of international affairs alike. Some changes are only recognised widely after long delay. Often, when it is recognised that changes have occured, their precise nature and duration are wrongly assessed. After catastrophes like the two World Wars and the Great Depression

everyone could see that great changes had taken place : the difficulties arose in differentiating what was temporary from what was
lasting among them. From the middle of the War until about 1950
funeral dirges were solemnly chanted over the great Europe of the
past : " decadence ", " decline ", and " decay " were favourite
words in the texts and sometimes in the titles of books which indulged
in moralisings based on the application to Europe of the theme of
" decline and fall " immortalised by Gibbon in another context. By
contrast an image was projected of a young and vigorous New World
replacing the tired old world of Europe—weighed down by feuds
beyond healing, and schisms beyond repair.

On the other hand, during and in the immediate aftermath of the
War, Asia, Africa, and tropical Latin America appeared to most
observers to be of only secondary importance. Eastern and south-
eastern Asia had been disrupted by the War and its mightiest and
most modernised state had been brought down, leaving behind
political and economic confusion over the whole vast region which it
had overrun and dominated during the War. The Indian sub-
continent was rending itself apart. China was ravaged by opposing
armies in a civil war. Western Asia and North Africa had been
overrun by the contending forces of the Great Powers, its peoples
helpless spectators of events beyond their control, forced to conform
to the will of external powers which used them as instruments in their
own designs, assuring them in the process that all was for their own
good. Tropical Latin America had been cut off from its main
sources of external supply and its economic life had been corrupted
by uncontrollable inflation, from which the few profited and the
many suffered, while social discontent deepened.

III. How do these impressions and interpretations, fashionable in
the immediate post-war years, appear in retrospect in the mid
nineteen-sixties ? Which of the changes then perceived were temporary interruptions of long-run tendencies, and which of them were
indications of a lasting transformation in the structure of international relations and in the distribution of power in the world ?
It is with these and related questions that the present study is
concerned.

To some students of international affairs such a wide sweep of the
international horizon may appear over-ambitious. The chief way
in which growing size and complexity are met, in a field of study as
in an administrative unit in business and government, is by specialisation. And in recent years this has been the actual practice in
international studies. Why, then, it may be asked, after stressing at
the outset the immensity and complexity of the subject, should an
attempt be made to cover such a large slice of it in a single study ?

The difficulty is serious and cannot be completely overcome. But it would be an evasion of the issue to seek refuge in further specialisation. Even if the student of international relations is free to do this, the statesman and the diplomat are not. Policies must be formed and actions taken which depend partly on comprehensive assessments of the international situation. Foreign Ministers must at least try to take account of the world position even when they are dealing with regional matters. I once heard a diplomat of long experience remark that whenever the Foreign Ministers whom he had served had attempted to review the world situation before Parliament, their speeches, in spite of contrary desires during the work of preparation, always took final form as a catalogue of the position in each area. He implied that they should have been much more, that the parts should have fitted into an interrelated structure running through the whole.

The Foreign Ministers who fall short of this aim may at least offer two explanations ; the first, that they and their leading officials are preoccupied with emergencies and with day to day routine, and the second, that candid public reviews of this nature would cause diplomatic offence by the roles which they assigned to some countries. The independent student cannot offer these defences, and if, from fear of criticism, he shrinks from a difficult task, there are no others to take it on themselves with the advantages that he has. The inescapeable imperfections must be accepted as an occupational risk. The attempt, from an independent point of view, to trace patterns of change in the recent past and the present and to estimate, however imperfectly, their significance for the near future, is the only effective antidote to the ever-present dangers of uncritical conservatism and stereotyped habits of thought. Those whose working lives have alternated between " inside " activities and " outside " observation and studies of international affairs can hardly fail to be impressed with the difficulties inside governments and international bodies of looking beyond the concerns of the moment in working hours occupied with a rapid succession of day-to-day issues on which improvisations have to be devised, compromises worked out, recommendations made and decisions reached. Under such conditions it is easy to drift into insufficiently critical acceptance of the orthodoxies of the day among " practical " politicians.

IV. To maintain that studies of world-wide scope are needed is one thing ; to devise and carry through such studies is another and infinitely more difficult task. The results are bound to be imperfect. The subject is not adapted to group studies. As in all studies of human societies, and more than in most, any attempt to interpret the whole field comprehensively will be affected by the particular experience, the equipment, and, in a less definable sense, the attitude, of the student. The subject matter lends itself to a variety of interpretations. It is not, and never can be, " value-free ". In addition, large parts of the field are little known and some of them unexplored.

These imperfections must be accepted. They should not deter us from attempting wide sweeps of the international horizon from time to time. An additional reason for attempting the broader view is that it is a necessary counterweight to the growth of specialised studies, including regional studies and strategic studies. Although specialised studies are an essential basis for comprehensive studies and also of high direct value, they tend to produce in those who fail to look beyond them a bias which obscures or delays recognition of underlying changes in the structure of international relations as a whole.

Consider, for example, strategic studies. Besides their direct value they help to remedy the tendency of " general " historians to neglect the history of the armed forces. Professor Michael Howard's excellent chapter in *The New Cambridge Modern History*, Vol. XI, Ch. 8 demonstrates the important role of developments in military technology and organisation in the international history of the period and may well make many readers conscious, some of them for the first time, of a serious gap in many histories of the period, both general and specialised. Now those who have observed the role of the tank and other armoured vehicles on the streets in the Middle East in recent years will not be disposed to neglect the place of arms in contemporary history. Again, however, events in the Far and the Middle East in the last few decades show that the military who wield the arms cannot long be segregated from the general population. Social history impinges on military history, notably in the emerging countries. In general, prolonged specialisation in strategic studies tends towards an over-estimation of armed power in relation to other forms of power, and, as a corollary, towards a disproportionate concentration on the great powers in relation to the medium and small powers. Both tendencies make against a comprehensive view of international relations, and the compensating influence of wider viewpoints is necessary.

V. Regional studies are an indispensable basis for wider studies, but they also tend to create a bias in those who work exclusively on them, particularly when they are combined with studies of doctrines. For example, the documents of communist parties, the reports of communist conferences, the writings of Russian journalists, and the machinery of Russian propaganda in Asian, African, and Latin American countries create the impression in many western circles of highly efficient activities which constitute a grave menace to those countries. But in some nine years of residence in areas of the Far and Middle East the picture which I obtained from experience on the spot contrasted sharply with the ideas derived from some of the western writers on Russian communism, from popular ideas in the West, and even from the upper classes in the countries concerned. These experiences have markedly influenced this study. I had learned that the output of leaflets, reports, and documents was not a measure of the degree of political influence exerted.

Similarly, my discussions of United States international policies have been much influenced by periods of residence in the inter-war and post-war periods and by an association—formed in Europe before the war—with the Hon. John Gilbert Winant, which brought me into his staff in London during his war-time ambassadorship, and into work at the United Nations in its first year. Though I returned later to university work in several countries, and to British citizenship, my outlook continued to be influenced by experience of the conditions in which those who form and execute the international policy of the United States carry on their work, and of the characteristics of mass public opinion in that country in respect to international affairs, which contrast sharply with that of the " intelligentsia " and is brought to bear on the government much more powerfully than that of the corresponding classes in Britain and the rest of western Europe, at the same time reflecting radically different aims and a different philosophy from those of the latter. On these matters it seems to me that misconceptions of " special relationship " still prevail widely in Britain.

VI. The present study is based on the premises that individual as well as group freedom, and cultural diversity, are desirable ends in themselves, and that international policies and measures should be examined particularly from the point of view of their bearing, positive or negative, on those ends. To define and analyse the ideas of freedom and diversity in the abstract would be impracticable here : It will be enough for the present study to postulate the desirability of at least that degree of individual freedom that exists, for example, in Britain and the Scandinavian countries.[1] Diversity must be interpreted in a reasonable manner ; in some cases it may, of course, be impracticable or even harmful. But it has a wide field of application to multi-national states and is of great significance in connection with the problems of integration and disintegration of states.

Having rejected ethical or moral neutrality I must add, however, that I have made every effort to avoid nationalist, racial, and other forms of group bias and prejudice. Those who may suspect that they

[1] Obviously this is not an exhaustive list, but I refrain from extending it because of ultimate difficulties over the border-line cases.

have detected any such bias should consider whether their examples may not be explained by variations in the extent to which different countries adhere to the ends here postulated as desirable in the interests of freedom and international harmony.   Moreover, since I share Acton's view of the corrupting effects of power on human societies, my appraisals of policies and measures may seem to increase in severity in passing from smaller to larger, weaker to stronger, states, reaching its height with the super-powers.   The same tendency may appear in discussions of the problems of integration within regions in some of which no state ranks as a Great Power on a world scale, but one state is much stronger than any of the others. The propensity towards imperialist expansion, whether by annexation or political and economic domination, has never been a monopoly of any particular race or group of peoples, nor—in spite of their refusal to acknowledge it—have continental peoples been any less prone to it than maritime peoples ; but opportunites have varied with variations in power.   The impermissible type of unacknowledged bias in the student of international affairs is that which arises out of his personal association with a particular group.

VII. In the ever changing international scene it may seem perilous, outside periodical literature, to discuss events so close to the time when the book will be first read.   In fact, however, the main theses of the study are concerned with tendencies, movements, and issues that are far from being transient, and that seem likely to emerge, in one form or another, from all the short-run changes and fluctuations of the near future.   References to events in the immediate past are designed, not to supply the reader with an up-to-the-minute account of the facts—which is the business of periodical literature—but to contribute to the exposition of the main theses which are concerned with longer period tendencies.   From the point of view of the future this study may be regarded as a statement showing how international issues and tendencies looked to an observer in the earlier nineteen-sixties with particular experiences of particular parts of the world and with particular oral and written sources to supplement them.   The risks of miscalculation are great and inescapable, but if we allowed them to deter us from attempting any general appraisal of the international scene in our own times we should be abdicating what seems to me to be an important function of international studies.   And after all, in this as in other fields of study even what are subsequently, in the light of newer knowledge in the future, seen to be our mistakes, may prove valuable to others who engage in the same task of trying to detect patterns and relationships in the bewildering flux of international events that ceaselessly confronts us.

POWER, DOCTRINES AND MORALITY
IN INTERNATIONAL RELATIONS

CHAPTER I

POLITICAL DOCTRINES AND BALANCE OF POWER

I

Contemporary Ideas of International Relations

THE historian of the future, looking back over the nineteen-fifties and probably the sixties, cannot fail to be impressed with the place given to political doctrines in the discussion of contemporary international affairs. In the eastern and in parts of the western world international affairs are popularly characterised as a relentless struggle between the governments of two contrasting political orders, each fearing and aiming at the overturn of the other, if not in open warfare, at least through doctrinal propaganda and underground conspiracy. As the suicidal nature of new weapons makes total war less and less likely, so the conflict is said to be shifting more and more to economic and psychological rivalries. But local armed conflicts, fought with old-fashioned weapons, in unsettled parts of the world, continue to be entangled in the doctrinal conflict between the two leading armed powers, and the danger is ever present that, through accident or miscalculation rather than by design, a local spark might set off a world-wide explosion. This extremely simplified picture of international relations is widely accepted in Russia and China on the one side and in the United States on the other : it is shared also by certain classes in western Europe, for example *la droite* in France, and by many in the newspaper-reading public generally.

The doctrinal split is at its sharpest between the United States, with its conservative-democratic political outlook, and the Russian and Chinese states, with their authoritarian-communist outlooks. Consequently it tends to place these three large states, and particularly the United States and Russia, in the centre of the international stage, as if the fate of the rest of the world depended mainly on them, and as if other states had little international freedom of action of their own. The predictions of those perceptive scholars— Alexis de Tocqueville and others—who, more than a century ago, foresaw that the United States and Russia, because of their size and vast potential power, within a century would far eclipse in many respects the states then foremost in world diplomacy, armed power, and influence, have been amply fulfilled. The popular vision of the

3

world of international relations today seems to make a mockery of the saying that " the meek shall inherit the earth".[1]

But we live in a world of change, and the popular current views of international relations may be as misleading as those of the mid-nineteenth century were for their day, either as a guide to the future, or even as an analysis of the present. It is my aim in this study to call in question both the role popularly attributed to political doctrines in international affairs today, and the view popularly held of the strength and influence of the Great Powers in relation to the rest of the world. Finally, I shall attempt to show the direction in which the real revolution in international relations lies—a revolution which is already under way and is destined to become the leading preoccupation of international statesmen in the near future.

II

The World Wars and Balance of Power

Up to, and during the greater part of, the First World War, international relations were conceived of mainly in terms of the distribution of power among independent states, some of them with attached political dependencies, in a world without an international authority or even, before the League of Nations, a permanent international political consultative body. Since there were differences in the interests of the different states, and no state was all powerful, it was necessary to establish relations with other states which had a sufficient area of common interests, with the object of maintaining a balance of power, or, if that failed, of gaining the greatest advantage, or suffering the least disadvantage, from any changes that took place.

It seems inappropriate to describe the aim of achieving a balance of power as a doctrine : at most it may be described as a principle dictated by the practical necessities of life in a world of independent states. It is, of course, based in the last resort on assumptions concerning human nature and man's proneness to abuse power, but these are not formulated as part of an abstract doctrine ; rather, they are derived from both everyday and historical experience. Nor does it follow that every independent state is obliged to align itself with a group in a formal alliance ; on the contrary, new alliances or changes in alignments sometimes tend to upset rather/maintain the balance of power. A small state may fit itself best into the scheme of world balance of power by maintaining " correct " though uncommitted relations with all existing alignments, and linking itself with

---

[1] In its extreme form it glorifies a pagan morality in which each side is convinced that it has a monopoly of virtue and its opponents of vice.

none. The balance of power applies in modern times to the world as a whole. In ancient and mediaeval times it applied in varying degrees to separate regions ; in modern times it still has limited regional applications, but never independently of the world situation. Often the survival of a small state depends on the balance of power among the large states on which the whole structure depends.

The idea that the principle of balance of power is in itself discreditable, even sinister, is one of the curiosities of the history of thought. Objections are often made to a particular balance of power established or pursued at a particular time, such as the kind of balance sought by Metternich. This merely means that a different kind of balance is desired : it might, for example, be one more favourable to liberal nationalism. But the recognition of the principle of nationality tends to increase the number of independent states, and, in a world without a central authority, this adds to the urgency, and sometimes to the difficulties, of establishing a balance of power.

The First World War destroyed the pre-war balance of power and the immediate post-war balance was precarious. It could not be expected that Russia and Germany would long remain in the positions to which they were temporarily reduced by the treaties of Brest-Litovsk and Versailles respectively. Thus the League of Nations was established in conditions of comparative power among its members, and between them and the non-members, which could not be sustained. After both the First and the Second World Wars the victorious Great Powers attempted to rearrange the world to their future advantage, but in each case events took a very different course from that which they had desired or expected. This has usually been attributed to their failure to continue in peace-time their war-time alliances and co-operation. But that is only part of the explanation. An equally if not more important reason was their failure to foresee the nature of the changes in the distribution and composition of power in the rest of the world, and to make the necessary adjustments to them.

These changes went in opposite directions. Among the victorious western Allies in each period there was a return movement towards the comparative positions of the United States and Europe which had existed in pre-war times and which had been disturbed when military operations devastated European without extending to North American soil. The second change, however, although its origins preceded the World Wars, was not a restoration of a pre-war balance, but a great acceleration of a rise of new powers in Asia, and, particularly after the Second World War, in Africa, together with new stirrings in Latin America. Within this movement, Japan did most to disturb the existing structure of power in the inter-war period, but after the Second World War the decolonisation movement took the lead in all these areas.

Thus, the balance of power which existed just after the two World Wars was soon disturbed by forces both old and new—those making for a return to the pre-war balance in Europe and North America, and those pressing on towards new roles in the world for Asia, Africa, and Latin America. The League of Nations and the United Nations were founded during two transient phases of the world balance of power. Far from dispensing with the need of a balance of power the international institutions could only perform their functions adequately if more comprehensive, and more stable yet flexible, balances could be established than those which existed when they were founded. In later chapters an attempt is made to analyse the nature of the moving equilibrium which is necessary for the realisation of the purposes of the United Nations, and the conditions to be fulfilled if it is to be attained. The failure of the western powers to pursue an adequate defensive balance of power in the nineteen-thirties was due not only to the inadequacies of ministers in charge of foreign policies but also to confusion in the minds of the public regarding the proper role of balance of power in the affairs of states.[1] Unfortunately, confusion has persisted, not only in the minds of the public but also among many students of history and of international relations.[2] The next section, therefore, contains a more formal outline of the sense in which the idea of balance of power is used in the present study.

III

The Idea of Balance of Power

The idea of balance of power is often a stumbling-block to the general reader, and sometimes a source of confusion to the student of international relations in his earlier approaches to the subject. A preliminary explanation, supplemented at appropriate points in later chapters, may best start by considering the position of the states-

---

[1] As one striking example see R. Bassett, *Democracy and Foreign Policy* (London 1952) for an illuminating analysis of the Manchurian crisis which, to those who read it, disposed of widespread misconceptions which prevailed for many years about the respective roles of the countries concerned. This work is a permanent contribution of a type of which we need many more in the field of international studies.

[2] After the text of this study had been completed my attention was drawn by Dr. Peter Lyon to a searching critique of " The Multiple Meanings of the Balance of Power " in a significant work which I had overlooked : Inis L. Claude, *Power and International Relations*, New York, 1962, Ch. 2.

POLITICAL DOCTRINES AND BALANCE OF POWER   7

men entrusted with the conduct of foreign affairs in any independent
state. Obviously their first concern must be the survival of the state
and the preservation of its independence. Even in the special cases
where it is desired to unite the state in question with a neighbouring
state, they have to ensure that the interests of their state are given
full weight in settling the terms of the union, after which responsibilities for safe-guarding the new and larger state must be assumed.

In meeting these responsibilities statesmen are obliged to take
account of the distribution of power in the world. They must strive
to establish such relations with other countries as will ensure that no
preponderance of power among the latter, singly or collectively, will
threaten their independence or encompass their downfall. In the
pursuit of this defensive aim they may decide, from time to time, to
enter into or form alliances with other powers, particularly when
those countries whose designs they fear are linked by treaty engagements. In other circumstances they may eschew all alliances, fearing that by entering into one they would provoke the hostility of a
rival group and be drawn into conflicts which they might avoid by
remaining dissociated from either group. Much depends on the
geographical position and natural resources of the state in question :
each state is unique in size, however defined, in resources, and in
geographical position in relation to other states. Consequently, the
precise measures appropriate to the maintenance of a defensive balance of power differ widely in the different countries. What is
common is the aim of survival.

A defensive balance of power is concerned in a broad sense with
the creation and maintenance of an equilibrium among the independent states of the world. But the idea of a stationary equilibrium
is useful only as an abstract reference point : in practice, it must be
reinterpreted in the sense of a " moving equilibrium ". Political and
social, economic and technological, conditions are continually
changing, and with them the comparative positions of independent
states. Thus the quest of a defensive balance of power is a continuous quest, calling for frequent adjustments and changes in groupings. There is no haven of rest for the foreign minister as the pilot of
the ship of state, no port where the ship can anchor long in tranquil
waters, sheltered from the winds of change and the tempests that
come with them.

But the defensive pursuit of a balance of power, conceived in
terms of moving equilibrium, is only part of the picture. It may
remain the sole concern of states which are too weak to pass beyond
defensive action, either on their own power or through their ability to
induce other states to join with them in the conduct of external
policy. But throughout history the more powerful states, and the
more powerful tribes before states were established, have not always

remained content with the defensive pursuit of a balance of power :
from time to time they have aimed at upsetting an existing balance
of power and re-fashioning it in a form that seemed to increase their
comparative strength in the world. Paradoxically, it has been the
attempts to overturn an existing balance of power that have brought
down the wrath of moralists on the heads of those students who have
approved of the conception in their writings on, and statesmen who
have applied it in the conduct of, international relations.

It is tempting, then, and some writers have yielded to the temptation, to reverse the position taken by those who regard the pursuit of
the balance of power as the root of all international evils, and to dis-
cover the heroes in those who have created and sustained, the vil-
lains of the piece in those who have designedly upset, the balance of
power. In substance this is still, broadly speaking, the position of a
number of " realists ", especially those who have little faith in the
development of the international organisations. They regard the
pursuit of a balance of power, mainly in an *ad hoc* fashion, but sometimes through the formation of alliances and understandings among
groups, as the best if not the only method of keeping the peace.
Admitting that it has sometimes broken down, they attribute the
failures to lapses and miscalculations and see the remedy in a more
competent and consistent pursuit of the same aim. At times they
appear to underestimate the difficulties in preserving a moving
balance or equilibrium under conditions of rapid change in world
conditions.

In the present study both these extreme positions are rejected.
The pursuit of a balance of power is unavoidable so long as the
statesmen in charge of foreign policy fulfil their responsibilities. But
in principle the term should be given neither a pejorative nor a
laudatory but a neutral sense—not as part of a " moral neutralism ", which is also rejected in these pages, but in recognition that
more than one balance of power may be sought, and the prospects of
peace, of the extension of freedom, and of the preservation of fruitful
diversities in the world, depend largely on what particular balance is
established and maintained.

The attempt to overturn a particular balance of power, by war if
it cannot be done by diplomacy, however undesirable it may be, can
be represented as a repudiation of the idea of balance of power only
when it is part of an attempt at world conquest. In the great majority of cases the aim is to overturn one balance of power with a view
to setting up another giving greater comparative power to the dis-
turbers of the existing balance.

But the line between a defensive and an offensive pursuit of a
balance of power is not necessarily a line between legitimate and
illegitimate aims, or between the pursuit of desirable and undesirable

ends. A balance of power may be attained in widely different forms and combinations, each of them with different effects on the prospects of peace, freedom, and diversity. The structure of all the balances of power before 1914 gave dominating positions to the Great Powers and encroached widely and deeply on the independence of the smaller countries, not only through colonialism but also through other forms of imperialism. They embodied large elements of hegemony which became intolerable after the spread and intensification of political consciousness beyond the Great Powers. It is part of the main thesis of this book that in the second half of the twentieth century we are in the midst of a far-reaching change in the balance of power, to which the Great Powers, including particularly the superpowers, will have to adjust themselves if grave conflicts are to be avoided. More than ever, if a balance of power capable of safeguarding world peace is to be established and upheld, it must be a moving and not a static equilibrium, and it must take account of all forms of power and not merely of armed power. The pursuit of a balance of power of this type is a respectable and indeed, if humanity is to survive, an indispensable pursuit, which is never completed and should constitute the central core of international life. Thus there is, simultaneously, a continuous pursuit and a continuous replacement of a balance of power, and the art of international diplomacy is gradually to displace the older by the newer without setting off an armed conflict in the process. In the nineteen-sixties the winds of change are blowing so strongly that even " gradualism " has lost its inevitability for a time. For a few decades international relations will be passing through their most difficult period in world history.

IV

Influence of Doctrines in International Affairs

Doctrinal elements have rarely been altogether absent from international affairs. In the nineteenth century various forms of autocracy and liberalism sometimes affected the groupings and policies of the Great Powers. Even in the early stage of the First World War these elements played a limited role. Autocratic, military, and monarchical elements dominated key positions in the governments of the Central Powers,[1] while Britain, France, and Belgium were governed by sovereign parliamentary institutions. Their willingness to accept an alliance with the autocrat of the East did not affect the

---

[1] It must be admitted that these autocracies were mild in comparison with those of the mid-twentieth century.

genuineness of their determination to preserve their own political liberties.

But all this was an element in a wider struggle over the balance of power among sovereign states, and, just as the Thirty Years War produced no clear-cut division between Protestant and Catholic states, so the First World War produced no clear-cut division between autocratic and democratic states. The aim, and for the time the achievement, were to prevent a militarised Germany from dominating all Europe. The most important territorial result was the elimination of the Austro-Hungarian Empire, and the substitution for it of a group of smaller states at odds among themselves, and some of them at odds with their neighbours beyond the group.

The other chief result of the War was the political and social transformation in Russia, largely influenced by new leaders professing Marxist doctrine, which introduced a new element in European and later in world politics. The Russian Revolution was something of a doctrinal anomaly : it came in a country which, according to the Marxist book, was unripe for it. This might possibly be met by a reinterpretation which, whatever violence it would do to the original doctrine, had at least a basis in actual accomplishment, which the pure doctrine had not yet attained. However, all this was of secondary importance at the outset, for the apostles of the day lived in expectation that the pure doctrine of the original revelation would be verified by revolutions in the advanced industrial societies of central and western Europe, beginning with Germany, which were ripe for the Day of Judgement. Hope was deferred but not abandoned for several years. But when no other country followed Russia, the idea of " socialism in one country " gradually gained practical acceptance, and with it the new force in international relations took on forms less divergent from and disruptive of the old order than its prime movers had originally expected and intended. Communism was forced to compromise with nationalism, and a communist state to live in a world of nationalist states, and to engage in diplomacy aiming at a defensive balance of power. Just as, in the twelfth century, Baldwin II subordinated his doctrinal zeal to the task of preserving the existence of the Kingdom of Jerusalem in the midst of neighbours of alien faiths, whom he had little hope of conquering and none of converting, so Stalin and his assistants placed the survival, and, on the borders of weaker neighbours, where possible the aggrandisement, of the Russian state before the advancement of communist doctrine. Ironically, it was unregenerate Germany, which the Soviet leaders had confidently expected, on the basis of Marxian doctrine, to be the first country after Russia to turn communist, which was most responsible for the reversion of Russia to balance of power politics in international affairs, first at the Treaty

of Rapallo in 1922, and, second, after Stalin had belatedly recognised
the menace of Hitler.[1] The Treaty of Rapallo was an advance sign,
hastened by injudicious Allied policies, of what would have happened sooner or later in any case.

The dream of a world revolution as a manifestation of inexorable
historical laws working in every society on Earth may be either dismissed as the prophecy of a visionary led astray by dogmatic adherence to a plausible doctrine without adequate empirical support, or
it may be interpreted as the herald of things to come, but, because of
the uneven development of the various societies, only to come in the
long run.   Between these two positions a great doctrinal gulf is
fixed, but the practice that follows from them differs little : in the
short run, which may last for many years even on Marxian assumptions,[2] the first aim of the existing communist state or states must be
to survive in a world of competing states.   As they do not occupy a
dominating position they must enter into the existing international
system or be left isolated, ringed around by potentially hostile forces.
For their followers this step must be made to appear doctrinally consistent : " Leninism " is dragged in to the aid of Marxism, and when
all else fails critics are denounced as " deviationists ".   In the days of
Stalin they were summarily disposed of.   In the end the communist
state is left to act in international affairs according to principles
hardly distinguishable in most respects from those followed by non-
communist states.   It is easy to find much continuity between the
foreign policy of Czarist Russia and that of Soviet Russia.

It does not follow that doctrinal influences are thus rendered negligible.   The doctrines of communism have proved to be a dynamic
force in the world far stronger than any pre-revolutionary doctrine,
probably stronger than any doctrines impinging on international
relations since the seventeenth century, when the doctrinal strife
between Roman Catholics and Protestants spread widely over
Europe.   The analogy, though limited, is useful.   The Thirty Years
War, or, more accurately, series of wars, was concerned mainly with
the balance of power in Europe, as, indeed, the statesmen of the day
recognised.   But religious divisions played some part in detail, and
the outcome of the wars had affected the distribution of the Roman
Catholic and Protestant churches, just as the World Wars of the
twentieth century, which were fought mainly over the balance of

---

[1] A useful study might be made comparing French diplomacy 1789–98 with
Russian diplomacy, 1918–34.

[2] But Marx's assumptions have been badly discredited by the failure of the
countries supposedly ripe for change to embrace communism. A central part of
the Marxian doctrine has collapsed beyond repair, and not all the tortuous
improvisations of his successors have been able to provide a convincing substitute
for it.   3

power in the world, affected the distribution of communist and non-communist states of various types. And in some of the military campaigns of the seventeenth century the rank and file, at least when they were not mercenaries in armies recruited and directed by private military enterprise on contracts with governments, believed themselves to be engaged in struggles on the outcome of which the destinies of men's souls as well as the fate of their bodies depended. This was a secondary influence, only sustained sporadically over the long period of conflict, but it was important where it occurred. Similarly in the twentieth century a number of movements, especially revolutionary nationalist movements which communists could not completely dominate, but which they believed would serve their aims in respect to the balance of power, and which, without their organising ability might have languished, have been given a drive, an *élan*, from the doctrinal zeal of communists within or on the fringe of their ranks, which they would not otherwise have been able to sustain.

But the influence of communist doctrine, though important, should not be exaggerated. For example, in the Second World War the armies of the Soviet Union, like the armies of an older Russia, seem to have been spurred on more by zeal to defend their homeland and chase the invaders out than by zeal for any kind of political doctrine, least of all one so complicated as " Marxism-Leninism-Stalinism ". The Second World War, like the First, and like the Thirty Years War, was criss-crossed by contradictory doctrines, of which most were represented on each of the opposing sides. If the democratic state was hardly[1] represented on more than one side, the totalitarian state was represented on both.

Since it is fashionable at the moment to divide states into " the communist world " and " the free world " I shall now examine in turn the role of balance of power and the role of political doctrines in determining international policies and actions, substituting, however, the term " non-communist world " for the term " free world ". The countries in which communism is not the official creed present a

---

[1] I say " hardly ", because notwithstanding widespread impressions in western countries, Japan was not a totalitarian state in the sense in which Germany, and, in a looser sense, Italy were. From democracy qualified by inadequate Cabinet control over the Armed Forces in the late twenties and the opening of the thirties, it gradually drifted into a large measure of militarist domination during the rest of the thirties. Misconceptions in the West led first to unnecessary indulgence towards Japan's external aggressions, followed by a sudden and drastic tightening at an inopportune moment, in the form of a demand in 1941 to a return to the position of mid-1931, accompanied by severance of vital raw materials. With greater knowledge and more intelligent Anglo-American diplomacy Japan could have been kept out of the Second World War, with incalculable consequences for Asia. See especially F. C. Jones, *Japan's Bid for Hegemony in Eastern Asia 1937–45*, a work of excellent scholarship and judgement.

variety of conditions and are governed by a variety of political forms. The term " free " when used in such a general sense, is too vague to illuminate or even describe anything of significance. The forms and degrees of political liberty vary widely in the non-communist world :[1] it is highly presumptuous and somewhat self-righteous to imply that the non-communist countries, or even the western countries alone, are uniquely " free ", although there are certainly fundamental differences between the structures of government and society and the position of the individual in the communist and part of the non-communist worlds. But within the non-communist world great changes are taking place—to be analysed in a later section—which constitute the heart of what I shall call the revolution in international relations.

V

National Interests and Balance of Power

Shortly after the Second World War it appeared to many observers in the West as if the communist world, strengthened by an important new member in 1949, was embarking on a new offensive through diplomacy, underground tactics abroad, and even local military operations. The uneasy wartime alliance between Russia and the West gave way to open diplomatic clashes and rising international tension. To complicate matters, in 1949 China emerged from a long period of turmoil with a firmly established communist régime ; bringing an accession to the communist fold of nearly a quarter of the world's inhabitants. The Korean War, costly in lives and economic effort, and the triumph of communism in China, which incensed American missionaries and their supporters, were followed by the rapid intensification of always latent fanatical forms of anti-communism and witch hunting in the United States, which hampered the conduct of American foreign policy. Fortunately the rest of the western world, including Canada, was untouched by these aberrations.

Notwithstanding these earlier years, when doctrinal warfare seemed, on a superficial view, to cast a deep shadow over international affairs, I would maintain that, on the whole, events since the Second World War have confirmed and reinforced the division and organisation of the world into independent sovereign states, each pursuing its own interests, or what it regards as its own interests, regardless of whether or not these interests crossed doctrinal lines of division. The Korean War had in it a doctrinal aspect, in

[1] This is also true, but on a different and lower plane, of the communist world.

the sense that, if South Korea had fallen to North Korea, an oligarchy of the left would have replaced an oligarchy of the right in
South Korea. Since it is generally harder to escape from the former
than from the latter, this would probably have worked against the
interests of the South Koreans in the long run. But from the point of
view of international affairs, and in the minds of its external insti-
gators, the Korean War was concerned overwhelmingly with the
balance of power in the Far East, both the Russians and the Chinese
resenting and fearing the intrusion of American forces and influence
on the Asian mainland, and each considering that, as a neighbouring power, it had a defensive and an offensive interest in the area
which it must assert against intruders from distant lands. Both
Russia and China, on a longer view, appear to have pursued historic
interests which had shaped their policies, when they were strong
enough to exercise them, under radically different pre-communist
régimes.

Four years after the Second World War a change of régime took
place in China, opening a new era. A new ruler appeared, under
new titles, after a chaotic period of internal strife, which had opened
the country to external interference. In his rise to power, Mao-Tse-
tung made free with orthodox Marxist doctrines. After his attainment of it, he tried to transform the structure of society, but continued to follow his own path, undeterred by precedent and with little
regard for external advice. The Chinese Revolution differed from
the Russian Revolution in being more self-centred and directed in
the main by men with little experience of other lands and peoples :
it was an indigenous achievement, owing little to Russia until a very
late stage. " The withering away of the state " seems as ludicrously
remote in China as in Russia, and not less remote are the prospects
that the two leading communist states will merge together, for all
their professed doctrinal unity or similarity.

Yugoslavia is also an independent communist state. It has shaken
off the satellite relationship which Russia, under Stalin, had
attempted to impose on it. It diverges widely from both Russia and
China in maintaining harmonious political relations with the
western countries and in allowing more freedom and decentralisation. Albania, much smaller and less important, has asserted its
independence in a very different direction, in doctrines clinging to
an older orthodoxy now outdated in Russia itself.

Since 1956 the line between independent and satellite communist
states has been slightly blurred. Poland, by skilful leadership, has
gained a very limited degree of autonomy and considerable freedom
of speech. Hungary, reaching out for more in 1956, lost all, for a
time at least, though it would be going too far to say that nothing
was gained indirectly in the longer run. Signs of independent ten-

dencies appeared in Roumania in 1963, and developed rapidly. Czechoslovakia and Bulgaria have shown signs of independence, but East Germany's attempts were crushed at the start.   These eastern and central European countries may be classed as Russian satellites in which communism as a doctrine has no deep indigenous foundation and the communist structure of government is an alien product, imposed by minorities linked with a powerful military neighbour capable of exercising sanctions if and when deviations in doctrine and policy exceed the limits which appear safe from the point of view of the balance of power between Russia and the West. In few, if any, of them would communist governments be likely to survive indefinitely if the possibility of direct Russian intervention were removed.   And such intervention, in turn, would result not so much from doctrinal zeal as from fears concerning the balance of power in a wider context.[1]

Thus the differences within the communist world have been wide, and each communist country seems determined to follow its own course so far, at least, as its geographical position permits it to do so. The communist world is, therefore, a world of separate political states, which, except to a limited degree among the satellites, maintain their independence of one another, as well as of the rest of the world, and between which doctrinal disputes are frequent and sometimes bitter.   But for the mistakes in the Far Eastern policy of the United States the outward signs of these differences would have been even greater than they have been.   Each of the countries claims to be the true interpreter of the gospel according to Marx and Lenin, and Dr. Edward Kardelj has held his own effectively against the Marxist high priests of both the other camps.

The differences within the communist world reflect far more than divergencies of doctrine about an orthodoxy.   They reflect wide differences in regional interests within the framework of world balance of power among communist and non-communist states alike.   No doctrinal explanation is needed to account for the more intransigently hostile attitude of China than of Russia to the United States, which has armed and supported a disinherited refugee from the throne now occupied by Mao-Tse-tung, on an island almost within artillery range of Chinese shores ; which kept Japan largely in the

[1] This seems to have been the main reason for Russian intervention in Hungary in 1956, just as it had been for Czarist Russian intervention a little over a century earlier.   In both cases the prospects were that Hungary would link itself with the powers to the West and would thus be a danger, in the earlier case to a Russia governed by a régime which happened to be of the " right ", and in the later to one which happened to be of the " left ".   Even if doctrinal alignments had been similar on both sides, considerations of balance of power would probably have been predominant, for both liberal and autocratic states often cherish imperialistic ambitions when they possess the power to realise them.

position of a satellite in respect to her external policies, which has maintained military bases there and in Okinawa ; and which, by underground methods in violation of the treaty of 1954, instigated the overthrow of the neutral régime of Prince Souvanna Phouma in Laos, and set up and armed a right-wing militarist government to take its place. All this, so far as China is concerned, is fully accounted for in classical terms of balance of power. Such doctrinal elements as may be found come mainly from the influence or pressure of anti-communist elements in the United States, but even these are intermingled with ideas in the Pentagon of military strategy conceived in abstraction from local political conditions in south-eastern Asia. Fortunately, President Kennedy went far to change the policy of his predecessor in Laos, but much harm had already been done.

Likewise, Yugoslavia's relations with other communist states are easily accounted for in terms of national interests and balance of power. As a direct neighbour of southern and central European countries, and as a developing country in need of capital, it was in her interest to maintain the fullest international economic relations, consistent with the maintenance of her independence, with non-communist countries. Since her interests and Russia's have not always coincided, and during Stalin's reign her independence was threatened, she desires a balance of power between the two great communist countries and the West. Like the heretical Christian sects in the Levant, which found economic relations with the Islamic world less burdensome than those with Byzantium, Yugoslavia has found her economic dealings with the West more advantageous and less open to sudden curtailment than those with her political co-religionists. There the analogy stops, for Yugoslavia's first aim is political independence of both communist and non-communist states.

If this interpretation meets objections on the ground that prolonged doctrinal disputes have characterised Russo-Yugoslav relationships, the answer is that these disputes masked real divergencies of interest which were not dependent, in the last resort, on doctrinal differences. Russia's policies towards the non-communist countries fluctuated from time to time in accordance with changes in what were believed to be the interests of the Russian state. Yugoslavia's external interests did not fluctuate as much or in the same way. Russia claimed to be the leader of the communist world by reason of her long experience and accumulated knowledge. But Yugoslavia asserted her independence as a state. Now there is nothing in the book to decide what ought to be done in a world of " socialism in four countries " which are interspersed with " capitalist " states. The Russian communists claimed that they had the right to call the tune at all times in international affairs. The Yugoslav communists asserted the sovereign independence of Yugoslavia. Naturally these underlying differences were overlaid by doctrinal coverings, to be fully appreciated only by those well versed in communist folklore. But the underlying reality is that the governments of additional countries converted to communism after the U.S.S.R. had been established, have asserted their independence against all countries, communist or non-communist alike, whenever their geographical position enabled them to do so.

The strength of nationalism, against which the weapons of communism are not able to prevail, lies mainly in differences in social heritage. It may be difficult to define these differences closely, but none can deny that Chinese civilisation differs widely and deeply from European civilisation, that it embodies a unique culture of its own. In some of the arts, in the education of its upper classes, and in some at least of the components of the standard of living, China probably maintained a higher level than Europe until well into the eighteenth century. But from about the seventeen-nineties it fell rapidly behind the western world and probably dropped below its own earlier level.[1] In one respect at least the Chinese remain what they have always been, inward rather than outward looking, determined to follow their own way which, however differently it may appear under different régimes, is always an indigenous way, contrasting in many respects with the ways of western man.

The Soviet Union is still mainly dominated by Russians, in spite of a façade of local " puppet " rulers (to borrow a term that came into wide use during Japan's attempts to dominate Manchuria) in her Asian territories. There are indeed oriental elements in the civilisation of the Soviet Union, but, since its centre of gravity of population is to the West, the European elements are still strong, and the gulf between western and central Europe on the one hand, and Russia on the other, is narrower than that between Europe and China. No one who has had direct dealings with Russians in negotiations over a considerable period of time could fail to notice the differences in background between the native of Leningrad and the native of points well to the east and south-east. Marx himself has been described, though the description may not command general agreement, as an offshoot of the European liberal tradition. In the heterogeneous collection of peoples in the Soviet Union the Russian elements tend to dominate key points, even in the territories of central Asia and Siberia.

Thus the divergencies in social heritage between the Soviet Union and China are profound, and no political doctrine can erase or

---

[1] All modern students, western and eastern alike, owe a steadily increasing debt to the great work of Joseph Needham and his associates, *Science and Civilisation in China* (Cambridge, 1954-62).

thoroughly transcend them. The conversion of China to communism was not an enlargement of a uniform communist world ; it was the creation of a new, politically self-contained unit, whose relationship to the other communist units was much like that of one non-communist state to another, except for the difference that totalitarian governments are less restrained than democratic states in their dealings with one another by the sentiments of the people whom they are supposed to be representing. This qualification, however, applies also to non-communist authoritarian states.

The extreme anti-communists used to retort that Russia and China (which Americans insist on calling " Red China " or " Communist China ", as if there existed another China of different hue) have shown no signs of genuine split, and that " reds " will always act like " reds ", working together to overthrow capitalism and private enterprise by force and " subversion ". It is, of course, as much in the interests of the fanatical anti-communists as of the fanatical communists to represent international affairs as, above all, the scene of an irreconcilable clash of doctrines.

This viewpoint, reiterated over and over again by those anti-communist vested interests which in the United States have struggled to keep China out of the United Nations, reveals a confusion of thought. The essence of the matter is that, in spite of doctrinal affiliations, Russia and China will act as independent, " sovereign " political states, each following its own interests as it sees them, with political doctrines in a secondary position.[1] Obviously, in view of the world balance of power at the present time it may possibly be in the interests of the two countries to maintain their alliance. Their common international interests have been strengthened by United States policy, independently of doctrinal considerations. Among the powers they appear as two neighbouring giant powers, on the flanks of each of which a third giant power has built up military and air bases in the territories of allies and satellites, from which it could stage offensive or retaliatory raids on their territories with weapons of deadly potency.

The picture in the minds of the majority of Americans, represent-

---

[1] There are many devices by which the outward adjustment of doctrines to national interests at a given time can be made. The commonest is that which represents it as a mere temporary change of tactics, adopted without prejudice to the ultimate aims. This device, however, tends to alienate the more idealistic rank and file when the supposed change of " tactics " involves a drastic change of principle, even amounting to a reversal, as for example, in the Russo-German treaty in August, 1939. In practice, means and ends are not so easily and completely separable as is sometimes supposed. But if two communist countries whose national interests diverge in a particular case both attempt to shape communist doctrines to justify the separate ways they have taken, a doctrinal row is sure to flare up.

ing the dangers from Russia and China simply as the outcome of their adoption of communist doctrines, is misleading. Are we seriously to suppose that the powers to the west and south-west of Russia would have trusted in Russia's benevolent use of her military hegemony over the European continent after the Second World War if she had not been a communist state ? Do we really believe that the powers to the south and south-east of China would have seen no cause for fear in the emergence even of a non-communist China as a potentially formidable military power, with almost illimitable resources in manpower ? Historical experience and common-sense preclude such naïve views. The European powers, faced with the historically intermittent danger of one power becoming strong enough to overrun the whole continent of Europe, would surely have acted as they have done since the sixteenth century, and sought mutual alliances for self-protection : this time, with the danger threatening from the East, and no strong, united central European power remaining, the western European powers would in any case have called in the New World to redress the balance in the Old ; and the New World, fearing the enhanced power of the great Eurasian Heartland, would have been left with no alternative but to respond in its own interests. China, on her part, would have had in any case a strong interest in preserving good relations with a powerful neighbouring country with which she has never yet been officially at war, and whose support would offset the western maritime countries that had encroached on her interests in the nineteenth century. On the other hand, to the southern and south-eastern Asian peoples China would have continued to appear as a danger, regardless of political doctrines. There has been far more continuity than is commonly realised between Chinese policy towards, and intrigues in, Malaya under the Kuomintang and that under the communists. The Kuomintang adopted an " anti-colonialist " policy with regard to the West and at the same time encouraged overseas Chinese to consider themselves as still Chinese[1] and yet demand the same economic rights as natives.

Even the type of communism adopted by China has been fitted at many points to her social heritage. The inward-looking tendency, and the antipathy to the West, that characterise the present régime long antedated communism : its roots are indigenous and no new doctrine was needed to plant them more firmly. Mao-Tse-tung's brand of communism has been shaped for domestic use with no great regard for the orthodoxies of western interpretations of communism except when it has seemed in China's interests to make opportunist

---

[1] Since 1955 the new régime in China has shown more disposition to change Chinese policies towards the overseas Chinese than the old régime did, especially in Cambodia and Indonesia.

use of " conservative " communism, as, for example, at the time of
the Hungarian revolt and again in 1961–2.

Notwithstanding a strong and indispensable area of common concern at the present time, the extent to which the interests of Russia
and China coincide is limited, and these limitations would have
become much clearer if British and French and not American political judgement had shaped western policy in the Far East in the last
decade. It is unnecessary here to go into the differences in detail
between the outlook, first of a more sophisticated second generation
of revolutionary leaders in Russia who are inescapably bound up
with the working of a bureaucratic government organisation and
party structure and are forced to go some way towards meeting the
demands of their newly created middle class of *functionnaires*, and,
second, the outlook of Chinese revolutionaries in the first flush of
power, zealots fired with missionary zeal, bigoted, intolerant,
humourless, and certain that they, and they alone, know what is
good for the people ; working, and forcing their followers to work,
at fever heat with the aim of fashioning overnight a new society of
their own pattern unlike any other society on earth ; disillusioned
from time to time with the gaps between aims and achievements,
and finding scapegoats at home and abroad to divert popular antipathies from the sources of miscalculation. It may be that, after the
passing of a generation, the outlook of these contrasting groups will
move closer together, but it is certain at least that the differences
today are a strain on the alliance and a source of friction only a small
part of which appears on the surface. They lead also to differences
of judgement over the correct course to be followed both towards the
West and also towards the neutral world. As we have seen, the
Chinese communists owed little to Russia in the course of their rise to
power. The ignominious dismissal of M. Borodin and his advisors
in the nineteen-twenties after their efforts to call the tune in the Kuomintang was followed by an indigenous development of the left that
was given its opportunity by Japanese aggression, with its disrupting
effect on the country, and by injudicious forms of American support
of a decaying Chinese régime. Stalin was late in recognising the
strength which Mao-Tse-tung had built up among the peasant
masses. It was not until 1955 that Russian troops left Port Arthur
and that the Changchun Railway was completely made over to
Chinese ownership.[1]

Now the Soviet Union maintains a position in the communist
world which differs from Britain's present position in the Commonwealth. It holds, and sometimes exercises, powers of coercion. It
claims the right to determine, and sometimes tries to enforce, ortho-

---

[1] In acquiring these privileges and relinquishing them later for political reasons
Soviet Russia was precisely following the pattern set by " capitalist " states !

dox doctrine and policy. It instructs, and asserts its authority to instruct, the communist parties of non-communist countries in the strategy, and even the tactics, which they should follow in their own areas. It has the power, and has occasionally used it, to apply economic sanctions to a member which deviates from its standard of orthodoxy.

The entry of China into the communist fold brought a revolutionary change in the structure of the communist world. Instead of one Great Power with a few much smaller powers, there were, after 1949 —potentially at least—two Great Powers. The new power was indeed weak in some respects : the masses were poor—in districts far from the transport system near the coast and from the main courses of the great rivers, they were miserably poor. But they were justly renowned everywhere for their untiring industry and perseverence, centred around the strong ties of a family system which had maintained cohesion even in periods of political anarchy and confusion. Their natural resources, though imperfectly surveyed, were known to be sufficient for an industrial development, not indeed comparable to that of Europe and North America, but capable of providing the sinews of a modern state which could not be safely ignored by the Great Powers. From the beginning it should have been clear that the entry of China would greatly complicate international relations both within and outside the communist world and in widely different ways between communist and non-communist countries.

Most observers have assumed, of course, that the entry of China into the communist world was a heavy blow to the western world as a whole. But we may provisionally leave this question on one side and usefully consider the more immediately important question whether, given the changes in China, the differences and rivalries as well as the co-operation between Russia and China will make the task of the Commonwealth easier or harder. The question is difficult because entries have now and will have in the future to be placed on both sides of the ledger, so to speak. Some of the potential disadvantages are obvious enough. As long as China is more intransigent than Russia, the Soviet leaders may tend at times to take up a stiffer attitude towards the West than they would otherwise do. Probably this has already happened in certain cases, notably over the breakdown of the proposed Paris conference at the " summit " in 1959, but a large share of the responsibility in this matter must be borne by President Eisenhower and his administrators, although the scope for conciliation on Mr. Khrushchev's part was narrowed by Chinese intransigence. On the other side, the scope for aggressive action by China has been limited sharply by Russia's power of restraint, and it may well be that, for example in the Indo-Chinese[1] peninsula, this has brought to the West advantages that more than outweigh losses in other directions. It appeared likely that, as long as Russia retained, and China failed to produce, atomic weapons, the ties between Russia and China would work more to the advantage than to the disadvantage of the non-communist world, unless they snapped altogether owing to new quarrels.

It is more difficult to envisage the changes that are likely to arise now that China has succeeded in producing atomic weapons. In the present stage of the Chinese revolution the possession of atomic weapons by China will probably increase her sense of world responsibility. Russia will remain the chief and most effective restraint on China, which could not hope to prevail in any conflict without Russian support. But even on the extravagant hypothesis that Russia and China together were prepared to consider seriously an armed conflict with the West, it is hard to believe that either would trust the other sufficiently to embark on a gamble that, if success were conceivable, would leave the survivors facing each other in the end in the almost unrecognisable remnants of the past world. One thing only seems certain : that if an atomic conflict began, the outcome would bear no resemblance to the intentions of its designers. This is the best ground for believing that there is only the remotest chance that it will be started deliberately, so long as no dictator of unsound mind comes to power and no false alarms are sounded.

Thus it appears that the existence of two large states in the communist world has introduced checks and balances which, though they may sometimes induce a competition in extremes—usually, perhaps, verbal extremes—seem, on the whole, to be a restraining rather than an aggravating influence, compelling frequent consultation and compromise and, on issues where the leading communist powers are at odds with a group of non-communist powers, creating a nearer approach to equality in respect of technical efficiency in negotiation and bargaining. Since communist philosophers, bound by the rigidity of their dogmas, failed completely to foresee such contingencies, the communist statesmen have had to improvise as best they could to meet them.

Whatever differences may exist between the two large communist states, the reality of their communism, and of the alliance between them, has never been challenged. Yugoslavia—smaller, but by no means negligible—is in a different position. At the outset the leaders

---

[1] I should not wish to press this particular case, however, since it was hardly in China's interest to risk another struggle like that in Korea, and, moreover, we have as yet little precise knowledge of the relations between China, on the one hand, and the Pathet Lao and South Vietnam guerillas on the other.

of the Soviet Union professed to be the supporters, the shield, and the protectors of Yugoslavia. On the U.N.R.R.A. Council and on other bodies concerned with economic aid they frequently accused the Allied powers of discriminating against Yugoslavia on political grounds. When the great breach came—one of the most significant events in communist history—they denounced the heretics, as they represented them, with bell, book, and candle, and from time to time since have treated them as outside the pale. But after Stalin's death they received them back into the fold for a time. The reconciliation has not been complete, and the relations between Yugoslavia and Russia have fluctuated with fluctuations in the international situation as a whole. Chinese criticisms have been stronger than Russian. Yet Yugoslavia remains a communist state in matters of doctrine, and, if allowance is made for the limitations said to be justifiable in the " transition " period towards communism, which in some degree apply to all communist countries so far, she has remained a communist state in domestic policy and practice, though much more humane and flexible than the other communist states. Judged by Marxist standards it may be said that, if the ruling Yugoslav groups appear to make more concessions to private enterprise than others do in the transition period, they also keep closer to the spirit of Marx in moderating the tendency, so pronounced in the rest of the communist world, to transform the dictatorship of the proletariat into the dictatorship of a self-appointed oligarchy *over* the proletariat.

VI

Interrelations of Doctrines and Balance of Power

It should not be supposed that the role of political doctrine is independent of the role of international balance of power. On the contrary, both revisions of, and reversions to, previously accepted communist orthodoxies are often if not usually connected closely with what are believed to be the interests of a communist state, which change from time to time with changes in world conditions. It would be difficult, for example, to interpret, in any other way, the sympathetic attitude of the Chinese leaders towards Mr. Gomulka's earlier unorthodoxies—from the Russian viewpoint—and their sharp swing to the " right " after the Hungarian uprising, which raised the threat of a secession of Hungary to the West. During his rise to power Mao-Tse-tung took such liberties with doctrine that we cannot possibly believe him to have accepted the verbal inspiration of the Marxist scriptures at any time : for him, doctrine must be adjusted to the exigencies of power, not the use of power to a literal application of doctrine.

This, however, merely strengthens and confirms the conclusion that, in international affairs, the role of Marxist-Leninist doctrine is subordinate to the role of balance of power, even in the minds of statesmen in the communist countries. As we have seen, the doctrinal heritage of communism was not originally designed, and has never been comfortably adjusted to, a world in which a small number of independent states under communist forms of government lie intermingled with a larger number of non-communist states—all the states, communist and non-communist alike, jealously insisting on their independent status and their national[1] sovereignty. The Marxist doctrines did not envisage such a development ; they underestimated the strength of nationalism and the enduring importance of differences in social heritage. The lines of a communist world of the future were not drawn with clarity ; they were hardly drawn at all.

It may, of course, be argued that Marxist doctrine was concerned with the conditions for the seizure of power rather than of its use after it was seized : nevertheless even the seizure of power is not wholly separable from its subsequent exercise when it comes in limited areas only, for the use made of it affects the prospects of its extension to other areas. Marxist doctrine, though not wholly an economic doctrine, has proved to be far too exclusively concentrated on economic structure to interpret the course of international developments. This defect would have largely disqualified it even if its ideas of economic structure and development had been less over-simplified and more far-sighted than they were. As it is, the attempt to apply the Communist Manifesto, and the descriptions of capitalism by Marx and Engels, to the prosperous industrialised western countries is ludicrous, and has no chance of overturning the western world from within. The most vigorous censorship is needed in Russia and China to keep the illusion and prevent the masses from grasping the truth about the world outside. And when Marxian doctrines are directed towards the countries where poverty exists on a large scale they misfire, at least in their original form, because there has been little industrial development in such countries and, though their agriculture is in need of reconstruction, it is in agriculture that the worse communist failures have taken place.

The communists of today are attempting to supplement the historical Marxist heritage by the experience gained through the

---

[1] It should be understood that this use of the adjective " national " is related to the noun " state " rather than the noun " nation ". Confusion was brought into the English language by the practice in some federal states of substituting " state " for " province " to designate an internal subdivision.

approaches to power in China and North Vietnam, which were based on the support of the agricultural classes rather than of an urban proletariat. The unorthodoxies of Mao-Tse-tung on the way to power, deviating from Russian methods of approach ; followed by the new unorthodoxies of Ho-chi-minh, deviating in some respects from both Russia and China, have widened the experience and broadened the armoury of the communist world. But the advances have been realised far more in the techniques of gaining power than in the realisation of the economic fruits of power.   Great claims have been made for the economic results obtained in China.   In some fields they are impressive, in others and notably in agriculture, they are to some extent a warning rather than an example ; but the Chinese, partly because of their family system, are industrious beyond most other Asiatic peoples, and are likely to remain so, within the limits of their opportunities, under any social system.   Further to the east the Japanese, with still more limited agricultural and mineral resources, have achieved far more, without a totalitarian political system, than the Chinese can hope to achieve for a long time to come with one.   Southward of China the peoples of south-eastern Asia inherit traditions and ways of life to which the regimentation in Chinese communism is alien and presents no mass appeal.   Even if it did, the fear of China as a powerful neighbour, tending to expand when not rent by internal strife, is supported by too much historical experience to be overshadowed by doctrinal influences.

Chinese imperialism needs no Marxian interpretation of its long history which began many centuries before modern industry appeared.   It persists independently of political doctrines—unless we assume that the Chinese conviction that they are superior to other peoples is itself a doctrine !   An aggressive attitude towards Tibet and on frontier questions has characterised almost all régimes : it weakens from time to time when the comparative power of the Chinese state has weakened, and it revives as soon as the power to press territorial claims or claims of overlordship revives.   Chinese claims to the possession of a superior way of life to that of their neighbours is in no sense dependent on, nor did it begin with, their adoption of communism.   Nor has Chinese communism superseded nationalism : rather, Chinese nationalism has become more intense and more widespread among the masses than ever before.   China is now in the early stages of a new dynasty, and as has happened so often in the last millenium under a variety of dynasties, it has entered on a period of effective central control and of the aggressive external outlook that has almost always accompanied strong central government.

Consequently in international relations the Communist world has taken on a similar form to that of the non-communist world. Considerations of the balance of power apply within the communist world as well as within the whole world. Doctrinal affinities, far from being a form of insurance against disunity, are an occasion for bitter wrangling among powers whose interests often diverge and each of whom interprets supposedly common doctrines to suit its own interests, exacerbating instead of reducing fundamental underlying national divergencies. The conflict between India and China brought support for India from western countries, but not for China from Russia or Yugoslavia. Even the most fanatical anti-communist can no longer seriously maintain that the ties of communism are too strong to permit genuine differences from ever arising between different communist countries or even to exclude the possibility of war between communist countries. In international affairs both national sentiment and the interests of the state as they are conceived by its rulers will continue to transcend political and economic doctrines.

The problem of coexistence is not, in the last resort, a problem of allowing rival forms of political doctrine and social organisations to exist side by side : it is a problem of adjusting differences in the interests of different states without resort to suicidal conflict. Coexistence should be interpreted as coexistence among states, not coexistence among doctrines. The problem of coexistence among doctrines is a domestic and not an international problem, allied to the problem of freedom of speech and inquiry. Alliances and counter-alliances are formed according to the interests of states, not of doctrines. The desire to preserve a doctrine at home sometimes contributes to the formation of alliances abroad with countries where opposite doctrines prevail.

CHAPTER II

THE NON-COMMUNIST WORLD

I

Failures of Communists in Non-Communist Countries

IN TURNING from the communist to the non-communist world we are
faced with wide variations in the respective roles of political doctrines and the balance of power in international policies.[1] The differences in the interests of these countries, scattered as they are over
all the continents, are very wide.

Those countries which we loosely call western, and which include
western and much of central and southern Europe and their past
offshoots overseas, are characterised by advanced economic development and high standards of living. They include the mature industrial countries which, according to the Marxian gospel, are ready to
enter the promised land. Ever since communist hopes of Germany
were shattered in the nineteen-twenties, it has become clearer and
clearer that Marx's vision, obsessed by the crudities and hardships of
the early industrial revolution, was distorted at a critical point in his
doctrine, and that a fight to the finish between vaguely defined
" workers " and " capitalists ", far from being inevitable, was more
likely to be an infrequent exception than the rule. Important aspects
of socialism could readily coexist in various degrees with private
enterprise. Those countries which, according to Marx, are supposed to be ripest for revolution are farthest from it. Communism
has decisively failed in the advanced western countries : except,
perhaps, for a short period in a few countries just after liberation
from the Germans, it has been little more than a local nuisance,
occasionally serving a useful purpose in exposing genuine weaknesses
or grievances.

Even in countries with only moderate standards of education,
communism is unable to obtain a dominating position in government. There are always a few exceptions, where men of high intelligence and attainment in specialised fields of learning become

---

[1] After this and other chapters concerned with the balance of power had been
completed, Mr. F. H. Hinsley's *Power and the Pursuit of Peace* (Cambridge, 1963)
reached me too late to take fully into account. It will be indispensable to students
of international affairs, notably for its historical analysis of the balance of power in
Parts I and II. My interpretation of the contemporary scene differs substantially
from that contained in Part III of Hinsley's work.

4

attracted to communist dogmas as to a sort of religion or substitute for religion. But, generally speaking, those who have a modicum of intelligence and knowledge of world conditions react with amused incredulity to the communist picture of the supposed state of the " capitalist " world, and of the comparative positions of Russian and western workers. The advanced western countries have conquered extreme poverty by a mixture of private enterprise and democratic socialism, representing piecemeal adaptations to changing conditions rather than the application of blueprints based on doctrines, without encroaching on the fundamental rights and liberties of the individual. In France and Italy, where communist parties have had considerable representation in the legislative bodies, large proportions of those who voted for communist candidates were not communists themselves, and the parties have no prospect of obtaining a grip on the machinery of state. The eastern European countries should be classified mainly as satellites of Russia, not as states converted to the communist faith by native or foreign missionaries. Even in Yugoslavia, where the communist movement had indigenous origins and is comparatively humane and civilised, there can be little doubt that the majority of the intellectual classes, if free to choose, would prefer social democracy to their present system. The existence of genuine opposition parties, free to criticise the government on all aspects of its policies, together with the opportunity and right of the electorate at appropriate times to change the government, including its highest ministers—these characteristics of the western political order, which, it should not be overlooked, are far from being shared in all the non-communist world, will never be exchanged voluntarily for the crude authoritarian régimes, as self-perpetuating as the most despotic monarchies of earlier times, and even more absolute in their claims. The dissatisfaction with the working of multiple-party systems in some countries has enabled ambitious heads of state to impose semi-authoritarian régimes, but even in these cases it has failed to convert the great majority to permanent acceptance of such forms and is on the defensive everywhere.

It follows that the cleavage in political practices between the non-communist countries which have maintained representative government and the communist and non-communist authoritarian states is sharp and irreconcilable, although it must not be supposed that communist countries are not subject to gradual underlying change.

On the economic side, the differences in form and structure are not as great as they are represented to be by the more extreme supporters of private enterprise. Britain has always rejected the claim often advanced on the continent that Marxism and socialism are synonymous and exclusive,[1] and has emphasised the largely inde-

---

[1] In the sense that there are conceived to be no other genuine forms of socialism.

pendent roots of socialism in Britain, where parliamentary democracy is and must remain the channel for socialist advance. The national health service and a wide range of social services, together with public ownership and operation of a number of productive and distributive services, have all been attained without any concessions to the authoritarian political machinery of the communist state. There remain large differences between communist and non-communist economic organisation ; for example, in the extent of economic activities directed by government organs, in the extent of freedom enjoyed by managers, in the scope and extent of central planning by government, in the freedom of trade unions and in the conduct of international trade. But Professor Tinbergen is justified in claiming that both the communist and western economic systems are " in permanent change " and that " several of the changes . . . are in fact bringing the communist and the free countries closer together ".[1]

The political and the economic cannot be wholly separated, and the cleavage between the communist and the western[2] forms of government are inevitably reflected in different degrees and forms of coercive elements in the economic systems of the two groups of countries. But these are secondary to the fundamental and irreconcilable divergencies between the methods of choosing representatives and ministries, their responsibilities to the people, the provisions for changing them from time to time, the existence of an independent judiciary, and the exercise of the rights of free speech and writing. The attacks on communism by western advocates of economic *laissez faire* are to some extent misplaced and tend to divert attention away from the fundamental political differences by identifying western societies with an extreme form of economic conservatism which at once presents a vulnerable target to communist snipers, and at the same time is unrepresentative of large sections of western opinion.

But if the non-communist countries will not voluntarily abandon representative government for communist autocracy, the question remains whether a well-organised minority could seize power by a surprise *coup d'état* and establish a communist state by force of arms. Czechoslovakia and some of the Balkan states are sometimes cited as cases in which communist parties came to power in this way.

---

[1] Jan Tinbergen " Do Communist and Free Economies show a Converging Pattern ", *Soviet Studies*, April 1961, pp. 333, 335. It will be noted that I have avoided the use of the term " free " economy, which, in a different way, is as misleading as the term " the free world ".

[2] " Western " refers to the countries of western Europe, their overseas offshoots, and a number of former dependencies which have now become independent. It does not refer to all the non-communist countries.

If a revolutionary group which is in a minority is to seize power in a modern state it must be able, first, to control the police and the armed forces at home, and, second, to safeguard the country against or open it to intervention from outside. But the police and the armed forces are usually commanded by senior officers with a comparatively conservative outlook and in all the non-communist countries they are a formidable obstacle to the seizure of power by revolutionaries of the extreme left. If they are ever found to be in collusion with revolutionaries it is only with those of the extreme right.

The seizure of power by communist parties in the eastern European countries other than Yugoslavia depended on the presence of large Russian forces within or on the borders of the countries concerned, which could be relied upon both to intervene in support of the communist parties when necessary and also to prevent non-communist intervention from outside against them. Beyond eastern and a piece of central Europe these conditions were not fulfilled, and communist parties were unable to attain power.

It is sometimes argued, however, that communist parties in the emerging and reawakening countries work in conditions much more favourable to the chances of successful *coups d'état*. The police and the army are less efficient and their loyalties less established than in the older countries. The practical difficulties of fulfilling the expectations aroused by independence lead to social discontent which helps agitators against the existing régime.

These questions are discussed more fully in a later chapter, but it may be said at once that, while social discontent works against the established order in the emerging countries, it does not necessarily work in favour of a communist order. When the army becomes disaffected it turns, not to communism but to forms of radicalism which, while aiming at social and economic changes, remain intensely nationalistic and resentful of any sign of interference from Great Powers either of the West or of the East. This is particularly characteristic of movements in which a prominent part is played by the " young officer " class. Such movements, and other radical movements based largely on sections of the middle classes in the towns, together with soldiers from peasant families, appear to be an outcome of uneven social change which leaves modern and mediaeval elements to coexist uneasily side by side in the same society. The radicalism of these movements aims concretely first at the removal of outdated forms of social and economic organisation and their replacement by modern forms similar to those adopted earlier in the present century by the advanced industrial countries. The stress on socialism and nationalisation reflects an impatience to accomplish the changes rapidly. The hostility to large landlords arises from a desire to remove what is believed to be a reactionary political force, and the antipathy to certain upper-middle-class elements, particularly large merchants, rests on the view that these were collaborators with, and profiteers from, the *ancien régime*.

These movements, which are difficult to classify in contemporary western political terms, are a compound of the radical " left " and the radical " right ". The early Egyptian nationalists of this type, like Arabi Pasha and his friends, espoused liberal ideas of representative government, but Colonel Nasir and his associates, who were also typical " young army officers ", established a military régime combined with a modern social policy in a number of fields, and, by substituting " Arab nationalism " for Egyptian nationalism, added intra-regional imperialism to their political aims. The aims of the Syrian and Iraqi Ba'ath have sometimes been described as " Fascism without Il Duce ", but this is misleading. Some of its members in principle have favoured representative government among an *élite* and strictly limited class who accept the doctrines of Arab nationalism and Arab socialism—a new variant of an old theme. Actually the Ba'ath has not been united on such questions. Western political labels are often misleading when applied to the Afro-Asian powers.

In addition there is, in many of the emerging countries, a genuine non-communist left, which desires social democracy with representative government. Unfortunately, it is poorly organised and finds great difficulty in making headway against authoritarian tendencies which often surround it.

Notwithstanding the wide differences among these movements they share one characteristic in common. Their foremost aim is political independence of the Great Powers, eastern and western alike. They are all uncompromisingly opposed to the establishment of communist states subject to instructions and interference from Russia or China. It follows that, contrary to ideas often uncritically accepted in western countries and in Russia and China, the *milieu* in which communist parties linked with Russia or China work in the emerging countries is a highly unfavourable one, and the chances that they will gain power are slender. There are serious dangers of autocracy in the emerging countries, but not, in my view, of communist autocracy.[1]

Thus communism is only of minor importance in the domestic affairs of the western world, and is unlikely to establish itself in the emerging countries. But this does not close the discussion of doctrinal influences on the international policies of the western world.

[1] The case of Cuba is often cited, but is unconvincing. It is discussed elsewhere in the present study. Broadly speaking, it may be said that Cuba was pushed towards Russia by the actions of the U.S. Government under pressure from anti-communist elements.

For, in Hegelian or Marxian fashion the communist thesis has given rise to its antithesis in the form of anti-communism, which in some parts of the non-communist world has evoked a fanaticism hardly less intense than that of the pioneering communists themselves. In 1924 a credulous public was influenced by the "Zinoviev letter" to dismiss Mr. MacDonald's Government in spite of his masterly handling of German and French questions and the transformation which he and M. Herriot effected in the European outlook. But a more balanced view soon reasserted itself, and anti-communist fanaticism never established itself in Britain. In France there has always been an intransigent element on the extreme right which, since the First World War, has included anti-communism among the political weapons with which it has attempted to influence foreign and colonial policy. In Germany anti-communism was adroitly used in the inter-war period on a humourless and credulous middle or small middle class, which had suffered from inflation, to place in power a fanatical leader of doubtful sanity for whom the destruction of communists and Jews and the subordination of the Slavs were the ultimate aims.

In the interpretation of the international history of the nineteen-thirties it has been alleged that doctrinal anti-communism, however slight its influence on the masses of British and French people may have been, played an important part in the policies of their governments towards Nazi Germany and Fascist Italy. It may, indeed, be agreed that, under Mr. Baldwin and Mr. Neville Chamberlain, British policy, for the first time in many years, no longer adhered to the aim of preserving a balance of power that would prevent the conquest of Europe by any single power or group of powers. This is not to say that Mr. Baldwin or Mr. Chamberlain and their French contemporaries desired any such conquest or would not have resisted it if it had been attempted. Rather, after the assassination of Barthou in 1934, their inaction, their lack of foresight, and the willingness of some of them to rely on verbal assurances from rulers obviously aiming at expansion, led them step by step into weaker and weaker positions from which their successors, with the help of allies, could only extricate them by a costly world war.

This is clear enough, and apologists for these statesmen have failed to affect the verdict. But the role of doctrinal considerations in "appeasement" remains doubtful. Some left-wing critics have maintained that certain British and French political leaders deliberately refrained from resisting German advances in the nineteen-thirties in the hope that Germany would direct her expansion to the East and destroy Russia. The motive was assumed to be doctrinal—the hope of destroying communism. Unfortunately the issue was clouded over with the characteristic exaggerations and embellishments of communist propaganda. The fiction of a scheming anti-Russian " Cliveden set " was invented and obtained considerable currency both at home and abroad.[1] No doubt suspicion of Russian motives was strong, and, in the case of Poland, well founded. A buffer state, lying between two totalitarian states, had only a choice of evils. In such circumstances, doctrinal considerations tend to follow the lead of nationalism : communism had, and, if Russian domination were removed would still have, no hold in Poland, if only because the communist state, as a going concern, originated with Russia, which had always threatened, and for long periods had destroyed, Polish independence. In his otherwise prophetic work, *Democratic Ideals and Reality*, Sir Halford Mackinder had ill-advisedly advocated a group of buffer states between Russia and Germany, allied to the West and ensuring that the Heartland would not be united against the maritime powers. Actually these successors to the Austro-Hungarian Empire were a source of weakness and not of strength to the West—an obstacle to the encirclement of Germany which, after the rise of Hitler, was the only hope of containing her. Nor was there any need for apprehension that, without the buffer states, the Heartland would unite against the rest of the world in the inter-war period. It cannot be supposed that two dictators, ruling two totalitarian states of opposite social doctrines and outlook from the rest of the world, would have agreed to unite their states, one dictator giving way to the other or adopting a secondary role ; or even that they would have trusted one another sufficiently to establish a firm, active alliance, based on combined and concerted operations against the outside world. Moreover, even dictators, with a few exceptions like that of Stalin from 1939 to 1941, cannot ignore public opinion and sentiment so far as to throw *all* doctrinal elements to the wind ; to do so would undermine the doctrinal claims that helped them to power.[2]

When all is said about the role of doctrine in the " appeasement " policy of the nineteen-thirties among western allies, it is difficult to believe that it was a leading cause of the Second World War. The fundamental factor, in broad terms, seems rather to have been the failure of the western powers to adhere to a policy of maintaining the balance of power, and for this the apathy of the public and the loosely pacifist tendencies representing a reaction to the horrifying slaughter of the First World War, together with the incompetence of the leading western statesmen concerned with international affairs during the nineteen-thirties, appear to have been mainly responsible.

[1] Even Mr. Maisky, who is the most objective of the Russian observers, appears in his recent memoirs to give undue credence to this view.
[2] This example illustrates the limitations of political geography when taken by itself in the interpretation of international events.

Even a working alliance with Russia to stop Germany might have been achieved by statesmen of the calibre of Clemenceau, Lloyd George, Barthou, and Winston Churchill.   No analysis of doctrines, social forces, and impersonal underlying changes can exclude the vital role played by the quality of statesmanship in international affairs, and in the nineteen-thirties it seems to have played a leading role in Europe.

These experiences of the inter-war period have had effects on the post-war policies of the West which have not all been beneficial. The old adage that men do not learn from history is ambiguous. They do learn from portrayals of history which are often inaccurate and almost always over-simplified.   Although a radical scepticism towards history would be disastrous, it must be admitted that it may sometimes be better to ignore history rather than adopt a faulty version of it.   In the post-war years, and especially in the nineteen-fifties, an over-simplified version of inter-war history led to dangerous and misleading analogies.   In the United States, reacting against its disastrous attempts to take refuge in neutrality in the nineteen-thirties, " appeasement " became a term of abuse directed indiscriminately against attempts to negotiate and compromise with communist countries.   This attitude overlooked the difference between Hitler and the Russian leaders, the first guided by the doctrines of *Mein Kampf* and the second ready in international affairs to temper doctrine with the interests of the state.   In Britain and France, although the public were little influenced by doctrinal prejudices, Eden and Mollet fell into one of the greatest errors of the post-war period in deciding to invade Egypt.   Eden's memoirs show that he was influenced by analogy with the pre-war " appeasement " of Germany, and Lord Salisbury, who, as Viscount Cranbourne had vigorously opposed the Chamberlain policy, apparently shared this view.   The analogy was faulty : Egypt's armaments were negligible, the strategic value of the Canal in the atomic age was slight, and, as the outcome showed, invasion was not the way to obtain free passage.

II

Influence of Extreme Anti-Communists

Since the Second World War by far the most important doctrinal influence on international policy in the non-communist world has been that of the well-organised and liberally endowed anti-communist groups in the United States which have maintained a continuous pressure on the Governments, on educational institutions, and on sections of the public.   Their aims have been to mobilise support for an anti-Chinese, anti-Russian policy, and for intervention in Latin America and south-eastern Asia, in order to forestall the supposed danger of communism in those areas. In the period when the late Senators Macarran and McCarthy were dominant, laws were enacted, practices were established, old vested interests in anti-communism were strengthened and new ones created, which have survived the passing of their creators and remain as a strong influence blocking the liberalisation of foreign policy. Humiliating inquisitions by committees of the Congress, the compilation of millions of dossiers on individual citizens by the Department of Justice, the intimidation of teachers and professional workers by the " patriotic " organisations, are strange characteristics of a country whose " Statue of Liberty " greets the visitor as his ship moves into harbour, and which is undoubtedly a democratic society.

Yet communism is insignificant in the United States as in most of the western world, and even in most of the less modernised countries. The idea that a handful of American communists could attempt " to overthrow the constitution of the United States by force and violence " is silly.

Extreme anti-communism in the United States has been responsible for the failure of the members of the United Nations to admit the Government of China, for the continued farcical representation of China by a group of *emigrés* who, by Allied connivance, were installed, and by United States arms maintained, as autocratic colonial rulers over the Formosan people ; and for the refusal of the United States, and, through pressure from the United States the refusal of a number of other countries, to extend diplomatic recognition to the Government of China. This policy is supported neither by logic nor by expediency, neither by self-interest nor by any coherent principle or strategy. It is a source of weakness within the western alliance, and of friction with other parts of the non-communist world. The exclusion from the United Nations of the Government of nearly one-quarter of the world's population is an anomaly which may well baffle future generations of students of international affairs who seek to explain it.

But if the refusal of the United States in the last twelve years to recognise the Chinese Government is by far the most important, it is not the only case in which a policy of " non-recognition " has been practised for political reasons. For more than twenty years the Soviet Union had no diplomatic relations with Switzerland.[1] A

---

[1] It was this which led to the establishment of the United Nations in New York instead of in Geneva. The U.N. Committee concerned with the site of the organisation had rejected " Europe " (which would probably have meant Geneva) by one vote early in 1946, the Russians voting with the majority. By the summer the Soviet Union had resumed diplomatic relations with Switzerland and had changed

number of Middle Eastern countries severed relations with France during the Algerian uprising. Japan, under severe pressure from the United States and through fear of losing her trading connections with Formosa, has refused to recognise her powerful neighbour, even though the future of the Far East depends on policies of coexistence between Japan and China. Australia also, contrary to her interests in the Pacific, followed the United States in refusing to recognise China, not from conviction of the wisdom of non-recognition but through fear of offending the United States : her whole policy in Asia was singularly short-sighted and unimaginative, after the departure of Lord Casey. In 1963 decisions were reached at the Addis Ababa conference of African states to commence a drive to expel Portugal and South Africa from the international organisations.

These and other cases of " non-recognition " of *de facto* governments have been, and some of them remain, serious hindrances to the development of international organisation. There is only one solution to this problem, and it is by adopting the simple principle that diplomatic recognition of states, and membership of the international organisations, should be separated completely from doctrinal differences, no matter what is the subject of these differences, no matter whether they are concerned with the nature of the domestic economic, political, or social systems, as with China, or with the practice of racial discrimination in a cultural backwater, as in South Africa, or with high-handed and humourless prohibition of criticisms of the chief of state, and suppression of the parliamentary opposition, as in Ghana. Neither in these nor in any other cases is any useful purpose to be served by the severance of official communication among states, and between states and the international organisation. Such penalties, when they are applied, are applied with gross inequity and with ulterior political motives that go far beyond the professed doctrinal grounds which, with much self-righteousness, are proclaimed as their original justification. Above all, the dangers of a hardening of attitudes, and of ultimate armed conflict, are immeasurably increased when direct official channels of communication are cut off.

" Non-recognition ", and exclusion from the international organisations, are dangerous practices the chief responsibility for which rests with the non-communist countries. The Middle Eastern countries have aggravated the position and some of the new African countries are showing themselves apt pupils of the United States in leading movements for the boycott of certain countries whose

---

its view on the site, being prepared to vote for Geneva. Other vested interests had developed by that time, however, and it was too late to go back on the earlier decision.

internal policies they oppose. Severance of diplomatic relations is an easy gesture to make. Unlike economic sanctions it costs little ; unlike political sanctions it can be used against a stronger power. It is high time for the western world to turn decisively away from it, and the French decision to recognise China in 1964 was a welcome if belated contribution to an important end.

In short, doctrinal fanaticism has not been a monopoly of the communist states, and the non-communist world has allowed its international policies to be hampered at a number of points by doctrinal considerations originating in groups on the extreme right or left.

From diplomatic conflicts let us turn to armed conflicts, and consider how far doctrinal considerations have affected the leading non-communist countries in the conflicts of the post-war period, of which the Korean War was on a much larger scale than any other, after China had been drawn into it. The circumstances which led to the initiative taken by the United States at the outset are reasonably well known. The appropriate divisions and committees in the U.S. Department of State held prolonged meetings to examine the available reports and to consider all their aspects and implications. They then submitted their conclusions and recommendations to the Secretary of State, Mr. Dean Acheson, in another meeting which again covered the ground fully. On the next day Mr. Acheson saw President Truman and presented the recommendations of the Department, which the President accepted. Here was no slapdash, impulsive action, no " talking off the cuff ", after the manner of Mr. Acheson's successor, Mr. John Foster Dulles, who seems to have made little use of the resources of the U.S. Department of State when great matters of state had to be decided.[1]

The decision reached may fairly be said to have been based on the idea of balance of power. Certainly a clash of political doctrines entered into the struggle from the beginning : the partition of Korea made this inevitable, but it might well have arisen in any case, for in pre-war days Korean political refugees spent much time in Russia and China. But the central consideration was that which had governed struggles over Korea for centuries—the strategic importance of the peninsula to the surrounding countries and sometimes to their more distant backers. Japan had indeed been reduced at this time to a satellite of the United States, but, in the first phase of the struggle at least, the action taken by the United States, and endorsed by the United Nations, was in accord with Japan's interest in forestalling Russian domination of Korea.

---

[1] This of course still leaves open the question how reliable were the reports coming to Washington regarding the situation at the frontier and the presumed intentions of North and South Korean forces respectively.

The position changed in the second stage of the Korean War, when China was drawn in. It seems probable that this stage would never have been reached if the armies of the United Nations had been content to drive the North Korean forces across the border and to leave it at that. The Indian Ambassador to China, the Sardar Panikkar, cabled to London and Stockholm, and his message was relayed to Washington, that the Chinese Foreign Minister had informed him that if the advance of the forces under General Macarthur continued towards the border, China would consider that her interests were threatened at a strategic point and could not remain indifferent.[1] This clear warning, if heeded, might and in all probability would have kept China out of the war. But the former President tells us in his memoirs [2] that the Sardar's warning was set aside on the ground that " he had played the game of the communists ". This flippant characterisation of a conservative Indian nationalist might be excusable if it came from " the man in the street " : it had tragic consequences when it represented the view of the head of state in the most powerful country in the world.[3]

The entry of China into the Korean War was thus in all probability a preventable disaster, ultimately due to doctrinal influences. As it was, it strengthened the forces of fanatical anti-communism, and prolonged the system of make-believe that shaped ideas about China in the United States. Thus, when the smouldering conflict in the Indo-Chinese peninsula flared up into serious local warfare, sentiment in some quarters in the United States came dangerously near to supporting large-scale intervention even at the risk of general war. A strong doctrinal element lay behind this sentiment.

III

Intermingling of Doctrines and Balance of Power

However, in examining the events of 1954 in south-eastern Asia, it is harder even than usual to draw a line between doctrinal influences and considerations of balance of power. The Second World War

---

[1] K. M. Panikkar, *The Two Chinas : Memoirs of a Diplomat*, London, 1955, Ch. IX.

[2] *Memoirs by Harry Truman, II*, p. 383. Further blunders were General Macarthur's insistence on using U.S. troops to advance towards the Yalu and Washington's ineffective attempts to control the General. But the responsibility for accepting the aims to reunite Korea by force of arms must be shared by the Allies. See esp. J. W. Spanier, *The Truman-Macarthur controversy and the Korean War*, Harvard Univ. Press, 1959—a competent and judicious account.

[3] If the United States had recognised China, this warning might have come from its own representative, and would then have been given more weight.

ad overturned the pre-existing balance of power in south-eastern
Asia, and the process of forming a new balance was still incomplete.
The movement of which Ho-chi-minh had emerged as the leader
was spreading southwards. To the doctrinaire anti-communist this
appeared as a rising tide, or, to use an analogy more appropriate in
a geographical sense, a torrent descending from the hills and threat-
ning to sweep all before it to the sea, leaving behind a large new
ccession to the communist world. To military circles in the
United States it appeared as a strategic threat to the interests and
he influence of the western powers in eastern and south-eastern Asia,
outflanking the lines of their sea and air communications across the
world, and endangering the links between different parts of the non-
ommunist world. If an attempt is made to express it in terms of
olitical geography, it might be said, with great oversimplification,
hat it represented an outward thrust from the Heartland, aimed at
reaking through and dominating the powers of the maritime fringe
n south-eastern Asia, thus extending the process which began when
he Soviet Union overran the Baltic states, which continued with the
xtension of its coastline at the expense of Poland, together with the
eduction of Poland to the status of a satellite, and which on the
ther side of Eurasia, was capped by the accession of China to the
ommunist world, linking the Heartland with the entire shore of
astern Asia, and abruptly expelling all traces of western power and
nfluence from this extensive portion of the maritime fringe of Eur-
sia. If the shores of the whole Indo-Chinese peninsula were to be
rought within the same control, the western maritime powers
would, it seemed, be in danger of losing all vestiges of influence and
ower on the mainland of Asia east of Singapore.

This way of looking at the matter, like most schemes that take
heir clue from Mackinder, is useful and suggestive within limits.
ts weaknesses, however, are serious, and arise out of ambiguities
nd implicit abstractions in the schemes of Mackinder himself, who
eft unanalysed the differences between the forms and methods of
hat unification of the Heartland which, he believed, would bring
world conquest in sight.

Unification might come either by conquest, or by voluntary fusion
nder a single government, or by a close alliance of governments by
reaty the terms of which bound them to a common external policy.
When the countries were already large, as Russia and Germany
were, conquest of one by the other was unlikely to create such a sense
f unity as would enable the conqueror to undertake further aggres-
ve action in the immediate future : the danger of uprising in the
vent of a setback was great. Voluntary fusion requires long pre-
aration and specially favourable conditions which never existed in
he case of Russia and Germany, and which do not exist now and are

unlikely to emerge in the near future in the case of Russia and China. The habits, the customs, the social heritage, the standards of living of the peoples in question are widely divergent and immense adjustments would have to be made if they were to be brought into one fold, under one shepherd.

This leaves only that degree of unification which can be attained by close co-operation, including the pursuit of a common foreign policy. To some observers this once seemed a genuine possibility in the case of Russia and Germany. It now seems wholly ruled out by the overwhelming evidence of the unpopularity of Russia among the German people. Even if Germany had not been partitioned, German sentiment and opinion would have been in closer harmony with its western than with its eastern neighbours.

The analogy between this case and that of Russia and China is not close. The " cultural " differences between Russia and China are far greater than those between Russia and Germany. So also are the differences in economic conditions and in economic power. On the other hand, political creeds and the internal political and economic systems are, in principle at least, similar in Russia and China. When we turn from principles to practice we find [1] the divergencies between the two countries so wide that fusion appears inconceivable. A considerable common element remains in foreign policy, based on a wide area of common interests which have been strengthened through the policy of the United States towards China. But divergencies of interest between Russia and China had already appeared in 1954 in south-eastern Asia, and since then rivalries between Russia and China in respect to their activities in Asian, African, and tropical Latin American countries have rapidly grown. It seems clear also that the communists of North Viet-nam, under Ho-chi-minh, have not always seen eye to eye with either China or Russia.

Thus the conversion of China to the communist faith did not effectively bring the power in the Heartland to the coasts of eastern and south-eastern Asia. The countries of south-eastern Asia will remain subject to pressures and rivalries from outside which will include rivalries within the communist world as well as those between communist and non-communist countries. Russia and China each desires to call the tune in south-eastern Asia and neither is likely to give way completely to the other. Russia claims pre-eminence in the communist world, ostensibly on the ground of its longer experience. But it would be contrary to Chinese traditions to acknowledge that China would accept indefinitely the predominance of Russia in practice. Rivalry exists, and will continue, between Russia and China, in respect to the control of communist parties and groups in south-eastern Asia. And since, on the other side of the Heartland

[1] Chapter I, pp. 17-21.

Poland and East Germany are reluctant satellites, it is clear that communism did not bring unification to the Heartland and is unlikely to create it in the future. As we concluded in the preceding chapter, the communist, like the non-communist, world is a nationalist world, with its own balance of power underlying the structure of the world balance of power.

The events of 1954 in the Indo-Chinese peninsula, therefore, are broadly explicable in terms of balance of power, not so much the maintenance of an old structure of power as the establishment of a new one to replace that which the War had irreparably damaged. But doctrinal considerations, both communism and fanatical forms of anti-communism, complicated the struggle over balance of power and gave it at times a more dangerous turn. It was to the lasting credit of Sir Anthony Eden and M. Pierre Mendès-France that doctrinal elements were subordinated to considerations of balance of power in 1954, and compromises were made which gave none of the interests concerned all that it wanted, but brought hostilities to an end and created a framework in which, if the outside powers had acted in good faith, the small states could have ordered their own affairs.

Unfortunately, these conditions were not fulfilled. The rivalries of the Great Powers reopened external interference. Communists within the Pathet Lao tried by intrigue to extend their influence. On the opposite wing, the United States, whose emissaries had worked their way, apparently in violation of the terms of the 1954 settlement, into positions formerly oocupied by France but which the French Government showed no interest in maintaining even to the extent permitted by the settlement. Movements encouraged by the United States military, aided by the U.S. Central Intelligence Agency, led to the fall of the government of Prince Souvanna Phouma, the only statesman capable of forming a government of ' coexistence "—the single alternative, in the conditions of the time, to fratricidal strife. Then followed a military dictatorship of the right, supported by American arms and subsidies. In this move the United States appears to have been influenced by an extremely simple idea of military strategy based on the assumption if Laos were not held as a potential military outpost of the United States it would fall to " communism ", and the West would be eliminated from south-eastern Asia.

The marked influence of military circles on the international policy of the United States after the outbreak of the Korean War inevitably created a division within the West on a number of important issues. At no time in history has the military mind been capable of grasping the subtleties of world politics. It is trained in a particular direction, and, although a few individuals can rise above their class outlook, military staffs and departments collectively cannot do so. No peoples in the world are less suitable objects of the simple patterns of military thought that prevail within the cloisters of the vast Pentagon building than the peoples of the Orient are. To make matters worse, the British and French Governments, although well aware of the dangers of the policy which the United States was following, failed to take a strong line against it as by the treaty they were entitled to take. In this period, British policy suffered from lack of informed criticism in Parliament, owing to a split in the Opposition over the British position with respect to the atomic bomb. France was so preoccupied with Algeria and the acute domestic issues which it aroused that she was equally ineffective, even though well informed on the dangers. Thus, through mistakes on one side of the Atlantic and negligence on the other, the fruits of the settlement in 1954 were thrown away and south-eastern Asia drifted again towards political disaster. At last Britain and France began to assert themselves, and President Kennedy, after taking office, with the help of Mr. Macnamara, took steps to bring the military and the " Intelligence " Agency under control. The competition within the communist world, together with the reluctance of local elements on the political left to forgo tactical advantages, created great difficulties for Prince Souvanna Phouma in his efforts to restore a balance that should never have been disrupted. No lesson seems harder for the leading western powers to learn than that ill-judged and simple-minded forms of " anti-communism " have presented gratuitous gains to Russia and China in the international manoeuvres over the balance of political power in the post-war world.

It is one of the ironies of the history of international relations in the post-war period that one of the chief architects of the settlement reached in Geneva in 1954 over Indo-China should himself, only two years later, have fallen into an error of political judgement second only to that which brought China into the Korean War. Sir Anthony Eden had rendered important services in international affairs during and immediately after the war in Indo-China—he had shown flexibility where flexibility was needed, as well as firmness where firmness alone was appropriate. He had been fertile in improvisation when difficulties over details impeded negotiations. Yet all these qualities left him in 1956.

It must be admitted that he had great provocation. From the beginning Mr. Dulles had vacillated. After rashly undertaking to support the Aswan Dam in the belief that, if the United States did not, Russia would, and in this way " bring communism into the Middle East ", he suddenly withdrew support in a manner which humiliated Egypt. The nationalisation of the Suez Canal Company was a direct riposte, and Mr. Dulles floundered ineffectively from one expedient to another until the British and French statesmen despaired of any concerted action.

But in international affairs a false step remains a false step, regardless of the nature and amount of provocation that preceded it. The resort to arms was a disaster from every point of view. It appeared in the eyes of the world, as in fact it was, an attack by two great powers on a small power which had only recently gained its independence. Granted that Egypt had broken international engagements ; other and stronger powers had also acted in arbitrary ways, and it had not been proposed that force should be used against them. Worse still, the attack on Egypt had been made to coincide with another by Israel ; and hostility to Israel—which was, and still is, regarded by Arabs as an " outpost of western imperialism "—was the chief issue on which all the Arab states were united. To Arabs throughout the Middle East it seemed as if Britain and France were attempting to reimpose an inferior status on a leading Arab country. In the post-war world there is no more delicate or more imporant task before western diplomacy than that of assuaging the resentments created by the inferior international status of most Asian, African, and tropical Latin American peoples in the past. British and French aggression over Suez offended against every canon of wise diplomacy in this sphere of international relations.

The attacks of the Opposition on the Government, the defections in the Conservative Party, even though only in the junior ministerial ranks, and the realisation that, for the most part, the permanent officials of the Foreign Office and of British missions to the Middle Eastern countries, had been opposed to the aggression, helped to qualify and soften the adverse effect on world opinion, and in the longer run it appears that the outcome of the affair was to hasten the process of psychological decolonisation among the British people which is an essential part of the adjustment to the revolution in international relations. Another less favourable outcome was the strengthening of the internal hold on Egypt of the " young army officers ", with Colonel Nasir at their head, who had replaced a dynastic régime by a military régime that blocked the growth of representative government even more effectively than the former had done.

Inconsistencies never cease in international affairs. By the time the breach among the western powers over British and French aggression in Egypt had healed, another breach was opened by the aggression of the United States in Cuba. Actually, this had already been foreshadowed in Guatemala, when the intrigues of United States agents against the government of President Arbenz, in violation of international diplomatic privileges, had overthrown the legitimate régime and substituted for it a puppet régime of the United States. Unfortunately, Britain and France, while not approving of this act, failed to oppose it publicly, and the military and "intelligence" agency which was behind the subversive activities was encouraged to carry them further. When a genuine revolution occurred in Cuba, and the new régime adopted policies disconcerting to the conservative American mind, and to the powerful business interests with Cuban properties, it was not long before the same processes of intrigue which had succeeded in their object in Guatemala were set in motion in respect to Cuba. This time, however, the new régime strongly entrenched itself at home and intrigue had to be centred mainly on *emigrés* abroad. There was a reversion to the characteristic forms of United States imperialism in and before the first two decades of the present century. Again, while the British and French governments disapproved of this aggression, they failed to take a public stand against it, such as the United States, in co-operation with Russia and other countries, had done at the time of the Suez affair, against British and French aggression. Fortunately, a number of private British and French observers wrote a high order of journalism on the subject and educated their public in the realities of Latin American developments.[1]

The aggression against Cuba stopped short of the aggression against Egypt. For this it seems that President Kennedy was responsible. It was all the more disturbing therefore that the greater restraint shown by President Kennedy than by Sir Anthony Eden was not matched by the American public or by the "opposition" party. In sharp contrast to the Labour and Liberal opposition and a large section of the British public over Suez, the Republican Party in the United States, and an overwhelming majority of the public, was critical of President Kennedy, not for lending himself to the aggression but for not carrying it much further !

The result was that intrigues against Cuban independence continued under the shelter of the United States, and the U.S. Government employed high-handed methods to gain an economic stranglehold over Cuba by boycott, and by pressure on countries trading with Cuba. Britain and other western European countries—except West Germany—refused to join in this, but they failed to take action in the United Nations with respect to the violation of international law by the actions of the United States. All this illustrated the primitive stage of development of the international community, particularly the existence in practice of one law for the rich and another for the poor states of the world. It was left to the Soviet Union, acting from motives of self-interest, to speak for the rights of a small

---

[1] A notable service was rendered by correspondents of *Le Monde* who visited Latin America.

country and to give economic assistance to Cuba. The whole episode was a grave setback to the growth of the rule of law in international affairs, on which the future of the world depends.

The sensational events in the autumn of 1962 strikingly demonstrated the dangers of neglecting abuses of power by great powers. The failure to grapple with the Cuban issue in the United Nations, in contrast to the prompt action over British and French aggression at Suez, might easily have led to world disaster, and but for the restraint shown by Mr. Khruschev in the hour of crisis, contrasting with his earlier dangerous interventions, it would have done so. His restraint was influenced partly by a realisation of the suicidal nature of a war but probably also by an evaluation of the comparative importance of the conflict over Cuba and that over China and her aims.

It remains to consider the respective roles of political doctrines and of balance of power in the genesis of the Suez, Guatemala, and Cuba incidents. Undoubtedly, doctrinaire anti-communism in the United States played a large part both in the initial offer and in the abrupt withdrawal of United States aid for the Aswan Dam which set off the train of events leading to Suez. With respect to Sir Anthony Eden's actions, the case is less clear-cut. The analogy of " appeasement " in the nineteen-thirties seems to have been uppermost in his mind. The unreliability of Colonel Nasir's word had already been demonstrated. Actually, of course the analogy with Hitler was misplaced. Germany had been a strong power threatening the existence of Britain : Egypt was a weak and struggling country which could only administer pinpricks abroad. If Sir Anthony did not grasp this, the rest of the world did. But Sir Anthony was misled into an exaggeration of Egyptian power : he believed, perhaps on expert advice, that the Canal was a life-line to Britain and control of it the only means to safeguard Britain's oil supplies. Subsequent events disproved this view but others besides Sir Anthony had held it. Thus it seems justifiable to conclude, that, although in the controversies that followed Sir Anthony stressed the dangers of Russian communism, he was influenced mainly by ideas of the balance of power.

It would be misleading to infer that the Cuban affair was a simple case of economic imperialism. The possibility would first have to be considered that the professional anti-communist organisations may have instigated and transferred the financial aid to *emigré* plotters, to say nothing of the role of the government's " intelligence " agency. Indeed, recent United States imperialism in Latin America seems to have its origin more in exaggerated fears of communism than in the activities of profit-seeking capitalists. It does not follow that the role of the latter is negligible, for there is no doubt that some business profits go to finance activities of the extreme right-wing organisations. The political and the economic are never wholly disconnected. But the initiative appears to have come more from anti-communists inspired by doctrinal zeal rather than from organised economic interests, and some of the contributions of business concerns appear to be given to avoid offending the " patriotic " zealots rather than out of an ardent faith in their aims and methods.[1]

The representatives in the legislature and the " patriotic " organisations are inspired by a militant mood against left-wing doctrines, but the executive, which is better informed about the outside world, is influenced more by fears of the spread of communist doctrines in Latin America, to the detriment of U.S. interests.

Thus the influence of doctrines did not replace the influence of balance of power : they distorted its application to concrete situations. Both the United States and Russia were using Cuba to serve their rivalries with one another. The Cuban leader, hard-pressed by the aggressive measures taken against him by the United States, and failing to obtain protection through the United Nations, forsook the policy of non-alignment which would have brought him the support of the Afro-Asian world. The Russian leader tried to turn this to account and shift the balance of power slightly in his favour. The doctrinal element in the struggle aroused the highly conservative U.S. public to a dangerous degree.

The differences between the United States and the other western countries, arising out of the political strength of the extreme right in the former, constitute a serious weakness in the North Atlantic Alliance which will not easily be remedied, and which will be discussed in later chapters.

In the continental western [2] European countries, as in Britain, doctrinal fanaticism appears to play only a negligible role in the international outlook of the government and the majority of the peoples. " La droite " in France is an exception, but their spirit of reaction goes much wider and they are often preoccupied with domestic political feuds. The devotees of " Algérie française " were influenced by fear of the Moslem population rather than fear of communism.

The smaller European countries are also primarily interested in the maintenance of a balance of power which alone ensures their survival as independent states. They have not all followed the same policy : their geographical positions and their traditions differ. Neutrality for Switzerland has been a long-standing tradition that could only be broken if a direct attack were made from outside, such as, for example, Germany planned to make if the Maginot line had held firm. So far, Swiss neutrality has been accepted by other

---

[1] I found a number of examples of this when living in the U.S. during part of the witch-hunt.

[2] Of course Portugal and Spain are not included in this category.

powers as being in the best interests of the world, and a beacon light of civilisation and humanity in the midst of the confusion and carnage of two World Wars. The neutrality of Finland and Sweden are related to geographical position. Countries on the borders of " super-powers ", like Finland, Sweden, Mexico, and Cuba, always have to take account of the dangers of imperialist encroachment from their towering neighbours.

This kind of neutrality is legal and " practical " rather than doctrinal. Thus the Swedish press is often more critical of Russia than the British press is, the Swiss Government sharper in its attitude to Russia than the British and French Governments are. There is no doctrinal neutrality in the neutral European countries, and no ambiguity or verbal juggling in their attachment to representative government. The essence of their neutrality is abstention from alliances and international political commitments other than those involved in membership of the United Nations.[1] It raises difficulties in the way of European economic unity, but methods have already been found of surmounting some of them. The stubbornness of West Germany over accommodation with Russia is concerned with historic questions of unity and with fear of powerful neighbours rather than with doctrines.

Thus it may be said that the fundamental differences among the powers in the post-war years have been primarily concerned with the problems of reaching a new balance of power in the world, and particularly in Europe and the Far East to replace the uneasy and crumbling balance of the decade before the War. Doctrinal cleavages have not displaced balance of power criteria, but they have aggravated and embittered international relations and increased the dangers of conflict.

Other causes of divergence within the non-communist world come more appropriately into the discussion of the non-communist countries that lie outside Europe and its overseas offshoots. To these let us now turn.

---

[1] Switzerland is not even a member of the United Nations.

CHAPTER III

MORALITY AND INTERNATIONAL RELATIONS

THE very idea of the pursuit of balance of power has often been regarded, not only by public opinion but also by several eminent statesmen, as immoral and discreditable. Others regard the pursuit of balance of power by each state as the only principle on which international relations can be soundly based. This controversy raises the broader question of the role of morality in international relations, and sooner or later an analysis of this question is indispensable to the main thesis of the present study.

International relations have always aroused strong passions, antipathies, and antagonisms. This is hardly surprising, since they comprise not only clashes of interests between evenly matched powers strong in armaments, but also the relations of the strong with the weak, of the more highly developed with the less highly developed peoples. Inevitably, moral questions have arisen and moral issues have been and still are hotly debated. Even when there was little or no political consciousness among native peoples, the moral sense of a number of outstanding personalities in the colonial or imperial countries themselves was aroused over the problems created by the impact of the peoples of European origin and their economic activities on the technically much less advanced native peoples. Las Casas, the Abbé Reynal, Philip in Cape Colony, the Quakers in North America, and many others approached these issues in terms of morality as well as of expediency.

Some scholars wish to make the study of international relations into a science from which ethics and morality are excluded except for the purely descriptive recording of moral influences that may have affected the course of events. The historian of international affairs should, they claim, refrain from moral judgements and adhere to a position of ethical neutrality.

On the other hand, in actual practice moral judgements are indulged in more freely than ever before in popular discussions of international affairs, and even government spokesmen for some countries have struck a moral note in many diplomatic exchanges. This tendency has been most pronounced in the United States, where, however, a few professional students of international affairs have sharply reacted against it, introducing a new adjective, "moralistic" in place of "moral", as a target for attack. But these critics, although they started on the right track, have usually

failed to clarify the general problem of the role of morality in international affairs, and have sometimes left an impression with careless
readers that they consider morality irrelevant to international affairs.

Occasional philosophers from the time of Machiavelli to the
present day have postulated a state in which power was to be exercised without any other check than that which comes of an estimate
of the strength of rival states ; in which every chance of successful
aggrandisement was taken, regardless of previous treaties and formal
agreements that might have stood in the way ; in which the end was
the expansion and glorification of the state, and all means that contributed to it were properly used without scruple. This can be
regarded either as an amoral view, based on the belief that morality
has no place in international affairs ; or as a particular form of
morality which separates the conduct of statesmen from the considerations that apply to individual human beings in their personal
relations with one another, holding that in international relations
that which seems to the statesman to contribute most to the aggrandisement of his state receives its own natural justification. It might
be summarised by taking the famous sentence, " In those days there
was no king in Israel, and every man did that which was right in his
own eyes ", and replacing " king in Israel " by " international
authority ", and " man " by " state ".

Many of the confusions in this theory have been exposed and there
is no need to work over them again. For present purposes it should
be noticed that its supporters have presupposed states governed by
despots. The Prince in Machiavelli's work was presumed in the
main to exercise a free hand in the conduct of external affairs.
Given this assumption, it is easy to slip into the habit of personifying
the " state ", giving it a life of its own, and treating relations between
states as relations between personal entities. But this creates a
dilemma. Morality is inseparable from personal relations, and in
the Christian era the moral sense in this sphere could never be
accommodated to the aims of arbitrary despotic power. Hence the
attempt to create a special morality for the relations between states.

This approach is an artificial one, poorly related to international
life in the twentieth century. A more accurate analysis lies in a quite
different direction. The " state " is an abstraction, not a being
endowed with personality. But the actions of statesmen are actions
of individuals who are not exempt from moral responsibility. The
real difference between the responsibilities of statesmen in personal
and those in public life are to be found in the different degrees of
choice open to them. In his private life the statesman has a wider
liberty of action and range of choices ; he may sometimes choose to
incur risks in the knowledge that only he would lose in the event of
failure. In his public life his responsibilities extend to all those on

whose behalf he is considered to be acting. This is seen most clearly in societies with representative forms of government, but is not confined to them : authoritarian rulers themselves claim in external matters to act on behalf of their peoples. When the ruled believe that the ruler in his international dealings is failing to act on their behalf and in their interests, under representative government they will dismiss him, unless they consider that his merits in domestic matters outweigh his failings in international matters. Under autocratic government the ruler may survive much longer when he follows courses abroad that do not commend themselves to mass sentiment at home. But he ignores such sentiment only at his peril, and it is a complete illusion to suppose that autocratic rulers can act indefinitely without restraint from and concessions to the public.

Thus, the international historian and the student of politics who examine the past actions of statesmen need not adopt a strained and unnatural pose of ethical neutrality. The statesman cannot claim exemption from moral obligations, either in his private or in his public life. But there is a duty on those who analyse his actions in retrospect to consider all the possibilities of action that were open to him at the time of each act. In the practice of diplomacy, responsibilities are unlimited and constraints often crushing. At times there is no satisfactory course open to the statesman. At home he may be precluded by public sentiment from making the drastic changes and readjustments which, on a more far-sighted view, would best serve the interest of his own and other peoples. Abroad he may be blocked by a legacy of past errors which have aroused such opposition and suspicion that unstable short-run compromises are all that can be obtained. Again, the growth of new and unforeseen forces in the world may so limit the alternatives open to him that he is forced into apparent inconsistencies between past and present actions. Thus, the statesman, whether in a democratic or an authoritarian state, is less free than is commonly supposed by those who have had no practical experience of international affairs.

The idea of morality has meaning only in relation to individual persons. The " state " or the " nation " is not a person and can, therefore, be neither moral nor immoral. But in the name of the state acts are committed, on some of which moral judgements are commonly passed. Such acts are not beyond the reach of moral considerations, since, in the last resort, they are the result of decisions reached by individual persons, singly or in concert.

But acts committed in the name of the state in international affairs are not always traced back easily to their sources. Under individual despotisms the source may be obvious ; under representative government it is often very difficult to specify it precisely. There are many types of authoritarian and of representative govern-

ment, and even the former cannot ignore public opinion and sentiment completely. Thus, statesmen often excuse themselves privately
or in retrospect for questionable actions by stressing the force of
opinion behind them which limited their scope for action and prevented them from adopting the most enlightened course of action.
When these excuses are genuine the attempt to assess responsibilities
leads beyond the immediate actors, perhaps to leaders of political
parties, government or opposition or both, who themselves can
claim equally that they are circumscribed by forces below them. So
the search goes on, perhaps leading to some form of mass sentiment
and opinion. If it be asked, then, what contributes to this sentiment
and opinion ; today the press, the radio, perhaps television, are
sometimes cited. The quest may end in some vague *collectivité*
within which it is difficult or impossible to assess individual responsibilities closely. The social psychology of different peoples
varies widely, and that of the same peoples changes from time to
time. It is extraordinarily difficult to define these differences in
national psychology, but no-one who has lived in a number of different countries in recent decades can doubt their continued existence, their importance in international affairs, and the constraints
which they place on the actions of statesmen.

It is this chain of responsibility, passing from the statesman to the
collectivité, that occasionally leads to the demand that a whole nation
should be held responsible for certain deeds committed by its government or its representatives. This demand is sometimes made even
when the country in question has been governed by a dictator : it
then rests on the assumption that all the people were responsible for
allowing the dictator to establish dominion over them.

The attempt to assess responsibilities in this way for international
acts regarded as aggressive and immoral cannot, in my opinion, be
sustained. It does, indeed, contain one valid element. When,
through apathy, cowardice, or sectional interests, many of those who
could have arrested a dictator's rise to power fail to take action in
time, they can fairly be said to share the responsibility for subsequent
international outrages committed at his instigation. There can be
little doubt that a surprisingly large proportion of the German
people willingly acquiesced in the policies of the Hitler régime. But
this gives no basis for later redress. It is impossible to assess such
general responsibilities among the large number who shared them,
but who are extremely difficult to identify as individuals. It is one
thing to bring individuals to justice for committing specific crimes,
either directly or through instructions to others ; it is another to
inflict penalties indiscriminately on a whole community for the
mainly passive acquiescence of an imperfectly informed majority in
the uncivilised actions of an autocratic régime. More important

still, there are inherent difficulties in any attempt objectively to assess motives and opportunities in such matters. Again, it cannot be shown how many people have had any opportunity to influence political events during the rise of an aggressive régime to power, even if—which is not always the case—they had realised the probable course of events. You cannot indict the dustman, the electrician, the shop assistant, for failing to intervene, for example, by staging mob riots. Skilled organisation and an unusual lull in the vigilance of the authorities are necessary conditions before there is any chance to " go out on the street " effectively. Finally, the dictator's road to power is crooked, and over long stretches of it he may pose as a supporter of democracy, and sometimes even of parliamentary government, against the real or alleged autocratic tendencies of the existing or previous régime. It takes a discerning public to see through such pretensions, especially in an age in which, following Lenin's advice, the dictators of the left, dutifully imitated by those of the right, deliberately confuse—often invert—the previously accepted meanings of political terms, in order to blunt their older appeal and steal, if possible, the emotions they arouse, transferring them by deception from the central parts to one of the extremities of the political spectrum. All these things add to the general political confusion of our age and leave the individual without stable points of political reference by which he can take bearings, determine his position, and estimate where the divergent currents around him are likely to lead.[1]

Let us return to the statesmen who held the posts of responsibility when international acts were committed for which it is argued that the people were responsible. How far can the statesman's claim that his powers were limited in face of pressures from below be accepted ? It can always be claimed that he should have resigned his position rather than agree to the act in question. But in reply it can sometimes be argued that if he had resigned a successor would have been appointed who would have supported still more extreme measures. When is the right time to resign ? Anthony Eden (now Lord Avon), Viscount Cranbourne (now Lord Salisbury), and the late Duff Cooper resigned in protest against aspects of Neville Chamberlain's policy. After the outbreak of the Manchurian aggression Baron Shidehara remained for a time as Japanese Foreign Minister in 1931, trying to curtail the Japanese military authorities. Japanese statesmen generally tended to stay in their posts as long as they believed they were of service to the state, even if this meant remain-

---

[1] Some of this seems obvious, but the idea of collective responsibility has been so persistently held and attempts have so often been made to apply it in practice, that a patient analysis of its elements seems to be the only way to place it in perspective.

ing while policies they privately opposed were in force. So long as their presence checked the fullest application of the policy forced on them they felt—rightly, if my observations in Japan at the time were correct—that it was better for the country that they should remain, even if they lost their reputations among liberal groups. Statesmen bear moral responsibilities for their international acts, but the ability of outside observers to assess these responsibilities accurately is limited. The statesman is always obliged to act with only a speculative know-ledge of the consequences of his actions, and what, in retrospect, may be judged reprehensible, in prospect may have appeared in a modified light.

Summing up, it may be said that moral responsibilities for inter-national actions taken in the name and by the representatives of the state are so diffused over many agents, and the motives of many of the agents are so obscure, and so intermingled with anticipations, frequently faulty, of the consequences of their actions, that the full assessment of the responsibilities is beyond human capacity. The trials of " war criminals " after the Second World War, and especi-ally those of Japanese statesmen and army officers, flouted the canons of justice—since the prosecutors and judges were of the same camp—and created a dangerous precedent for the identification of military victory with the right and the good, a return to the super-stition of trial by combat.

This conclusion in no sense implies that morality is irrelevant in international affairs, or that the " state " is " beyond morality " in the sense that acts committed in its name and by its representatives are self-justifying. The philosophies which have attempted to represent political states as super-entities acquiring a sort of personal-ity of their own, exempt from the moral considerations that apply to human personalities, may have supplied useful apologetics for aggressive and ambitious statesmen and dictators, but at best the object they try to create is an idol which attracts only superstitious veneration—a perversion of nationalism and a source of fratricidal strife within the human race.

Thus international relations cannot in any sense be divorced from morals and ethics. They are concerned, not with the morals of any abstract super-entity, but rather with those of many individual actors, each limited in the scope of action open to him and in his understanding of the nature of the forces with which he is dealing, and, in much more difficult and at times obscure ways, with the inaction of those who might have acted if they had so willed.

It follows that there is no valid basis to support either those who argue that international relations is a scientific, non-moral subject of study, or those who, at the opposite extreme, would use it to frame indictments of whole peoples or of whole classes on moral grounds.

Both Machiavellian [1] cynicism and " moralistic " indignation are out of touch with the realities of international life.

At the present time " moral indignation " against colonialism has reached an extraordinary height, particularly in Africa and Asia. It has become a potent political force, and essentially a negative force. It is based largely on distortions of history and damages relations between countries which, in a more objective view, have many common interests in the present and will have still more in the future. Paradoxically, the end of the colonial relationship leaves the former colonies in greater need than ever of international interchange— economic, technical, cultural—with the former colonial powers, this time on a basis of political equality. The ritual outpourings of moral indignation against colonialism, fostered by Russia and China to serve what they conceive to be their own national interest, encourage the masses to look backwards in anger instead of forwards in hope and determination. But indiscriminate anti-imperialism and anti-colonialism cannot be met effectively on their own ground. Attempts to set up a defence on the same plane as the attack lead to endless recrimination. For as a corollary of the preceding analysis it is clear that the attack is based essentially on the mythical assumption of states with collective personalities of indefinite lifetime. The realities are quite different. Imperialistic expansion, leading to conquest and absorption or to colonisation, has been the result of the decisions and actions of numerous individual personalities, influenced by a variety of motives. We can only unravel these gradually by laborious historical research. The great majority of the individuals concerned are beyond the reach of either moral indignation or commendation coming from the present generation. Their successors were presented with *faits accomplis*, and had to make decisions of a different nature.

If we approach the subject from this point of view we shall find no ready-made collective targets for the " righteous indignation " of " anti-imperialists " and " anti-colonialists ". Neither shall we find any figures in white array around which the apologists for imperial expansion and colonisation can throw a protecting screen. The realities are far more complicated and inconclusive, more suited to be the objects of investigation and analysis, rather than those of passion and invective or praise.

---

[1] I refer to the Machiavelli of *The Prince*, not of the *Discourses*. In the latter he appears to share the concern for liberty on which the present study is based.

PART II

INTERNATIONAL RELATIONS AND THE WORLD-WIDE SPREAD OF POLITICAL CONSCIOUSNESS

CHAPTER IV

CHANGING POLITICAL GEOGRAPHY

I

General Characteristics of Recent Changes

THE preceding analysis of the roles of political doctrines and of balance of power in the communist countries and in the western countries of the non-communist world leads to a decisive rejection of the idea, held most widely and tenaciously in the United States on one side, and Russia and China on the other, that the central issue in international affairs today consists in a struggle between communism and non-communism. The non-communist world is described and interpreted in many ways. Doctrinaire communists call it a system of " capitalism " or " monopoly capitalism ". Some western spokesmen call it " the free world ", others " the free " or " the private enterprise system " : others make a rough separation between the economic and the political, finding the fundamental cleavage between the communist and non-communist worlds in matters of political rather than economic freedom. I have preferred to adhere to the term " non-communist " world, because I can find no such homogeneity in it as exists in the communist world, which, for all its internal quarrels over interpretations and its practical divergencies, possesses a recognisable unity in doctrines and in a considerable range of practice. The rest of the world has no such doctrinal unity, and in my view it is out of the diversity of the non-communist world that the most important changes in international affairs are now developing which will revolutionise the international scene in the near future, cutting across and to a considerable extent overshadowing the cleavage between East and West.

The revolution has its conservative side. It is concerned largely with a change in the scope, rather than in the nature, of the forces that shape international relations ; with a revolutionary geographical extension, which has already begun, and will go much further, of the system of balance of power, taking in the countries of every continent instead of being dominated overwhelmingly by a few large countries of northern Eurasia and North America. The countries of western, southern, and south-eastern Asia, central and south America, and Africa, will increasingly assert their independence, no longer content to be grouped formally or tacitly behind the older large powers. The balance of power will be more geographically dispersed, the political manoeuvring within the United Nations more complicated, with groupings and re-groupings that will cross the conventional lines of the past and shift with new changes in the distribution of power. There will be not two, but a number, of " blocs ", probably held together more loosely than those in the past. All this will constitute a revolutionary shift in scope and scale.

The second aspect of the revolution is a wider, though not a complete, break in principle with the past. It is concerned with the nature of power. Some readers may have been disposed to challenge what I have written of the wide changes in the balance of power. It is true, they will admit, that a large number of independent countries are being added to the world of states, but how much power do they really have ? The revolution in armaments has placed them more than ever at the mercy of the Great Powers, notably, Russia and the United States. The U.S.—Russian clash over Cuba in the autumn of 1962 may seem to have reinforced that view. Indeed, the extreme right, citing also the experience of India with China, has revived the contention that the lesser powers should group themselves behind the super-powers, rather than gamble that the rivalries of the Great Powers will indirectly protect them by making each Great Power fear to take aggressive action against small powers lest it bring another Great Power into a nuclear war to prevent a territorial change from disturbing the balance of power.

Variants of the argument had a considerable and, as I think, a dangerous influence on international policy for some years after the Second World War. Following the U.S.—Cuban and Sino—Indian affairs in 1962 attempts have been made to revive doctrines which, with differences in detail, broadly follow these lines.

In examining this view, it may first be agreed that the two great wars of the twentieth century finally demonstrated that armed power has come to be concentrated overwhelmingly in large and highly industrialised states. Neither a technically advanced small country nor a technically backward large country can hope to amass enough armed power to prevail in combat against large industrialised countries, well endowed with natural resources and manpower. The coming of atomic energy, following the scientific foundations laid in Cambridge earlier in the century, has carried the concentration of armed power to a point where at the moment only the two continental states can deploy enough resources to be considered as major armed powers.[1]

---

[1] Scientific knowledge is unconcerned with the boundaries of states. The development of atomic energy was essentially an international effort. The original conceptions and experimental work seem to have come from outside both the super-powers.

But it is another matter to deduce from these developments that the old-fashioned system of balance of power has been replaced by a simple alignment into two camps, each led by a " super-power ". All variants of this point of view are rejected in the present study ; they depend on the fallacious assumption that power consists merely in armaments and that therefore the distribution of total power corresponds to the distribution of armed strength. This assumption is as far away at one extreme from the facts of international life as the pacifist's assumptions are at the other ; it is further away than it was at the beginning of the century, for the development of atomic energy has made armed power so deadly, and fraught with such dangers to those who use it as well as to those against whom it is used, that the possessors of the new weapons do not dare to use them unless the same types of weapons are first used against them. Stalemate has been reached. The more deadly the weapons, the less usable they are. Paradoxically, therefore, we are in a stage at which the countries with the greatest armaments are least able to risk war, and the power derived from other sources than armaments takes on increasing significance. The U.S.—Cuban and Sino—Indian conflicts have not modified this conclusion.

Armed power is a means of defence or coercion. As a means of coercion of states weak in armaments the new forms of armed power must be set aside. Thus the main armaments, using up great economic resources of the super-powers, are significant only in relation to each other. For the rest, if they seek to coerce by arms, they must fall back on newer types of weapons of the Second World War. But if they wish to use these, they are faced with two dangers. First, one super-power may provoke the other or others into retaliation, and the danger of ultimate atomic warfare may arise. Second, even if they succeed in keeping a conflict localised, they have to reckon with widespread political hostility, not only among the masses of people in the country coerced but also in other countries in the same region, and countries friendly to the latter in other regions. Radio and press denunciations, resolutions in the international organisations, threats of boycott, and other signs of disapproval, are not to be treated lightly in international relations today, even if they cannot be backed with arms, and even if the offending country is overwhelmingly superior in arms to all the countries opposing her actions verbally and diplomatically. Third, the hostility and disapproval of large numbers of poorly armed countries whose peoples are above all passionately attached to the idea of political independence, and who fear that successful coercion of any one of their number will be followed by demands on them, will tend to draw them informally closer to the other Great Power or powers not involved in the act of coercion. Although this will not bring a large accession of armed strength to the latter, it will weaken the influence of her rivals and affect votes in the international organisations in the same direction.

Nor can the use of arms be altogether ruled out in such cases. If the area in which the Great Power in question has exercised coercion is suited to guerrilla activities, small arms may be smuggled in surreptitiously through neighbouring states, and an underground conflict carried on in remote and difficult terrain may be prolonged. If twentieth-century warfare has established the supremacy in arms of a few super-powers, which alone have the resources needed to produce the latest weapons of destruction, it has also given new methods and more effective small weapons to guerrilla fighters. The possibilities of guerrilla campaigns depend partly on the nature of the terrain and the position of the area with reference to external sources of supply, but in a number of areas guerrilla and other forms of underground campaigns have been kept alive for several years and have engaged disproportionately large forces of well-armed troops attempting to suppress them. The Great Power which becomes involved in such conflicts faces a serious risk of weakening its military position with respect to other Great Powers.

Thus the armed power of the super-powers has become too powerful to use ; pitched battles of armies are becoming unlikely ; and military operations seem now to centre largely on guerrilla warfare. On the other hand, forms of power other than armaments have grown in strength and variety; they are more organised and concerted, and based on immensely more effective means of communication, than in any previous age. They can no more be ignored by great than by small powers. They play, and will continue to play, a leading role in the revolution in international affairs, associated with the reawakening of the newly independent states of Asia, Latin America, and Africa, and their assumption of an active role in international affairs.

International relations during the rest of this century will be largely concerned with far-reaching adjustments in the relations between the countries of Europe (including Russia), North America, and Australasia on the one hand, and Asia, Latin America, and Africa on the other. There will be numerous cross-groupings, subgroupings, shufflings, and reshufflings, affected at some points by the balance of power in the North Atlantic, eastern European and northern Asian areas. But the primary aim of the western, southern, and south-eastern Asian, the Latin American, and the African powers will continue to be the attainment, where it is not already attained, of political independence, and its jealous preservation where or when it has been attained. Their attitudes to the western world are still influenced by past relations of dependence. This passion for independence is, and, I venture to predict, will continue to be, the key to the interpretation of policies and events, and we must turn at once therefore to a consideration of its origin, its nature, its strength, and its significance for the western powers, and particularly for Britain and France, because of their past historic relations with Asia, Africa, and the Caribbean area, and for the United States, because of its historic relations with Central and South America.

II

Geographical Characteristics of Changes

The political geography of the world is in an early stage of revolutionary change. The previous era out of which we have been passing has been described by the late Sir Halford Mackinder as the Columbian era and by the Sardar Panikkar as the Vasco da Gama era. The former era was said to have ended at the turn of the century, with the completion of geographical discovery, and the latter soon after the close of the Second World War. Each date is justifiable in relation to the purposes of the writers. The Columbian era is said to have ended when, with all the world known and linked by transport and communication, a disturbance in any one part quickly produced its effects on other parts. The Vasco da Gama era is said to have ended when the tide of European expansion and political influence that began with the Portuguese discovery and domination of routes to and across the Indian Ocean began to recede sharply during and after the Second World War, and a dominance based largely on sea-power ended with the attainment of independence of the countries along the routes.

The Columbian or Vasco da Gama era itself started with a sharp break from the past. When the age of discovery opened, Europeans were hemmed into a series of peninsulas on the west of the great Eurasian land mass. Arab imperialism had thrown a half circle around them, most of which was later taken over by Ottoman power. The Crusades had failed to break through to the east, and on the west the seemingly illimitable ocean shut off escape and expansion.

Vasco da Gama is the symbol of the breakthrough to the east, and Columbus of that to the west. The first outflanked Ottoman power and Arab trading interests, and opened a new route to lands, peoples, and civilisations, some of them known already, though vaguely, through spasmodic communication by hazardous combined sea and land journeys. The second, possibly starting with the same object as the first, accidentally opened up a new world, inhabited by hitherto unknown peoples. Neither the peoples of

Europe nor the peoples of the areas reached by the new discoveries were united. European civilisation, though real and original, did not bring political unity to Europe. Local rivalries were often more intense than rivalries with distant peoples, and alliances and alignments often cut across the boundaries between European and native peoples. Europeans in that age conceived of trade in terms of monopolies, which inevitably linked trade with warfare—among themselves as well as with Asian rivals.

Doctrinal warfare was interwoven with struggles over the balance of power in Europe and sometimes among smaller kingdoms in the Asian territories invaded by European peoples. Its incidence was uneven. The Portuguese and Spaniards embraced it with crusading zeal, the Portuguese sometimes to their strategic disadvantage. The French, Dutch, and English held aloof from it, aiming at trade and power rather than religious proselytism.

Even in the mediaeval and still more in the early modern period Europeans carried their European rivalries beyond Europe itself. The actions overseas can often be interpreted only in the light of the distribution of power within Europe itself. The argument now heard that British schools and universities should give more attention to Asian history is valid, but only on condition that the study of European history is intensified rather than diminished. The history both of imperialism and of colonisation must be interpreted in relation to the balance of power within Europe without reference to which some aspects of it are unintelligible. From the later eighteenth century the United States embarked in earnest on its empire building and must be added to the European picture : like Canada, Australia, and New Zealand, it was an offshoot of Europe ; its empire was destined to overrun the richest natural resources within any comparable area in the world.[1]

In the sixteenth to the eighteenth centuries Spain and Portugal established a wide hold in Latin America, and Spain, Portugal, Holland, France, and Britain acquired a number of scattered and far-flung commercial posts in Asia and Africa. Meanwhile, Russian imperialism moved eastward overland across Eurasia, trading interests again leading the way. Commercial penetration in unsettled areas led to political penetration. But the European and North American populations, and, still more their economic resources, remained too small for large-scale empire building until the nineteenth century, when the growth of population, the indus-

---

[1] See especially Richard W. van Alstyne, *The Rising American Empire*, Oxford, 1960. " The War of American Independence was conceived and fought under the spell of an imperial idea, an idea inherited from the remote past of the seventeenth century. It was the idea that the continent of North America belonged, as of right, to the people of the thirteen colonies of the Atlantic seaboard." (p. 78).

trial revolution, and the application of mechanical power to transport gave a new impetus to commercial, financial, and territorial expansion and empire building, both in Europe and, accompanying an immense transatlantic migration, in North America. Britain, France, and Holland extended and consolidated their power in Asia, and the United States in the Caribbean, Central America, and the Phillipines. The consolidation of empires in these areas had only been accomplished after wars among the colonising powers. But, in the last quarter of the nineteenth century, Africa, the last of the continents to fall under extensive European domination, was partitioned into spheres of influence and colonies without war, not so much through economic rivalries as through inter-European political rivalries and considerations of balance of power. By the late nineteenth century, when the whole interior of Africa was annexed, the weapons of war had become more deadly, and the rival Great Powers were not anxious to risk a full-scale war over the disposition of territory of doubtful value. Yet none of them was content to be left out of the colonial picture, since overseas territories might have an important bearing on the distribution of power within Europe and North America, and colonies were regarded in some circles as essential for Great Powers.

Thus, on the eve of the First World War, Europe and its offshoots in North America, Australasia, and South Africa dominated or controlled southern and south-eastern Asia, tropical Latin America, and almost all Africa. No continents were left for further expansion. High tide had been reached.

After high tide comes the ebb or recession. The same influences which rapidly accelerated the later stages of the processes of expansion and colonisation hastened the processes of contraction and decolonisation once they had started. If the earlier centuries of colonisation resembled a sluggish incoming neap tide, the nineteenth and twentieth centuries may be likened to a rapid spring tide reaching its height near the First World War and retreating rapidly after the Second.

None of this should have come as a surprise. Alien rule, whatever benefits it brought to many areas, inevitably provoked resistance sooner or later. Colonial rule is by its very nature temporary : it is a strange but widespread delusion that leads the peoples of colonial powers and privileged European or American colonists living among native peoples to think otherwise. The revolutionary advances in transport and communication which hastened the later colonisation also brought the colonial areas in closer touch with the outside world and opened them to the European ideas of nationalism, independence, and self-determination. When the radio was invented, and propaganda techniques developed, even the illiterate masses could be roused to a crude form of political consciousness. But the tide would have turned more slowly, and more time would have been left for fuller adjustments, if the two World Wars had been avoided. Thus, if rivalries among the European and North American peoples were a leading factor in territorial expansion and colonisation, they were also an important factor in hastening the reversal which would have come sooner or later in any case.

Yet the World Wars were symptomatic both of the processes that led to expansion and colonisation and to those that are leading to contraction and decolonisation. They arose out of disturbances in the balance of power within Europe. Although rivalries over North Africa had nearly created a crisis in 1908, neither the First nor the Second World War was the outcome of colonial rivalry. Hitler's determination to subjugate the Slavs and expand to the east for *lebenstraum* was of course an attempt at imperialistic expansion and annexation,[1] but this was in a different category from overseas colonial rivalry, which Hitler rejected as no substitute for overland expansion into contiguous territory. But, although the origins of both World Wars were to be found within Europe itself, the wide economic and political links with other continents transmitted shocks from European upheavals to the rest of the world. The independent offshoots of Europe, like the United States, Canada, and Australasia, as well as the European colonies, were affected in various ways, all of them in economic and social matters, and some of them by military operations, which in the Second World War caused widespread upheaval in south-eastern Asia.

The spectacle of the colonial powers of Europe and North America locked in deadly combat with one another, and drawing other parts of the world into the fray, lowered western prestige in Asia, Africa, and Latin America, and aroused resentment against the western world collectively, especially in the rising younger generation. It gave birth to nationalist movements in some areas, and hastened their gestation in others. The colonial powers themselves inadvertently gave an impetus to the move for decolonisation by stripping the defeated powers of their colonies, alleging that the latter had acquired them arbitrarily and ruled them oppressively. The crowning absurdity came in the Yalta communique in 1945, in which it was announced in righteous tones that Formosa had been " robbed

---

[1] Mr. A. J. P. Taylor in his recent work, *The Origins of the Second World War*, contends that Hitler did not really want war. Obviously Hitler would have preferred to reach his objectives if possible without war, but to suppose that he would have shrunk from war if he found himself unable to attain them otherwise seems an untenable thesis, which would require us to write off *Mein Kampf* as a false statement of his aims and of the psychological mainsprings of his actions. This appears incredible. For a critique of Taylor's work see P. A. Reynolds, " Hitler's War ", in *History*, October, 1961, pp. 212–17.

from China " and would be returned to her. Actually, Formosa was annexed by Japan in 1895, with the acquiescence of the European and American powers, and each of the countries which signed the Yalta communique had annexed a number of territories several years later with no more justification.[1] The self-righteousness of the victorious powers towards their former enemies was less convincing to the overseas world than to themselves.

But a number of western writers, and a considerable section of opinion in political circles and among the public, had long opposed the acquisition of colonies or at least their retention after maturity, on various grounds, some political, more economic, and many humanitarian. With the rise of modern education, and the admission of able students in dependent areas to western institutions of higher learning, these views spread to the colonial peoples themselves. Nationalist agitators, in dependencies where attempts were made to suppress them, often took refuge abroad to carry on their agitation from the outside, sometimes from western countries.

Colonial powers reacted in different ways to the rise of nationalism in their colonies. In many British dependencies limited forms of representative government introduced by instalments began early, especially in the West Indies. In some colonies native peoples were excluded entirely from political life, while forms of representation were allowed to overseas settlers. This worked against the interests of the native peoples ; overseas settlers in dependent territories generally lag behind the advances in thought and practices in their homelands except, perhaps, in some of the productive and distributive skills. In the vast territory of the Belgian Congo both the native peoples and the European settlers were excluded from political life, in favour of a paternalistic rule by agencies of the colonial power.

There are also a number of modern European powers without colonies : to them Canada must be added. Yet the urge to colonise, whether by direct settlement or by establishing rule over alien peoples, is an old one, and even in modern times non-European peoples, when given the opportunities, have responded to it as readily as European peoples have. Japan followed the same line as the western powers.

With all the divergencies of outlook among the western countries, it was inevitable that decolonisation, like colonisation, once it began, would be hastened by competition. As we have seen, the occupation and colonisation of a number of areas in south-eastern Asia and Africa were carried out to forestall rival western powers rather than from motives of direct economic gain. The rapid occupation of

---

[1] I believe that the hypocrisy of this communique was unconscious—a startling commentary on knowledge of international history at the " summit " and even among advisers !

tropical Africa can be largely explained in this way. In the process of decolonisation Britain led the way in most regions, although the pace was slower in the areas containing European settlers than in other areas. The United States and Russia, posing incongruously as virtuous anti-imperialistic powers, used such limited influence as they had to encourage and hasten European decolonisation in Africa and south-eastern Asia, while themselves seeking to maintain accommodating rulers in territories in which one or other of them claimed special interests in Asia and Latin America. Hypothetically, competition for the favour of the new governments and the peoples of the former colonies might be a constructive force in helping to overcome local inertia : in practice, the delicate and complex nature of the problems to be resolved in areas where populations were not homogeneous was insufficiently understood, and the difficulty of ensuring that the transition would be effected without bloodshed and excessive loss of efficiency was underestimated. Pressure from outside, therefore, sometimes brought more harm than benefit, while, on the other hand, it appeared largely ineffective in cases, such as those of the Portuguese and South African colonies, where the colonial power stubbornly dug itself in and defied the rest of the world.

Finally, the movement towards decolonisation was complicated by the introduction from outside of strong doctrinal elements from countries of opposing thought and practice. The two largest powers, whose leaders conceive themselves, sometimes melodramatically, as carrying the torches of " free enterprise " and " communism " respectively, have attempted to impress on the peoples of dependencies who have passed or are passing from colonial to independent status the alleged virtues of the economic and political systems practised in their countries, each of them in different ways representing the system of the other as oppressive, inefficient, and doomed to failure, and each endeavouring to enlist the emerging and reawakening countries on its side. Both Russia and the United States have intervened high-handedly in some areas, each intensifying pressures on weak countries not to associate with the other. On the other hand, the competition between the two powers has also brought benefits to the weaker countries in the form of economic aid.

CHAPTER V

IMPERIALISM, COLONIALISM, AND NATIONALISM

I

Characteristics of Imperialism and Colonialism

PROFESSOR W. K. Hancock, who has written brilliantly on Commonwealth history, has stated that imperialism is no word for a scholar. This is certainly true of the term in the sense in which it is used by political propagandists in the mid-twentieth century. Unfortunately it is difficult to banish the term from our vocabulary and find generally acceptable substitutes for its legitimate descriptive uses. I shall therefore use it, first, to denote annexation of territory and expansion of the boundaries of a state by other means than voluntary union. But it is impracticable to stop rigidly at that point, and I shall extend it to include incomplete, less direct, and less formal encroachments on the independence of states which are comparatively weak, by those which are comparatively strong, in armed power. Such forms of imperialism may be exercised by a combination of political and economic pressure, or even by political pressure alone. Thus defined, the boundaries of imperialism are rather fluid and blurred at some points. The neo-Marxist theories of imperialism are, of course, carried to extremes, sometimes treating all forms of foreign investment as imperialism ! While summarily rejecting these absurdities of propaganda, however, I do not think it would be useful or practicable to confine the term wholly to outright annexation, particularly since the growth of newer methods of political control in recent times over " puppet " states and " satellite " states. Thus Russian imperialism in eastern Europe did not end with the Czarist régime but reappeared in a somewhat less direct form in other régimes.

" Colonialism " is the policy of acquiring colonies ; that is, territories ruled by separate local governments subject ultimately to the central government of the occupying power. There may be limited forms of representation in colonial governments and in a few cases, as in Algeria before independence, some representation in the legislature of the colonising power, but the political representation of the people of the colony is inferior to that of the people of the colonising power : sometimes there is no genuine representation at all.

Obviously there is overlapping between the two terms. Imperialism may result in outright annexation and immediate extension of the same laws and representation to the peoples of the annexed areas as the peoples of the colonising power already possess. Or there may be a colonial phase between annexation and complete absorption, as in Hawaii, where colonialism lasted for sixty years. British imperialism was necessarily overseas and, apart from indirect control and influence, took the form of colonialism instead of annexation and absorption.

The results of these two forms of imperialism differ widely. Annexation and absorption are aimed at forcing the peoples of the annexed territories into the same mould, the same culture and ways of life, the same political structure, as those of the expanding country. If the annexed peoples are small in numbers compared with the expanding peoples, only a deeply rooted culture of their own will enable them to resist complete absorption, and even then they may be outnumbered in time by immigrants from the expanding power. Such was the fate of a number of peoples who stood in the paths of the expanding Russians and Americans. Usually this occurs in imperialist expansion overland, but in the case of the Hawaiian Islands it crossed nearly 2,000 miles of ocean. There is a strong chance that, owing to economic pressures and interests, Puerto Rico may be engulfed. The cost incurred in the sacrifice of variety to a dull uniformity is often very high in such cases.

Colonialism leaves more scope for the retention of indigenous characteristics. While many valuable borrowings from colonising powers have been usefully absorbed into the cultures of a number of former dependencies, it has been possible in most colonised areas to retain enough of the distinctive characteristics of indigenous culture to enable nationalism to develop in the twentieth century. Once this is assured, annexation with absorption becomes almost impossible without ruthless and costly repression.

Consequently, colonialism is by its very nature a temporary political relationship. In earlier years, when nationalism was unborn or only in its early infancy, the masses of people made no sharp distinction between one set of authoritarian rulers and another. Often the " native " rulers had themselves come from invading peoples, and rulers of European origin were merely incidents in a series of foreign rulers. While these conditions lasted, colonial rulers were sometimes able to benefit the colonial peoples in a number of ways, although they did not always use their opportunities. From the later nineteenth century, however, with advances in transport and the means of communication, leading ultimately to radio broadcasting, the distinction between foreigners and native peoples was sharpened, and nationalism, with its demand for domestic self-government and often for total independence of the imperial powers, gathered such strength that the days of colonies were numbered. However, all this was only a question of time : it is mere common sense to conclude that no peoples, when they have become politically conscious, will consent to be ruled indefinitely from outside by what to them are foreign governments. Colonies were bound either to be swamped by the greater size of the imperial power and annexed and absorbed, or to be granted self-government by the imperial powers which, like Britain and France, had attained sufficient political wisdom to sense that more was to be gained by relations of friendship in independence than by relations of enmity in dependence.

Thus colonialism has at times performed an important function in human history by preserving diversification of cultures and leaving the way open for the development of future self-governing areas, when annexation and absorption would have prevented both these developments in the long run. It has reduced the dangers that accompany those forms of imperialism that lead to annexation and absorption. And, though absorption through genuine voluntary union must be distinguished from imperialistic annexation, the boundary between the two is not always easy to draw. If an area with a climate tolerable to peoples of European origin, such as Hawaii or Puerto Rico, is acquired during imperialistic expansion, and is then opened to an extensive influx of capital, business enterprise, technicians, newspaper and magazine publishers, and traders of all sorts, from the imperial power, its entire economic life may become so dominated by and dependent on the latter that, within a few generations the economic interests involved, together with the cultural propaganda from the imperial power, will submerge the foundations of the native culture and leave nothing but an insincere façade, maintained to appeal to tourists and serve as advertising material. This has been the fate of Hawaii and may yet be the fate of Puerto Rico.

Colonialism intended as a stage on the way to absorption, however, has met insuperable obstacles in a number of areas. French colonialism, which in principle has resembled U.S. colonialism in a number of ways, faced a strong distinctive culture in North Africa, where Islam provided a cohesive influence strongly resistant to absorption into an alien culture. French culture has, indeed, a strong attraction for many educated Africans and Asians and has been a constructive influence of lasting value. But the intransigent attitude of the " colons "—the majority being of French adoption, not origin—who clung tenaciously to their privileges, excluded all possibility of reconciling Arabs to a future common society. In any case such an outcome was highly improbable : a society in North

Africa whose Islamic roots go back more than a millenium differs radically from a society of easy-going Pacific islanders.

Colonial government, on the other hand, without the aim of annexation and absorption, with frank recognition of different cultures, often consciously avoided undue interference with local traditions, and left the way open for political evolution towards representative government, culminating in independence, in some cases with the retention of links with the colonising power. In these cases, diversity has been preserved but informal links have been created which help to offset the dangers of fragmentation. If our goal should be that of unity underlying diversity, colonialism has been a useful stage towards it in some parts of the world. In these iconoclastic times it is often difficult to conserve on a basis of equality relationships which grew slowly from origins in which inequality prevailed. Yet resentments against past inequalities, established in generations now dead, are a poor basis on which to frame the future relations of peoples now politically independent of one another but sharing that inescapable interdependence which is the condition of human survival. The Commonwealth and the French forms of association are contributions to the preservation, on a new basis of freedom, of some of the accompaniments of older relationships now outgrown.

Finally, a more long-drawn-out complication of colonialism has left its mark in our times on Latin America, which is wrestling with different forms of the general problem of decolonisation. The attainment of independence in the first few decades of the nineteenth century severed political ties with Spain and Portugal but left the colonists of Spanish and Portuguese origin in control. This was part of a general change wrought by the discovery and occupation of the American continent by Europeans. The native inhabitants, loosely designated as " Indians ", were far inferior to the invaders in armed power. In the temperate regions of North and South America they were massacred in large numbers by a combination of treachery and superior weapons. This infamous chapter in the history of Europeans and their overseas descendants has received scanty attention, doubtless because most histories have been written by peoples of European origin. Fortunately, in mainland tropical Latin America, partly through the efforts of the Catholic priests and of Spanish governments, a considerable proportion of the native peoples survived. But they would not undertake all forms of labour, and Negro slaves were brought in their stead into parts of the continent. In the absence of " Anglo-Saxons " and Germans, colour prejudice seems to have been slight, and widespread, though incomplete, racial intermixture has characterised the modern Latin Americans.

Independence, when it came, was dominated largely in some areas by the " colons ", if the term may be used to include the offspring of mixed racial unions. Over a considerable area, economic divisions have corresponded to a large extent with the division between European colonists and their descendants, on the one hand, and the native Indians and people of African descent on the other. The lines, though blurred by racial mixture and softened by the comparative insignificance of colour prejudice, have not been obliterated everywhere : poverty falls disproportionately on the descendants of Indians and of African slaves. For long they were quiescent, accepting with fatalism a low status in society. Now the political upsurge which has rapidly spread over Asia, Africa, and the American continent south of the Rio del Norte has affected all classes in Latin America, and turbulence and assertiveness are replacing apathy. The old order cannot last. The cleavage between the generations is particularly wide. In the mid nineteen-sixties the foreign policies of the majority of these countries are in most cases in the hands of conservatives of the older generation, or of moderate " middle of the road " political leaders, who cannot ignore the strength of the vested interests and the traditional elements but who realise the explosive nature of the new forces from the left which seek revolutionary solutions rather than " gradualism ".

Imperialism appeared long before nationalism, and, in principle, nationalism and imperialism seem contradictory, but in practice the one often leads to the other. The reason is simple. A group inspired by the sentiment of nationalism which is able to realise its aim increases its power in the process. If it becomes strong enough in relation to its neighbours and to overseas states, there is a temptation, for various reasons which will be analysed later, to continue the process of state-building at the expense of others. Most groups are more concerned for their own independence than for the independence of other groups, and are ready to believe that their rule is beneficial to others, especially to those who have been badly ruled by their previous governments. In some cases their aim is to convert the " conquered " peoples to their own nationalism : this has characterised much of U.S. imperialism. The tendency of the comparatively strong nation states to expand has been so widespread in the past that we may suspect the states which shunned it to have remained virtuous from lack of opportunity rather than from lack of desire.

II

Effects of different Forms of Imperialism

An extensive literature exists on imperialism and colonisation, and a variety of theories, not to say dogmas, have been constructed to explain or interpret them. Attempts at economic interpretation have taken a foremost place since the later nineteenth century. It is obvious that empire-building has its economic side and that no theory can be formed that has no economic bearing or economic elements in it.

Let us first consider the pioneering activities which opened the way to ultimate political expansion.

Colonial expansion overseas, and a part of imperialist expansion overland, were sometimes initiated through the activities of traders, who were concerned not with political domination but with commercial profits. On some routes the traders formed commercial companies, which represented not governments but private interests. The chief companies received charters from governments, and in this sense had an official link which served their monopoly interests. But usually the traders, however they were organised, led the way with a view to private profit rather than the creation of empire. When, in this pursuit, the supplies of the goods in which they traded fell below the demand for them, they acquired an interest in the organisation of production, and in the maintenance of old and sometimes the creation of new transport routes, which often led, in areas of political instability and internal strife, to interference in the internal affairs of the peoples, followed by the establishment of administrative machinery designed to secure production and deliveries. But commercial companies, intent mainly on profits, were not easily adapted to the performance of political functions, and abuses gave rise to scandals which brought the governments of the trading countries into an active role.

Thus commercial imperialism sometimes led to territorial imperialism, and British rule was established in India, and British, Dutch, and French rule in parts of south-eastern Asia. From the beginning these forms of imperialism and colonialism were complicated by the commercial rivalry among the traders of the European powers, joined in the nineteenth century by those of the United States and Japan.

The overland expansion of the European settlers in North America and that of Cossacks and Russian traders in Eurasia—the westward movement in the New World and the eastward movement in the

Old World—were in part led by traders and trappers. Just as the maritime commercial imperialism in southern Asia was based on the desire for tropical products that could not be produced in the mild temperature latitudes of the European peninsula, so the trading vanguard of the eastward and of the northern parts of the westward imperialist expansions overland were based on the desire for furs and other products of the cold northern latitudes. Thus it was that the uneven geographical distribution of the gifts of nature, arousing the desires and the acquisitive instincts of localised groups of men for that which lay beyond their borders in other climes, set off migrations that brought cycles of strife and development, of confusion and reorganisation, and finally, in our own time, is bringing a general awakening in nearly all quarters of the globe.

The role of governments in the overland, as in the overseas, expansion was a mixed one. Private trading interests often acted without official sanction in areas far from the central government. They sometimes gained support from outlying government officials, but found it much harder to induce their central governments to incur new obligations and expenses. Occasionally individual leaders of outstanding energy and an expansionist turn of mind, such as the Russian minister, Count Muravieff, and the British Colonial Secretary, Mr. Joseph Chamberlain, were ready in central governments to push the claims and support the actions of men in distant spots who were advancing into areas regarding which the overwhelming majority of people in their homelands were completely indifferent.

The historian who tries to unravel the tangled and complicated chains of events that led to the establishment of European and North American control over dependent countries of Asia, Latin America, and Africa will find it necessary to study at least the forms of commercial organisation, the conditions of demand for and supply of tropical and far northern commodities and their substitutes, the links between trading interests and governments, the characters and abilities of individuals in high places in trading concerns, in government posts abroad, in central governments at home, and, not least, the contemporary setting in the world of the Great Powers at the time of each act of expansion in the Vasco da Gama era, and the relation of acts of colonisation or annexation to the shifting balance of power among the colonising countries. In many cases, notably in tropical Africa, this last factor was much more important than all the economic influences combined. And just as, in international economics, decisions must be based on expectations of the conditions of supply and demand in the near future, so, in international politics, they must be based on expectations of the distribution of power in the near future. In both cases foresight is imperfect and expectations may be at fault. The historian has therefore to appraise actions in the light of the imperfect knowledge available at the time when they were taken.

Before analysing the full implications of these conclusions, something must be said of the rival theories, based on economic determinism, which would treat all these doings of chartered monopolies, private traders, explorers, diplomats, political leaders, missionaries, and others concerned, as mere symptoms of, and incidents in, an inexorable process of development through conflict and struggle from one social and economic order to another, the individual being carried along in the stream, with power only to modify slightly its rate of flow and its eddies and turnings. These theories followed on the disappointment of the mid nineteenth-century hopes of the free-traders who looked to commerce under free conditions as a great force for world peace and liberation, superseding colonialism by free economic interchange that would retain the benefits of association with overseas territories, while dispensing with political domination over them, and thus, by a great increase of trade, diffusing prosperity over the world, and reducing geographical inequality of economic opportunity. To the left-wing critics of this view, observing the gains of protectionism in the closing decades of the century, commerce under capitalism and private enterprise brought, not free trade or peace, but monopoly and the sword and gunboat ; not liberation or diffusion of opportunity, but the imposition of external rule and exploitation, which, whatever temporary benefits they might bring, inevitably bred resentment and aroused opposition.

Neo-Marxian theories, building on the writings of J. A. Hobson, have represented the competition for colonies as an outcome of " monopoly capitalism " and surplus value—which is supposed to have forced the capitalist countries to seek markets abroad because of the inability of the exploited workers to absorb the goods at home. As we have seen, the Chartered Companies in the east, and Spain in the west, precipitated conflicts out of their claims to monopoly. But this began long before the industrial age, and decayed during the early industrial revolution, while rivalry over colonies increased.

Rarely can economics and politics be completely dissociated, but the correct association is not to be found by making the one wholly a consequence of the other. The primacy given to particular economic factors in the economic theories of imperialism would make imperialism and colonisation a modern development arising simply out of a particular economic structure. It is true that the forms and directions taken by imperialist expansion, colonisation and other kinds of domination, may be affected by changes in technology and economic structure. A treaty was made by Britain with the Sheikh of Kuwait when the chief British interest was the safety of the route to India and the protection of its flanks. Much later, when outstandingly rich oilfields were discovered, an economic motive was added to the political motive which, by this time, had considerably weakened. However, in spite of the growth of the area in economic importance, the tie with it has been made weaker and is now mainly confined to protection against direct outside attack. Again the motive has been political.

A fundamental underlying reason for colonial rivalry lay in the struggle for political power in a world of more or less independent states. Political power cannot be divorced from economic power, and there were obvious economic aspects of the political rivalry among colonial powers. But, given the same political framework of the world, these rivalries would have existed whatever the nature of the economic systems in the countries concerned ; they would have been reflected also in the working of the international economic order as by-products of international politics.[1] Tortuous attempts at explanation in terms of class struggles, and intricate theories of value forged at a high level of abstraction, divert the eyes of the student of international relations away from the main highway into side turnings which, however interesting may be the vista opened up on some of them, at best give no more than a partial glimpse of conditions in limited areas and periods of time.

Now in almost all cases the expansion of the European peoples and their overseas offshoots in Asia, the Americas, and Africa in the Vasco da Gama era was achieved partly through a technical superiority in arms over the peoples of the areas annexed or colonised. This helps to explain how the European peoples broke out, or, in the more vivid language of Mackinder, how they raised the siege imposed on them by the Arab and then the Ottoman Empire. The latter were sometimes as well equipped as the Europeans and superior to them in military organisation. Mahmud II, as late as 1453, prevailed at Constantinople largely by the strength of his artillery. But once the Europeans had begun to outflank their immediate south-eastern neighbours about half a century later, they found no such military force in their way as that of the Ottoman Empire. This does not fully explain the foothold which small forces of Europeans gained in Asia and the Americas. After a point, lack of numbers offset advantages of military arms and technique, and

---

[1] This follows from the premises on which the present study is based. It has ample confirmation from recent events in the communist world. With the virtual completion of geographical discovery there is now less scope for old-fashioned territorial imperialism, but a rivalry has now grown up for favours from the former colonial areas, and between none more than between Russia and China ! Moreover, it is ironical that China turned to Canada for imports of grains, including barley, while Russia was undercutting local suppliers of barley in some Western, including British markets !

annexation or the establishment of colonial rule was only possible in the end by the fluctuating internal distribution of power among disunited native peoples. The possession of superior weapons had to be supplemented by skilled diplomacy, leading to alliances with one group against another. In commercial imperialism, indeed, often the aim was only to tilt the internal balance of power in favour of those indigenous groups that would grant or create the most favourable trading conditions.

The phrase " divide and rule " has often been used misleadingly, as if a colonising power deliberately, with Machiavellian cunning, created divisions among the indigenous peoples. In most cases this cannot be established. Twentieth-century students too often read back into past history conditions and concepts familiar in their own times but which were remote a century or more earlier. Before mechanical power was applied to transport and communication, unity over any large area was extremely difficult to achieve. Political authority was widely dispersed and often fragile. Divisions were there already and had not to be created. The entry of the Europeans was at first no more than the arrival of a new group to complicate the balance of power among existing groups, which were often as anxious to use the newcomers for their own purposes as the newcomers were to use them. But they overlooked the special dangers of attempting to use in their internal conflicts an incoming force armed with superior weapons and whose verbal engagements were unreliable.[1]

The effects of European expansion overseas on unity and fragmentation among the various peoples over whom they established their rule can only be estimated in general terms. We cannot tell what might have happened if all Europeans had stayed in Europe. But the oft-repeated allegation that territorial imperialism hindered or prevented unification that would otherwise have taken place is generally misleading. It may be valid in some cases, chiefly where rivalries among colonial powers led to agreements on dividing territories in certain regions. Even here, however, it seems more correct to say that arbitrary boundary lines were laid down than to say that small dependent countries were established in place of large independent countries. Without European penetration, modern forms of transport, communication, and public administration would have been delayed : in their absence large states are difficult to establish and still more difficult to maintain. And in a number of outstanding cases European occupation created unification which might never

---

[1] Some Europeans, whether from downright treachery and villainy or from religious fanaticism, or perhaps by affecting the latter as a screen for the former, held that there was no obligation on them to keep their engagements with " heathen peoples ".

have otherwise occured.   India, as a national state, was a creation of the British Raj.[1]   Nigeria seems to be in a similar category.   External rule, or the threat of it, or the struggle against it, has been one of the greatest influences in the creation of psychological unity and national consciousness.

III

Imperialism at the Receiving End

The preceding examples illustrate the importance of a study of the internal conditions of the countries which were brought into dependency in the Vasco da Gama period.   In many of these areas the imperial governments and the colonisers alike had little knowledge at the outset of the conditions they would face if they established a " permanent " occupation and thus had to take over the responsibilities of government, either openly or through " puppet " rulers. To some extent the same limitations apply to the work of European, North American, and Australasian historians who study colonial history : they have been generally much better equipped to deal with the part played by influences within the imperialist powers, and by the effects of struggles over the balance of power among them on imperial expansion and colonisation, than with the part played by developments within the countries penetrated, in the periods immediately before and during intervention.   In time this bias may be corrected by future Asian, African, and Latin American historians, but in the near future there is little sign in most of these countries, except India and Japan, of the establishment of modern historical studies on an objective basis.

Again, historians, in dealing with the expansion of Europe and the United States, have sometimes tried to account for apparent changes in policy towards expansion largely in terms of changes in the expansionist countries themselves.   According to a theory fashionable in the first half of the twentieth century, and which has not yet lost all its influence, a dividing line came in the late nineteenth century when true, conscious modern imperialism really began in deliberate territorial aggression, claims for special privileges, and other encroachments on the independence of weak countries.

Attempts were made to explain the transformation largely by reference to changes in the psychology of the masses in the western world, following the spread of universal primary education, the birth of the " Yellow Press ", and other internal developments.   Some

---

[1] I do not imply that it could not have developed from within, but it is hardly conceivable that it could have occurred without prolonged delay.

historians and popular writers have gone so far as to represent modern imperialism as a creation of the late nineteenth century.

This viewpoint is now collapsing under extended historical research. From lack of space, I am here mainly concerned, however, with one only of the flaws in it, namely, the neglect of changes both in the countries into which the western powers had already penetrated before the later nineteenth century and also in those into which they penetrated during that period. The countries into which the western powers were drawn were already undergoing internal changes. Two cases should be distinguished. The first is that in which there had been no previous western interference from outside. Professor Max Gluckman, in an introduction to Mr. Gann's *The Birth of a Plural Society* (p. 4), remarks :

> I have myself argued that the kindly reception and lavish help given by Maklolo chiefs to David Livingstone for his explorations can only be understood when we see that Livingstone was of critical importance in their foreign policy. As he was Robert Moffat's son-in-law, and Moffat was friendly with the Matabele king, they seem to have argued, if *he* settled among them he might induce them to make peace with them. Without an understanding of Makalolo politics, the historian of this period, or biographer of Livingstone, is handicapped.

Missionary activities were, of course, followed later by more widespread western penetration. But this illustration shows convincingly that, even under comparatively primitive conditions, there is an internal balance of power which will be affected by impacts from outside, particularly, it may be added, if new techniques are subsequently introduced unevenly among the groups concerned in the existing balance of power. Often, historians have concentrated on the effects of rivalries among imperial powers on the course of colonisation, with little systematic study and analysis of the political structure of the areas penetrated and subsequently colonised, whether inhabited by tribes, or kingdoms or petty principalities. In respect to Africa the historian who felt at home in dealing with European, North American, and Australasian conditions found himself in strange surroundings when his materials impinged on such peoples as the nomadic peoples and the riverain cultivators of the Middle East and the tribes of central Africa. In some areas a second difficulty arose out of the necessity of mastering new and sometimes difficult languages, and searching for materials in unfamiliar places, if the Asian sources were to be examined as thoroughly as the western. The larger part of the historical work dealing with western imperialism in eastern Asia, for example, was done without reference to Chinese, Japanese, or even Russian source materials. It was not until after the Second World War that serious attempts were made to expand Oriental studies in recent and contemporary international relations, and even now the resources devoted to this aim in the western world, and especially in Britain. are meagre and often concerned with narrowly specialised topics.[1]

My second example of early western contacts with unfamiliar worlds is concerned with Egypt. Britain's intervention in Egypt has been the subject of debate for over eighty years and an immense literature on it exists, particularly in English, French, and Arabic. But we are a very long way from exhausting the materials and still further from agreement on the judgements to be derived from them. The recent work of Robinson, Gallagher, and Denny concludes that it was the occupation of Egypt in 1881 that touched off " the scramble for Africa ".[2] Even apart from this possibility, its long-run strategic and above all its psychological effects on the Middle East were of immense importance right up to the time of the Suez affair in 1956. No-one who has lived in the Middle East is likely to underestimate the role played by the British occupation of Egypt in fostering anti-western types of nationalism. The initial steps came after prolonged hesitation and procrastination, and sharp internal conflicts of view which were never resolved to the satisfaction of any of those who took part in them. The issues then debated were wholly modern and have lost none of their relevance in the twentieth century.

The misjudgements of the liberal imperialists in President Kennedy's entourage, on Caribbean and Central American affairs, show striking similarities to the misjudgements of the liberal imperialists in the Gladstone Ministry of the early eighties on Egyptian affairs.[3]

The bombardment of Alexandria and the decisions which led to Tel el Kebir came at a time when new forces were stirring within Egypt, the outcome of external influences, such as French cultural relations beginning in Napoleon's day, and of western interference in

---

[1] It is a grave error, however, to suggest that too much attention is and has been given to European history. On the contrary, Europe has been, and I believe still is, the chief motive power in world development. The world regional imbalance in the study of history must be corrected by an increase all round, covering every region.

[2] R. E. Robinson, J. Gallagher and A. Denny, *Africa and the Victorians* (Cambridge, 1960).

[3] In both cases the imperialism was of the type that encroaches on the independence of smaller countries without formal annexation of territory. Although in the first case commercial interests had some influence, the main aim in both cases was to preserve monopolistic " spheres of influence ". The autonomy and interests of the smaller powers were subordinated to the rivalries among the great powers.

respect to the debts incurred by the Khedive Ismael, interwoven with internal political and economic issues, among which arbitrary despotic rule and the poverty and helplessness of the peasants, attracted the greatest attention of reformers.

Nothing could be further from the realities of the British interventions which led to the occupation of Egypt than the conventional ideas of Arab nationalists of today, who see in them the aggressive designs of hostile imperialists who aimed at suppressing and exploiting Asian and African peoples to maintain their economic advantages and political privileges in the world. On the contrary, the desire even of those who favoured direct interference was for " intervention, reform, and withdrawal ", and all but a very small minority desired and expected very early withdrawal—that is, within a year or so. A few " realists " did not believe early withdrawal to be possible, but even they did not desire annexation.

The " realists ", of whom the Marquis of Hartington (later, Duke of Devonshire) was perhaps the most typical, were correct in two important points : first in the necessity for a firm decision in place of wavering and procrastination ; second, in the belief that it might, and probably would, take several years to achieve the aims of the intervention which, nevertheless, they advocated.   Where, as I believe, they showed mistaken judgement was in advocating intervention at all.

Historians have been quick to expose the confusions in the Gladstone Cabinet and the lack of foresight which it showed in Egypt and the Sudan.   But they have generally stopped short of a systematic analysis of the precise issues and the alternative courses of action open to the Cabinet, given the limitations of its knowledge and the conflicting advice offered to it.   One consideration which played a large role was the security of the route from Britain to India through the Suez Canal—which had first arisen only a few years earlier.   But this was hardly separable from the wider problem of " containing " Russia, which had repudiated the clauses of the Treaty of Paris restricting its naval rights in the Black Sea.   How important was the control over Cairo and over the Canal for this purpose ?   An analogous question arose in 1956 under very different techniques of warfare.   Then it was not the route to India so much as the route along which indispensable raw materials were brought to Britain that was deemed indispensable.   Similarly, it might be asked in the contemporary world how important especially in the atomic period is the retention of Panama as a puppet state, resulting from earlier United States imperialism, at the cost of Latin American goodwill.   There is no space to analyse these questions in the present context, but at least it may be said that the contemporary judgement of the strategists in each of these cases is open to serious doubt.

But in addition the viewpoints of western strategists have been subject to a fundamental weakness, whenever Asian, African, and Latin American territories have entered into the picture. They have practically left out of account the sentiments, the wishes, and the internal political structures of the peoples concerned. The necessities of imperial strategy have been taken as overruling local views of local interests affected. The self-assurance of the imperial powers that their mission in the world subsumed the interests of lesser powers, whether or not the peoples realised or acknowledged it, seems to have remained unbroken up to 1956, and still stands in the way of psychological decolonisation in the United States.

Army spokesmen commonly reply to such criticisms by maintaining that they are concerned only with the strategy of armed power, and that it is the business of politicians to pacify alien peoples who fail to appreciate the benefits thrust upon them by the Great Power or Powers which have assumed the burden of protecting the world against this or that menace.

This contention, however, demonstrates that strategy cannot be left to the armed forces. They may be qualified to decide on strategy in terms of armed power alone, but other kinds of experience and knowledge are necessary to assess strategy as a whole. The reactions of other peoples to strategic measures of the Great Powers which affect them should be the first, and not, as it has been so often in the past, the last consideration in forming a strategy of defence. At times it may have been necessary to override local interests in wartime emergencies, as, for example, in parts of the Middle East during the Second World War. Even there, however, a good case can be made for the view that, in certain instances, diplomacy might have been substituted for force [1] with better results. And in peace-time the western powers can no longer afford to neglect the local interests of the smaller countries.

---

[1] For example, in Iraq over the Rashid Ali al Gailani affair in 1941. The military history is excellently written by I.S.O. Playfair, *The Mediterranean and the Middle East*, London, 1956, Vol. II, Ch. IX. General Wavell twice urged that a settlement should be sought by diplomatic negotiation, and also that a Turkish offer to mediate should be accepted. But the Chiefs of Staff took the view that, " There could be no question of accepting Turkish mediation . . . the Defence Committee could not entertain any settlement by negotiation except on the basis of a climb down by the Iraqis, with safeguards against future Axis designs on Iraq. They considered that Rashid Ali had been hand in glove with the Axis powers and had been waiting for support from them before exposing his hand " (p. 185). For an account in English from a different viewpoint, see M. Khadduri, *Independent Iraq, 1932–58*, Second edition, London, 1958, Chs. VIII and IX. The British demand for Rashid Ali's resignation seems to have been an error in tactics. London was also poorly informed on the Baghdad political situation. There is a field for further research in Arabic materials on the subject. General Wavell's judgement may yet be justified.

But strategy is not all. The outstanding misjudgements in the eighteen-eighties go beyond the short run. They are above all concerned with the failure to appreciate the new stirrings of political consciousness in Egypt, and their future significance. The conditions in Egypt at the time of occupation differed fundamentally from those in India both at the time of penetration by the East India Company and at the time when the British Government assumed direct responsibility. These differences seem never to have been fully appreciated by British administrators in Egypt. First of all, British intervention suppressed a new popular movement representing the early stages of a rising nationalism, and suppressed it with the object of maintaining a régime which had fallen into deep discredit. This was acknowledged even by the administrators, such as Sir Evelyn Baring (later Lord Cromer) and Sir Auckland Colvin, who subsequently became apologists for the occupation, and reluctant to relax it. Colvin wrote in 1906 of the trial of Arabi Pasha and his associates that,

> The prisoners, in common with all Egypt, had suffered under the tyranny of Khedive Tewfik's father, as the generation before them had suffered under Muhammad Ali. But for British intervention the prisoners and their friends would have thrown the whole house of Muhammad Ali, bag and baggage, into the Red Sea. The Khedive could not be allowed, under benefit of the intervention of a civilised power, to make himself the arbiter of their fate. All this was unanswerable, and public opinion in Great Britain was disposed to show itself generous. There came the rub. The third party was the Khedive. The cost of British clemency had to be met by Tewfik Pasha, and the eclipse of the Khedive's authority was to be the measure of that cost. The British had landed in Egypt, not to destroy the authority of the Khedive but to restore it, and to retire. . . . It was generally believed in Egypt that . . . they had adopted, curiously enough, the one course calculated to prevent the restoration of his power.[1]

Like Sir Evelyn Baring, Colvin was in no doubt that but for British interference the old régime would have been displaced by a new one. The following passage summarises the judgement of another observer on those who would have led the new régime if British intervention had not caused their downfall with a loss of thousands of lives on the battlefield and a future legacy of resentment against and distrust of Britain among the politically conscious peoples of the area :

[1] Sir Auckland Colvin, *The Making of Modern Egypt*, London, 1906, pp. 25–6.

Arabi was by no means the only Egyptian nationalist of character and capacity. He certainly possessed the best qualifications to lead, but others showed more than ordinary ability in giving practical effect to his plans. Mahmoud Sami's letters and official documents are evidence of no mean intellectual powers. Yacoub Sami was unquestionably an excellent administrative officer, with a great facility for arrangement and organisation. Ali Fehmy and Abd-el-Al were both good soldiers and Mahmoud Fehmy the best engineer Egypt could boast of. . . . My own personal impressions of Arabi and his friends leave little doubt on my mind that if they had only received that sincere and hearty co-operation of their immediate sovereign which they once expected, and had escaped the misfortune of an armed foreign intervention, they could have satisfactorily accomplished, in their own way and according to their own lights, the mission which all Egypt confided to them.[1]

How successful Arabi and his friends would have been in the absence of outside interference in 1884 is a subject only for speculation.

As things were, the British occupation brought important advances in agriculture. The administrators, who had the advantage of experience in India, grasped the importance of irrigation and the position of the peasant. Baring, who became Lord Cromer, and others, including Lord Kitchener, showed a greater concern for the peasants than any Egyptian rulers had done. But the British régime, because it was alien, could never hope to win the support of the rising urban classes, already touched by modern influences, and increasingly imbued with national consciousness, which would never be content with any status less than that of independence. Lord Cromer was a great administrator of the highest integrity, but it is a measure of his limitations that he failed to understand the strength and significance of the new forces in urban life, neglected the educational development which would have directed them into more constructive channels, and repressed manifestations of the inevitable and natural desire for political independence.

There are no final judgements on historical events, but from the point of view of the relations between Britain and the western world on one side, and Asian, African, and Latin American countries on the other, which is the main theme of the present study, the bombardment of Alexandria, the military campaign which ended in the battle of Tel-el-Keber, and the subsequent occupation of Egypt and

[1] A. M. Broadley, *How we defended Arabi and his Friends* (London 1884), p. 451. See also William Scawen Blunt, *Secret History of the English Occupation of Egypt* (London, 1907).

rule through a puppet régime, were the result of a failure to detect the existence and appreciate the significance of internal changes that were taking place in Egypt and leading to the dawn of political consciousness analogous to that which had developed earlier in Europe and its overseas offshoots.   Its central aim was political independence.   The original aims of the Gladstone Cabinet, as we have seen, had been to intervene, reform, and retire.   The first has always been easy for a Great Power facing a Small Power.   The second and the third become more rather than less difficult with the passage of time, unless the administrators are willing to identify themselves with the people and are able to convince them of their good faith, meanwhile prodding their governments to provide the resources to assist in social and economic advance.   Cromer and his successors, in spite of valuable achievements, failed to work with, educate, and encourage the rising nationalist movement.   The opportunity to repair the misjudgements that led to the initial intervention was lost, the capacities of the indigenous peoples were underestimated, and, although gains were made, and useful legacies left behind, they only postponed the day when the plunge had to be taken.

It must be frankly acknowledged that if we could recall the spirits of the chief actors of the early eighteen-eighties, and reveal to them the events since their deaths, the resulting debate would still be inconclusive.   Assuming that the judgements of Mr. Broadley and Mr. Blunt on Arabi and his aides, based on personal experience, are accepted, it does not necessarily follow that when it came to reconstruction after revolution, the abilities and the administrative capacities of the leaders would have proved capable of dealing with the formidable tasks that would have faced them at home and abroad. Much would have depended on the actions of the powers with respect to the external debt of Egypt, and on the ability of the new rulers at home to collect taxes, curb landlords, and develop irrigation.   France had declined to intervene in England's company earlier, but if Arabi had repudiated the debt, which would seem to have been the only satisfactory economic solution, the French bondholders might have succeeded in provoking French intervention. We may argue over the " might have been " indefinitely.

A more profitable approach is to consider what was the soundest approach at the time, with the limited knowledge available.   The first step should obviously have been to seek the views of Europeans who were acquainted with politically conscious Egyptians outside the Khedive's entourage.   Blunt was one of these, and instead of dismissing him as a " dreamer " or " poet ",[1] his personal know-

---

[1] For some unknown reason the British administrators seemed to regard the writing of poetry as an eccentricity that disqualified the writer from saying anything useful on public affairs.

ledge of the liberal nationalists, like Mohammed Abdu and Arabi and his friends should have been treated as weighty evidence. Next, a sound principle to follow in such circumstances is that reform must come from within if it is to endure : it was a major blunder, after nationalism had already taken roots, to subject the country to foreign occupation and dictated reforms through a puppet government. In the long run the real " dreamers " were the " realists " like Hartington among the politicians, and the former India adminis-trators among the officials.[1] The danger of unilateral intervention by France if Britain had left could have been met by diplomatic means. Moreover a friendly Egypt would have been one of the best safeguards for the Canal route, and diplomatic pressure, backed by a strong fleet, against attempts by any other power to dominate the Canal would probably have found a good response among the Powers. As it was, the occupation of Egypt set off a series of far-reaching repercussions among the Powers, even, according to the ably argued thesis of Robinson, Gallagher, and Denny,[2] leading to the partition of Africa as a by-product. Their conclusion is appro-priately qualified : " . . . without the occupation of Egypt, there is no reason to suppose that any international scrambles for Africa, either east or west, would have begun when they did ".[3]

The revolution in transport which was showing its effects on a world-wide scale after the eighteen-seventies would in any case have brought Africa out of isolation, and, in the existing state of inter-national organisation, it is difficult to see how western rivalries for influence in Africa could have been avoided. Whether the results would have been more or less favourable to African development we cannot tell. It must be admitted that the actual " scramble " was remarkably peaceful on the whole, and that the beginnings of modernisation came much earlier than would have been likely if Africans had remained isolated.

[1] In justice to Lord Cromer it should be added that he would almost certainly have moved faster than his successors did in extending the use of Egyptian officials in administration.

[2] *Africa and the Victorians* (Cambridge, 1960), Chs. VI and IX–XIII.

[3] op. cit., p. 163. This part of their thesis is vigorously disputed by a number of scholars of Africa. See especially Jean Stengers, " L'Imperialisme Colonial de la fin du XIXe siecle ; Mythe ou 'réalité'", in *Journal of African History*, III, 3, 1962, pp. 470–97. M. Stengers makes an impressive case, and my own argument that the Egyptian occupation was a false step in our history does not depend on the view that it started the scramble for Africa. On that question far more study is needed. The establishment of the *Journal of African History* and the high quality of its early issues are encouraging evidence that future work on African history in the late-nineteenth and early-twentieth centuries will be less " Euro-centric " and will give more attention to the internal conditions at the time of European intervention. See also J. D. Hargreaves, *Prelude to the Partition of Africa*, London 1963.

Even in Egypt there was much more in common between the ideas of Cromer and those of present-day nationalists in the Middle East and Africa than an Arab or African nationalist could admit publicly today without being reviled. He was concerned for the improvement of the conditions of the *fellah* and regarded the land lords as parasites. He believed that reform on western lines was the only hope for Egypt and that above all an improvement in material conditions must be hastened ; he used all the funds he could obtain for this purpose.

But it is a central thesis of the present study that, once an indigenous political consciousness has been aroused, and the foundations of nationalism have been laid, an intervention from outside cannot succeed in reconciling the people to foreign rule, either direct or indirect, by means of material improvements.[1]   Nor is it possible in such conditions to attract and train the ablest local talent to take over the eventual administration of the country. Once nationalism has taken hold among the politically conscious classes and is spreading through them to the masses, all those who co-operate with foreign rulers lose influence among their own people. Therefore the aims to " intervene—reform—retire " are an illusory combination, only practicable in earlier societies, like India during the eighteenth and a considerable part of the nineteenth century, before nationalism had emerged. When imperial rule was established during such a period, it was probably advantageous in the long run to prolong it during the earlier stages of the subsequent development of nationalism, so long as resistance to it was not strong enough to lead to serious conflicts, and so long as progress was being made towards self-government, and the indigenous people were being brought increasingly into the public services. In such circumstances national unity was forged through unity in resistance to external rule, and at the same time the resources and the organisation and leadership necessary for successful self-government were created, and the danger of breakdown in the transition from dependence to independence was avoided.

In the mid-twentieth century, however, the time for gradual transition has passed. It is to the great credit of the British and French Governments that they have recognised this and acted on it. If, as I believe, the Gladstone Cabinet showed faulty judgement, and adopted the wrong alternative when they ordered the bombardment of Alexandria, the Wolesley expedition against Colonel Arabi,

[1] In the present context I am leaving aside those cases in which occupation is followed by substantial immigration and import of capital. United States and Russian imperialism shows many examples where this placed the original populations either in a numerical minority, or in a minority position with reference to the key positions in government, administration, and economic enterprises.

and the subsequent administration of Egypt through a puppet régime, any analogous policy today would be even more damaging in the long run, for it would encounter a far stronger nationalism than had yet appeared anywhere in Asia or Africa in the eighteen-eighties. Yet, as we shall see, there are striking analogies between actions of British liberal imperialists in the early eighties in Egypt and recent attempts of the liberal imperialists in the United States in the early nineteen-sixties to maintain a dominant position in Central America and the Caribbean.

More generally, the course of imperialist expansion and con-traction, of colonisation and decolonisation, has been determined, not merely by conditions and personalities within, and rivalries among, the Great Powers, but also by the personalities and changing moods and conditions within the areas in which intervention took place. However weak in armed power these areas may have been, they were inhabited by societies which were rarely static or stagnant, some of which were passing through significant changes, and which cannot be dismissed as mere passive instruments in the hands of the Great Powers.

IV

The Rise of Political Consciousness

If, in his international dealings, the statesman is limited by public sentiment at home, he is also constrained by public sentiment abroad. In a biological analogy we might say that here lies one of the chief nerve centres of the international organism, and that the leading characteristic of the twentieth-century revolution in inter-national affairs is to be found in the growing sensitivity of this nerve centre. The masses of people in most of the Asian, African, and Latin American countries had neither time, nor knowledge, nor inclination to concern themselves seriously and directly with inter-national affairs until very recently. Even now many, and probably the great majority, would prefer to be let alone in peace rather than to become involved, as some of them have been, in international conflicts exacerbated by the rivalries of would-be leaders at home and of the Great Powers abroad, and tinctured with doctrinal fanati-cism. Nevertheless an active minority, generally guided and stimu-lated by leaders educated in the West, will set the pace in the whole community and the majority will acquiesce even when many take little active part in the movement for independence, external as well as internal.

It is hardly necessary here to enlarge in detail on the influences which have contributed to the rapid rise of political consciousness in Asia, Latin America, and Africa in the twentieth century. The example of the rise of Japan was perhaps the first major influence at least in Asia,[1] the disturbances of the First World War the second the indirect effects of the Great Depression then played a part which was still incomplete when the Second World War brought an upheaval of vast dimensions, overturning many landmarks in the Middle and Far East and in south-eastern Asia, and indirectly affecting tropical Africa and Latin America, particularly through its economic ramifications. These events brought sharp and sudden changes in the ways of life of millions of people ; the changes were bound up with international and not merely domestic events, and men were constrained as never before to look beyond the borders of the countries in which they lived. In the two World Wars the peoples of Asia, Latin America, and Africa saw western civilisation rent apart from within, divided into armed camps locked in a death struggle, each camp trying to draw the outside world into its own orbit, and use it for its own purposes. The prestige of the West faded, the magic touch had gone, the claim to moral superiority lost its foundation, and the rising generation of educated Asians, Latin Americans, and Africans set as their goal, much more strongly than before, the control of the destinies of their own peoples, free of external domination. The keynote was, and remains, that of independence.

But in rejecting the tutelage and political domination of the West they became, in most areas, more and more western in their material outlook and aspirations. Thus the *avant-garde* broke, not only the western tutelage and leadership, but also with many of the traditional elements in their own countries, and internal as well as external strains and stresses were set up which greatly complicated the search for means of reconciling the aims of the West with those of the newly awakening peoples of Asia, Latin America, and Africa.[2]

These developments are not a complete explanation. The *avant garde* of young nationalists were at first a small minority, and though the Wars and their aftermaths gave them opportunities which they would not otherwise have had until much later, it would have been difficult for them to arouse mass support and infuse an *élan* into their movements if new means of communication had not been invented. The masses were so illiterate in most of the areas concerned that the printed word had little power over them. But the

[1] However, as we have already seen, Egyptian nationalism was already emerging in the 1880's.

[2] At the end of the First World War, for example, there were sharp differences among British advisers in the Middle East regarding the best means of establishing new governments in the Arab territories of the former Ottoman Empire.

ansmission of the human voice over radio revolutionised political
ommunication and enabled political appeals to be conveyed per-
uasively and fervently in the languages of the masses, as intelligible
> the illiterate as to the literate, directed to undermining the *status
uo*.   And the range of broadcasting was such that, when the
uthorities in any area censored utterances, international rivalries
nsured that " Voices " would be beamed into the area from outside.
n recent years, day in and day out, an unceasing stream of propa-
anda has been poured into the ears of the masses in Asia, Latin
merica, and Africa in their own languages ; consisting in some
reas of unending torrents of abuse of the existing governments and
ie established order of society, in distorted versions of the history of
ie recent past, in incitements to revolution and occasionally even to
ie assassination of rulers ; in other areas, consisting in more artfully
isinuated criticisms of the existing authorities, restrained and per-
uasive in form, and affecting a pained air of regret calculated to
ppeal to listeners of moderate views who would be repelled by crude
enunciations.   It is an error to suppose that most of this war of
rords comes from communist sources ; nationalist sources, and
ationalist-imperialist sources are no mean rivals to communist
urces, either in extent or in virulence.   Today the radio " Voices "
arry political agitation into the houses and streets of villages on the
inges of deserts and high in mountain ranges as well as in the large
entres of population.

And always the destructive note carries greater appeal to the
rowd than the constructive note.   " *Écrasez l'infame* " strikes as
ympathetic a chord as ever.   To find the source of present ills in the
ersonal villainy of the rulers of today, the obsolescence of existing
istitutions, and the domination exercised by foreign powers ; to
romise and to expect that the assassination or dismissal of the
ilers, the destruction of the institutions, and severance from foreign
ominion, will bring, if not a new Heaven, at least a new Earth—
iis approach to the sufferings of the present time has the force of
implicity, the advantage of relieving those who accept it from the
iborious and exacting, though creative, task of converting the
resent order, piece by piece, into an order adapted to changing
iodern conditions, and serving the interests of all the people.
Liberation " is its keynote, and what lies beyond liberation is
llowed to remain below the political and economic horizon.

Unfortunately, the new order passionately desired does not come
i this way ; the empty, swept, and garnished rooms are not
efurnished without careful thought, infinite labour, and adminis-
ative skill, all of which make exacting demands on the individual
nd give little scope to the emotional release and excitement of per-
onal denunciations, of underground conspiracies, and of mob

demonstrations. The task of the statesman who tries to lead an
guide in the reawakening or newly emerging countries of Asia, Lati
America, and Africa is extraordinarily difficult. He is beset by pi
falls at home and abroad. Behind him he has a small literate an
semi-literate group leading or attempting to lead a mass of illitera
people on the land and in the towns. The illiterate, most of who
have far more intelligence and shrewdness than the literate con
monly realise, are not in themselves ill-disposed towards publi
order, but may become formidable obstacles to it when they ar
exploited by contending factions of the literate and semi-literate.

In his international dealings the statesman in such a country ha
an equally if not more difficult task. The people, whatever faction
differences may divide them in domestic affairs, are united in a su
picion of outsiders, and particularly of outsiders who have rule
them, directly or indirectly, in the past. In some cases there a
solid grounds for suspicion ; in others there were solid grounds in th
past but they have now disappeared ; in others still, as in the case
some mandates and trusteeship agreements, suspicions were nev
firmly based. But the statesman must take account of them, regar
less of their basis or lack of basis. The Burmese leaders, at the tim
of independence, realised that it would be in the interests of Burm
to remain in the Commonwealth. But the mass of their followers, i
the course of the struggle for independence, had been worked up
such a pitch of hostility to those who had occupied their country i
the past, that the retention of any external connection, howev
innocuous or even beneficial, would have aggravated an already pr
carious domestic political situation, and brought a threat of renewe
outbreaks of violence. Britain wisely refrained from pressing th
matter, and when Burma decided to remain outside, continued t
co-operate with her in practical ways when opportunities aros
Before long, excellent psychological relations were establishe
between Burma and Britain, and such arbitrary acts as the Britis
annexation of Upper Burma in the eighteen-eighties were forgotte
or regarded dispassionately as a mere episode in past history. Th
full and ungrudging recognition of political independence sometim
works psychological wonders—if it comes in time.

But the more completely independence is achieved, the great
the practical and political difficulties which face the statesman in th
emancipated country. Relieved of the struggle against powers an
principalities outside, he has no ready scapegoat at hand which ca
be conveniently blamed for the delays and setbacks that still hind
the improvement in the material conditions of life. His mass follow
ing, deprived of the chief outlet for its passions, but reluctant t
subside into political passivity, and ill qualified to appreciate th
difficulties of transforming a society, may turn its emotions towar

domestic issues, ushering in a turbulent political era at home that may leave the ordinary working family worse off for a long time, in respect of goods and services, and of personal security, than it had been under the old régime.

Navigating these wild currents, the statesman is prone to turn in any direction that may promise easier sailing, or bring at least temporary relief. He may, for example, erect an artificial scapegoat in the form of " the imperialists ", who are allegedly plotting secretly against the independence of the country. He leaves it to his hearers to make any application they like of his vague general denunciations of these monsters, and himself often carefully omits proper nouns to avoid unnecessary offence to other countries. It does not follow, of course, that all actual denunciations of imperialists abroad are without foundation. Both Russia and the United States have engaged in clandestine operations aimed at the overthrow of governments in smaller countries and their replacement by régimes subservient to one or other of these Great Powers. Britain and France tried to overthrow the Nasir régime in Egypt in 1956. Egypt has attempted to overthrow by underground means régimes in Tunisia, Jordan, Syria, Iraq, and perhaps other parts of the Middle East. But in a number of small countries not facing these dangers, generalised denunciations of imperialism have been used mainly for reasons of domestic politics. Such utterances should not be taken at their face value, and in the Commonwealth and western Europe we would often do well to ignore them, and to regard with sympathy, and assist where possible, those whose domestic difficulties lead them to resort to this device.

The explosive political forces within the newly emerging and the reawakening countries of Asia, Latin America, and Africa are the most important and least calculable development in the international relations of the mid-twentieth century. They are likely to remain so well into if not through the twenty-first century. These countries are in the process of changing the whole balance of power in the world, even though their armaments are negligible in a world setting and of local significance only, and even though their political life remains stormy for years to come. In the future, no Great or Medium power will be able to ignore them or alienate them with impunity.

The power of mass sentiment, organised and developed by small groups of educated or semi-educated people, extending over immense geographical areas among populations exceeding many times the combined populations of western Europe, North America, and Australasia, is a striking confirmation of the view that armaments are only one item in any accounting of the sources of power, and that, the more destructive armaments become, the less power they represent among the sources of power as a whole. Armaments are

8

too deadly to be used in conflicts between the Great Powers : armed interference by one of the Great Powers in the emerging and awakening countries might draw in a Great Power ranged on another side, or start a local war which, like the First World War, would quickly become a general war. Equally important, it is difficult to hold down by armed force large populations that above all things passionately desire independence, resent the enforced dependency of the past, and prize above all else the freedom they have won by past effort. Even the most heavily armed powers cannot afford to dissipate their armed forces over large areas of the world to hold down resentful populations which prize independence even above material gain. Nor can they afford the unpopularity in the rest of the world which such actions brought to Russia in Hungary, to Britain and France in Egypt, to China in Tibet, and would bring on the United States in Cuba if her repressive measures were successful. Such interventions may or may not be applauded at home but they are almost universally condemned abroad. The people of the United States are increasingly coming up against the power of mass sentiment, the mass desire for independence, in Latin America. As yet they are only beginning the process of psychological " decolonisation ", and a long period of disillusionment awaits them. Only when they recognise the impotence of armaments, and the necessity of restraint and patience, in dealing with Asia and Central America, and only when they are ready to treat Latin Americans on an equal footing and genuinely recognise their independence regardless of the nature of their internal régimes, can they hope to earn the esteem and goodwill of the younger generation of their neighbours.

Britain and France cannot afford to take up an attitude of moral superiority in these matters : in the past each of them has at times intervened in Asia and North Africa without due regard to the interests of the inhabitants. And the colossal error over Suez is too recent to be explained away by the morals of an earlier generation. None the less, Suez, Indo-China, and Algeria have brought Britain and France out of the era of colonial psychology and have opened the way for the establishment of relations with Asia, Africa and Latin America on a footing of equality, respect, and non-interference.

CHAPTER VI

THE PSYCHOLOGICAL NECESSITY OF DECOLONISATION

I

Decolonisation and Personal Freedom

IN THE long run decolonisation may be expected to add to the sum of human liberties. At its best, colonial rule can only lay part of the foundations on which self-government can be exercised in genuine democratic institutions. It can create institutions, local and central, through which the indigenous peoples can gain the political and administrative experience without which self-government is always in danger of lapsing into autocracy. But colonial rule, by its very nature, cannot complete the edifice of political liberty. Its ultimate seat of authority is external, and sooner or later is bound to come under challenge, to which it can respond only by using force or by granting freedom. But freedom can only be granted to the *collectivité*; it does not ensure the firm establishment of individual freedom within the *collectivité*. In the long run, however, we may cherish the hope, and hold to the faith, that political communities will not submit permanently to tyranny from their own kind any more than they will submit in our own time to the continued exercise of authority from outside.

But in the short-run the outlook is less favourable, and Latin American experience shows that the " short-run " may last for many decades, possibly for centuries. It is too early yet to tell whether or not the movement for decolonisation will add to the sum of individual liberties at all in the short-run. At the time of writing the reverse appears to have been the case so far. The ancient saying, " My fathers chastised you with whips ; I will chastise you with scorpions ", has lost none of its relevance, if we substitute " predecessors " for " fathers ". Domestic tyranny has often been more intense, more deep-rooted, and more difficult to throw off, than foreign authority. The grant of political independence, having been made to a *collectivité*, represented at the outset by a small ruling class among the indigenous peoples, does not ensure that this class will continue to hold office at the will of the people. Many of the new states are threatened by the attitudes both of the ruling class and of the people. The former are often tempted to maintain themselves in office by demagoguery and military power, and the latter have not yet acquired a deep respect for the "legitimacy" of the new institutions.

In practice it probably matters little whether the newly independent state derives its legitimacy from the act of the colonial power in granting it independence, or whether it ignores or replaces this act by a formal resolution of a new national assembly presumed to represent "the people", and thus attempts to create a new and indigenous source of legitimacy,[1] sometimes described as autochthony.

Such distinctions may appeal to nationalistic lawyers and politicians but it can hardly be expected that the masses will appreciate them or that opposition groups will be induced by them to accept more readily the constitutional changes which the first independent governments may make in order to prolong and strengthen their tenure of power. Even when the new governments do not abuse their powers, the psychological acceptance of their legitimacy by the masses may be slow in coming, and this adds to the difficulties of establishing representative government.

Hypothetically, it might be argued that the analysis in this study has shown that in some areas the retention of colonial rule by force would maintain greater individual freedom than would be left by a decolonisation that opened the way for a domestic dictatorship. However, this is a shift of ground. The statement that decolonisation might reduce the sum of individual liberties implies a comparison between a past and a present or future condition. The argument for refusing decolonisation can only rest on a comparison between two future conditions. The difference is critical. As we have seen, the two World Wars, the spread of western education, and the revolution in the means of communication, have aroused the peoples in the emerging and reawakening countries to the point where they are no longer content tacitly to accept western rule, direct or indirect, as many of them were in the past.[2] Nationalism has been a comparatively late growth in these countries, as it was in the West before the French Revolution. British colonial rule could then leave substantial freedom to the individual, and even increase the sum of individual freedom by introducing the machinery for law and order and the peaceful and just adjudication of disputes.[3] The gains then made in many colonies were impressive.

---

[1] See especially Kenneth Wheare, *The Constitutional Structure of the Commonwealth*, Oxford, 1960, pp. 89–114.

[2] It has often been pointed out that the British military force in India was insignificant in comparison with the immense population. The same may be said of a number of other areas.

[3] Seeing this process at work in Kuala Lumpur in 1925, I obtained a lasting impression of the vast gain in freedom when impartial adjudication took the place

But those days are over. The demand to throw off what is felt to be foreign rule, direct or indirect, has spread to all the corners of the earth. It has shaken the foundations of empires, eastern as well as western. It must be accepted voluntarily or repressed bloodily— there is no third way to meet it. Britain and France have chosen the first response to it, Russia and China the second, though Russia has loosened its hold in some areas since Stalin's death. In the fifties and early sixties the United States, as the Guatemalan and Cuban affairs showed, has been poised uneasily between the two.

Consequently, it is impossible to project into the future the comparison we may legitimately make between the degree of individual freedom under the best British colonial régimes on the one hand and that under the new independent régimes on the other. In the face of hostile underground activities, aided by external sources, encouraged by external agitation, and defended in United Nations debates, colonial régimes could only be maintained against the will of the peoples by repressive measures and censorship that would continuously violate freedom of speech, of assembly, and of publication, and leave little or no room for the individual liberties which many British and French colonies have enjoyed in the past, and which rested on tacit consent to colonial rule in the days when nationalist sentiment was in an early stage of development.

The art of government and the art of international diplomacy and international relations depend on the ability to forsee and anticipate the " winds of change ". The Union of South Africa is still following static policies, depending on repression to turn back the winds of change. China is also, by more ruthless suppression, trying to change the underlying conditions in Tibet, destroy Mahayana Buddhism, and force the people into conformity with the Chinese Empire.

How long the totalitarian powers will be able to maintain their imperialist domination of outlying peoples who wish to follow their own ways of life is not yet clear. But repression is out of the question for western Europe, most of all because the peoples of western Europe and the " Dominions " and India would not permit the continuing use of measures abroad in flat contradiction to the principles and practice of their governments at home.

---

of arbitrary and fluctuating methods of adjudication often influenced by personal favouritisms and corruption.

II

The Problem of Timing in Decolonisation

The late nineteen-fifties and the early nineteen-sixties will go down in history as a time of earnest debates in Britain and France over the dilemma confronting both countries in the territories on the verge of independence which contained substantial numbers of settlers of European ancestry who had occupied privileged positions.

To select one illustration of these debates : Miss Perham, a leading British authority on African politics, in a letter to *The Times*, criticised the Government in 1961 for going back on their original proposals on the constitution of Northern Rhodesia.[1] The letter drew some temperate, reasoned, if biased, replies which stated well the case for going more slowly, and pointed out the dangers coming from the crudities and inexperience of the nationalist movement, the presence of extreme groups over which, at the time, Mr. Kaunda's effective control in Northern Rhodesia was doubtful, and the intimidation practised against dissenters from the nationalist demands. No serious student could dismiss these charges as based on pure prejudice and selfish interests, and it would show disloyalty to the ideals of freedom on which the case for self-government rests to dismiss as irrelevant the dangers of terrorism and victimisation practised against dissidents. It was well that those dangers were given publicity and that the force of outside opinion should have been brought to bear on the conduct of the nationalists as well as on that of the colonising powers. The Rhodesian case was mild in comparison with the Algerian : the supporters of the F.L.N., in its campaign of terrorism, did not always shrink from massacre of the innocents, designed to intimidate those indigenous peoples who did not support it.

Yet Miss Perham was substantially right in diagnosis and prescription. The generally statesmanlike record of Mr. Macmillan and Mr. Macleod in respect to Africa in the late nineteen-fifties was marred by fumbling over Northern Rhodesia. It was probably true that an African majority in the legislature was inevitable in the near future, and the Africans would have done well in their own interests to gain some political experience before plunging into the responsibilities of office. But to defend the actions which the Government then took was to misunderstand the psychological conditions of the

---

[1] Their position, of course, was changed later : I discuss the position in 1961 because it brought out the significant issues of wider relevance that underlay the whole controversy over early or immediate independence—the time and speed of transition.

time and place.   It was hopeless to try to convince the nationalists
and their mass following that their interests would be served by concessions to the pressures exerted by Sir Roy Welensky against
Mr. Macleod's original plan.   To attack Sir Roy personally was
pointless :   he was the elected representative of the population of
European origin or ancestry, and he had therefore to represent their
point of view or resign office.   If he had resigned, his successor would
probably have been even less favourably disposed than he was himself to the rapid political enfranchisement of the indigenous population.   But if Sir Roy was sincere in holding to his viewpoint, so also
were the indigenous political leaders :   they had followers to
represent, who circumscribed their freedom of manoeuvre even
more narrowly than the population of European descent circumscribed that of Sir Roy.   They had experienced racial discrimination
and inferior status—mild, indeed, by comparison with the position
in the Union of South Africa, but enough to create distrust of the
motives and intentions of the local population of European descent.

Just as Sir Roy was more moderate and intelligent in outlook than
the majority of the population of European origin, so Mr. Kaunda
was more moderate and intelligent in outlook than the majority of
his followers were.   Actually there were wider divergencies, not only
between Mr. Kaunda and many of his followers but also among
different groups of the latter, than there were within the population
of European descent.   Hence, in a statesmanlike approach to the
problems of central Africa it was of supreme importance to create the
conditions which gave the greatest scope, and offered the best opportunities, to those leaders and potential leaders who desired a reasoned
and constructive solution which would allow future co-operation of
races in a society where all individuals would have equal rights under
the law, and which would leave the way open for economic
co-operation with the rest of the world, including the former colonial
powers.   Not all Africans desire such a solution, and to rebuff those
who do, and whose aim was to seek peace and ensue it, consistently
with justice, was to strengthen the hands of those rival would-be
leaders who, disbelieving in the possibilities of a peaceful attainment
of what they considered to be justice, wished to set in motion the
resources of underground warfare—arson, murder, economic sabo-
tage—creating the psychology of terror and the ever-present apprehension of sudden death, cutting off the just as well as the unjust, an
offence against the laws of God and man, but one from which
nationalist political warfare has not shrunk in our century of declin-
ing civilisation.[1]

Since the " European " population was small, the African large

[1] As one of those whose youthful military experience began in Ireland in the
spring of 1916, I do not in the least imply that Europeans have a better record

and the use of peaceful or violent methods among the Africans hung in the balance ; since violence on one side would engender violence on the other, and on both sides the consequences would fall on the just and on the unjust alike, it was the part of statesmanship to make concessions to, and thus strengthen the hands of, the nationalists who sought a peaceful solution. Miss Perham was therefore right, even though most of the facts stated by her critics were correct when taken by themselves. To act otherwise would have been to fall into the same error, in principle, as Parliament in Westminster fell into in 1909, when it debated and passed the South Africa Act, giving precedence to the interests of the white minority of European origin over those of the Bantu majority.[1] The points at issue in the two cases were widely different. Parliament's concessions to the population of European origin in South Africa fastened a permanently inferior status on the rest of the population. The Government's concession in 1961 to the population of European origin in Northern Rhodesia would only have delayed for a short time an African majority. Nevertheless, the failure to grasp the psychological consequences of the second of these errors might have brought results hardly less disastrous in the long run than those which the framers of the South Africa Act, having less experience to guide them, failed to foresee.

British Governments fell into three errors within a decade in central Africa. The first was to complete the grant of internal self-government to the population of European origin in Southern Rhodesia ; the second was to sponsor and push through Parliament the legislation establishing the Central African Federation against the wishes of the native peoples ; and the third was to retreat for a time from an arrangement accepted for the transition period in Northern Rhodesia. Each of these three false steps arose out of the same error of principle, that of ignoring, or giving insufficient attention to, the feelings, attitudes, and opinions of the population of African descent.

These events illustrate well one of the key notes of the present study, which applies to practically all the emerging and reawakening

---

than Africans and Asian peoples. Even the dreadful Western Front to which we passed on in the summer of that year followed certain rules of the game which are disregarded in civil strife. It is a salutary experience today to be reminded of these events in C. D. Greaves, *James Conolly : His Life and Times*, London, 1960, and to see that the uncivilised acts were not confined to one side. One cannot read without a deep sense of shame and loathing the circumstances of Conolly's execution (pp. 335–41).

[1] ". . . The South Africa Act received its second reading in a thin, practically empty House of Commons (the attention of Parliament was absorbed by the struggle over Lloyd George's Budget). . . ." *Cambridge History of the British Empire*, Vol. III, p. 274.

countries. The revolution in international relations requires above all a revolution in western psychology with respect to the Asian, Latin American, and African peoples. Nothing less than psychological decolonisation will do. The most dangerous malaise affecting international relations today is that of patronising, " superior ", and ' stand-offish " attitudes among populations of European origin, wherever they are situated in the world, on the one hand, and the fierce resentments arising out of what, for want of a better phrase, may be called an " inferiority complex " on the part of many of the Asian and African peoples on the other.

The material basis of this psychological tension may be found in the wide and apparently growing disparity between the two worlds in wealth and in the standards of living of the masses. Its historical basis, over part of the vast area concerned, lies in intermittent relationships of dominance and dependency in the last few centuries. The extreme nationalists attribute the material disparities to western exploitation, and the historical retardation to western dominance. The realities are infinitely more complicated. The balance sheet of colonisation varied from area to area : in the long run posterity will probably accept as the best criterion, in judging these varied records the extent to which in each case the indigenous peoples were afforded opportunities for political and social development. No outcome of colonisation can be more disastrous than the sudden accession of independence without previous opportunities of gaining experience in the art of government.

But it does not follow that at this stage independence can be postponed until the peoples are judged by the colonising power to be prepared adequately for it. The opportunities for a gradual enlargement of the role of indigenous administrators and legislators, in preparation for eventual self-government, still existed earlier in the century, but the revolutionary psychological changes since then have ended them. In the mid-century we are not living in an age of " gradualness ". The best that could be expected after the Second World War was a time-table which proceeded by fairly rapid stages, each extending the areas of responsibility of the elected indigenous representatives. The Webb's phrase, " the inevitability of gradualism ", remains relevant in certain economic fields : many apparent departures from it are departures mainly in name rather than in underlying realities. But in the political aspects of colonial policy it is otherwise : there, the only discrepancies between changes in name and changes in substance lie in the retention of " advisers ", who in fact for a time are rather more than advisers in their spheres of competence. However, this hardly differs fundamentally from the early stages of modernisation of some countries, for example, Japan and Turkey, that never came within the colonial orbit.

III

The Problem of the " Colons "

The path to independence in territories containing significant numbers of settlers of European descent has been strewn with pitfalls. It would seem that the difficulties of psychological adjustment to the revolution in international relations tend to vary inversely with distance from the colonial territories. Long after the populations in the former colonising countries have reconciled themselves to the passing of the colonial age, their compatriots in some of the colonies themselves have striven desperately to delay or prevent the passing of power into native hands. No groups in the world have been more short-sighted than they, or have clung more tenaciously to lost causes. Their attitudes have contained the seeds of tragedy : they have been self-defeating, tending to make the break, when it came sharper and more thorough-going than it need have been. The fanaticism of the adherents of " *Algérie française* " fomented divisions that disrupted the French army, damaged its morale, and deprived the French Government of part of its bargaining strength when the time came to negotiate with the rebels. In some, though fortunately not all, colonies, the settlers who once enjoyed a privileged position seemed incapable of foresight.

Liberal observers in western countries have tended to treat the *colons*, as the French aptly call them, with impatience, anger, and contempt. Yet there is no good reason why *colons* should not be objects of systematic, impartial study. As it is, we have surprisingly little detailed analysis, social or psychological, on the subject. From what elements among the *colons* did the active supporters of intransigence spring ? Through what means did they exert their influence on their compatriots ? What background, upbringing, and institutions did most to favour an intransigent outlook and a far-sighted outlook respectively ? What means were open to the governments in London, Paris, and Brussels to bring home to the rank-and-file settler the nature of the changes in world forces and the impossibility of continuing the former social and political relationships ? Little attention has been given to these questions. Yet it has long been known that many settlers, and in France some politicians left their homelands with liberal views but, after experience on the spot, were assimilated to the viewpoint of the settlers. This would appear to establish a prima facie case for analysis of the external influences which had been brought to bear on them and the personal characteristics that shaped their responses to the change of environment.

Much popular discussion of this difficult issue has shown signs of irresponsibility. At one extreme the cause of the settlers of European origin has been defended uncompromisingly, without regard to the position of the indigenous peoples. It has been argued that they and their predecessors settled in the area in good faith, in the assurance that their interests would be permanently safeguarded. At the opposite extreme, the settlers [1] have been denounced as reactionaries, and it has been argued that they should all be forcibly repatriated if they were not willing to take their chances without guarantees from the new régime.

Obviously, neither of these views was tenable. The colonial powers have held responsibilities for the well-being of all the peoples in the territories which they governed directly or indirectly. They could not justify policies which subordinated the wishes of the large majority of the inhabitants of a country to those of a comparatively small minority, as British Governments did on three occasions in the nineteen-fifties. On the other hand, those who speak as if the settlers of European origin were of no account, or even a sheer hindrance to the future of the areas in question, also betray a lack of understanding. The position varies in different areas, but in all of them one of the paramount needs in the near future is that of economic development on modern lines. The whole future of the emerging countries as independent states depends essentially on their ability to meet the needs of rapidly growing populations from fixed areas of land. The populations of European origin have contributions to make which are out of proportion to their numbers. A small section of the population possessing skills far above the average in the territories concerned, and directing activities which are on a higher technical level and more productive than those of the majority, makes an economic contribution to the community as a whole far beyond what would be expected from its size. The newly independent governments can ill afford to throw away this contribution in the difficult days ahead, though some of them have gone far towards doing so. The economic difficulties which have faced some of the new states are such as would daunt the most experienced western civil servants and economists. How much more formidable must they be for the comparatively inexperienced political leaders and civil servants in new, untried régimes. In such circumstances it is folly to throw away economic assets unnecessarily. Political independence is worth some economic sacrifice, but if economic deterioration goes too far chronic political instability will set in. Either the emerging country will become dependent on gifts from abroad, which are not often

---

[1] This common term is seriously misleading when applied to *colons* generally, for by the mid-twentieth century the majority of those so designated were natives of the countries concerned and had known no homes outside them.

given unconditionally, or the new government will be tempted to meet rising discontent by the suppression of liberties, and individual freedom will decline below the level attained under colonial rule. The new rulers, if they sincerely desire to link independence with liberty, would do well to refrain from alienating unnecessarily the minorities within their frontiers who are making, or are capable of making, exceptional contributions to the economic development of the country.

This is what made the situation in a number of African territories so dangerous in the nineteen-fifties and early sixties. The *colons* in Algeria clung to privileges that became anachronisms in the twentieth century. They showed a suicidal intransigence in face of President de Gaulle's far-sighted statesmanship.[1] They competed with the revolutionaries in deeds of violence and in the massacre of innocents.[2] It is not surprising that they aroused widespread resentment and distrust among the Moslem population. But resentment is no basis on which to shape a policy for the future, and the removal of distrust is an essential condition of success in the establishment of a new state. Reconciliation and co-existence between the Moslem population and the population of European origin was the only alternative to partition or to exodus of the latter and return of the Algerians in France, either of which was fraught with economic dangers. The price of indulgence in the destructive and foolish passions of the past was too great to pay, on either side. Unfortunately the mischief was already done and a mass exodus of the " French " population created grave economic trouble in Algeria.

The settlers of European origin in the Rhodesias and in Kenya came a long way in the political sense. They have shown less intransigence than the adherents of " *Algérie française* ". But in the Rhodesias they lagged behind in the nineteen-fifties, when it was essential that they should have gone at least as far as Sir John Moffat was already willing to go, and, in addition, to end social discriminations which reserve separate facilities for " whites ". Later, Sir Edgar Whitehead courageously undertook this but it could not be effective without the day-to-day co-operation of the settlers who later rejected him and his policies. As the experience of the United States demonstrates, such discriminations are an insuperable barrier to harmonious racial relations, and enlightened opinion will properly insist on their removal on the continent of Africa. Those members of the population of European origin who clung to the idea that the

---

[1] Doubtless only a small minority carried out these acts. But the majority were unwilling to run risks by opposing them.

[2] When de Gaulle came to power in 1958 it appears that the colons, as well as many of his supporters in France, believed that he would support " *Algeria française*."

discriminations of the past could be continued in the future were moving about in a day-dream.

It by no means follows, however, that all the fears of the populations of European origin as to the capacities and the goodwill of future African governments were necessarily ill-founded. If greater efforts had been made at earlier stages in the history of these colonies to advance native education and political and administrative experience, there would have been firmer ground for future confidence. As it was, some of the potential leaders of the nationalist movements had already begun to seek popularity by the most primitive appeals to anti-foreign sentiment and did not hesitate to meet prejudice with counter-prejudice, and concessions, when they came, with new demands. The precarious economic structures of some of these countries, and the dependence for export earnings on the enterprise of the population of European descent, exposed as dangerous folly the substitution of a new race prejudice and exclusiveness in the opposite direction to the old. But the position was not hopeless, provided mutual confidence could be established between responsible indigenous and " settler " groups, and capital and technical skills needed in economic development were forthcoming. These conditions could not be fulfilled unless the population of European origin were willing to make the necessary psychological adjustments, and to incur the necessary risks of accepting a position in which the peoples of African descent would have equal legal and political rights with them, and equal access to public services and facilities. Those peoples of European origin who are given the opportunity, and take it, to assist the emerging African peoples in their first steps to establish themselves on equal terms with the peoples of other continents will be playing a great and unique role in history, and adding a new item on the credit side of Europe overseas, an item more glorious than any their ancestors contributed by penetrating and occupying the land. The time fast approaches when the newly emerging political class of African descent must decide whether to harbour or set aside resentments over the past and whether to revert to the backward-looking cry of " Africa for the Africans ", or to keep the way open for the population of European descent and, under suitable control, European capital to continue within an independent Africa those activities without which the land might revert to its old conditions of self-sufficiency at a primitive level of subsistence.

CHAPTER VII

COMMUNISM, ANTI-COMMUNISM, AND
LE TIERS MONDE

I

Misconceptions of the Extent, Role, and Significance of Communism

A COMMON attitude in western countries has been to represent *le tiers monde* [1] as a battleground of ideas in which the western countries are engaged in a life-and-death struggle with the eastern countries for the souls of the emerging and reawakening peoples. Russia and China, it is said, are carrying the gospel of communism to politically inexperienced peoples, whose older customs, traditions, and faiths are collapsing and who are seeking new faiths and new ways of life to fill the resulting void. The West, it is often said, is absorbed in the pursuit of material gain and has no buoyant faith, no inspiring ideals, no concerted aims, comparable in appeal with the lure of communist doctrines and their application.

This is the note of the evangelist, and if the issue were determined by political evangelism and political crusades, the prospects would be gloomy.

But the present study is written in the belief that this approach misses the central issues and fails to represent the actual flux of events and play of interests and ideas in the emerging and reawakening countries. The realities are infinitely more complex and confused. The transition from the older world to the world of the second half of the twentieth century takes place unevenly among the various groups in each emerging country, setting up stresses and strains that burst out from time to time into internal conflicts which spill over into international relations. The one thing in common which unites the emerging and reawakening states is the passionate desire for political independence, which, though it is sometimes compromised, in the states as they are now bounded, by sentiments of regional kinship, applies without exception to their attitude to the outside world, both West and East. The chief stress has been laid on independence of the West, merely because the emerging and

---

[1] I am applying this designation to the developing states of Asia, Africa, and tropical Latin America, omitting, in Asia, China, Japan and Asiatic Russia.

reawakening states were formerly under western rule or in western spheres of influence, and the non-Russian and non-Chinese peoples now under Russian or Chinese rule have had little or no opportunity to make their voices heard. Already, as we shall see, where communist parties linked with Russia, but beyond the reach of Russian troops, have gone beyond giving assistance to nationalist movements and endeavoured to interfere in a contrary sense, they have been quickly halted and sometimes suppressed altogether. Such episodes have generally brought disfavour on the Soviet Union and as they tend to rebound to the advantage of western countries the Russians have a strong motive for avoiding them as far as possible.

Those movements which work below as well as on the surface are not easy to appraise, but after some years of experience and reflexion I believe that, while the communist movement in the emerging and reawakening countries is important within limits here and there, its scope has been greatly exaggerated, its nature widely misconceived, and its future prospects greatly overestimated. This is not surprising. The proportion of western people who have any direct knowledge and experience of the ordinary people in the emerging countries of Asia, tropical Latin America and Africa is extremely small. The class divisions in Britain, the significance of which today seems to be exaggerated for political and literary purposes, fade out of notice by comparison with the international class divisions between the West and most of the emerging countries. These divisions are exacerbated by the luxurious conditions in which western people of all shades of politicial opinion live when they are in the countries in question—sometimes more luxurious than those which they normally enjoy in the countries from which they come. Asceticism in any form seems to be as much out of fashion on the political left as on the right, and there appear to be no counterparts of the late Mr. Gandhi in the West. Many find creature comforts so indispensable, and have become so over-sensitive in matters of hygiene, that they tend to exclude themselves from direct relationships of any kind with the vast majority in the emerging countries.

Consequently, among western people who visit the emerging countries, most of the information and ideas about the feelings and opinions among the masses and even among local students are derived from listening to small numbers of comparatively well-to-do people, such as government officials and ministers, merchants, landowners, and business men, who speak a western language and live more or less in western fashion in their homes.

From such sources a biased picture of what is happening in the countries is usually derived. In countries under right-wing rule a misleading and exaggerated view is obtained of the extent, the role, and the importance of communism. Popular discontent, particularly the unrest among students and the younger members of the professional classes, is loosely attributed to "communism", and, most misleading of all, a variety of dissenters from the existing régime are described as "communists", who have very little in common with each other except a dislike of the government, and a tendency to attribute to its shortcomings everything they believe to be wrong with the country.   Early in the course of residence in Asia my curiosity was so aroused by sweeping allegations about communism that subsequently I took considerable trouble to make my own estimates on the matter in circles in which I had many close acquaintances.   In widely separated areas then and since I found that a large majority of those described loosely as communists were neither members of the party, nor in the confidence of the party, nor disposed to accept Russian domination in their countries.   There was a small number of extremely active communists with considerable skill in organising, or helping to organise, agitations against the régimes in question, and against the western countries which, according to them, used the régimes as tools and instruments of imperialist aggression in the world.   Such successes as they obtained were chiefly negative : they helped to intensify opposition to the government, but it existed independently of them.   The overwhelming majority of the anti-government groups had no wish to replace the régimes they disliked by communist régimes, or to align their countries, directly or indirectly, with Russia.

These conclusions seem to be in harmony with the chequered history of the communist parties in Asia, Latin America, and Africa. If the communist position had been strong, if the doctrines of communism had possessed an appeal comparable to that of the sentiment of nationalism, and if the spectacle presented by the countries which had already embraced communism, or had been forced to adopt it or acquiesce in it, had demonstrated convincingly its capacity to produce a better, freer life than is enjoyed in the advanced western countries, then it would have been reasonable to expect that the peoples in the emerging countries would have been strongly attracted to it.   But none of these conditions has been fulfilled.   Even in the disturbed—in some areas the anarchical—conditions of the war and early post-war periods in south-eastern Asia, the communist parties, which might have been expected then to reap a better harvest from political agitation than at any other time, failed to take over government in any areas except in North Korea and North Viet-Nam, in both of which they received outside help across a common border with communist countries.   In North Vietnam their successes were only gained by adopting unorthodox practices, independently of China and Russia, and communist rule was only maintained subsequently by reversing the more orthodox communist agricultural policies which they had first attempted to impose on the peasant.[1]

Russia and China have still less of a foothold in Africa and little prospect of obtaining an important one. Most of Africa is far removed from either of the two great communist powers ; it has very limited relations with them, except in some countries through students, and although economic relations may be expected to increase gradually, there seems little likelihood that African political relations with the East will be very close, if only because the emerging African countries are above all concerned to assert their independence and to form their own policies.

The central point may be stated in simple terms. As we have already seen, the emerging and reawakening countries regard independence as the first and foremost aim in their policies. In the course of history they have sometimes fallen under the rule of Europeans but, for geographical reasons, never under that of Russia or China. Although Africa has benefited in many ways during the Colonial period, Africans cannot be expected to look at history from the European point of view, nor was western rule an unmixed blessing. As we have seen, the motives of colonisers, and the effects of colonisation in the light of possible alternative forms of development, have been extraordinarily diverse and are subjects of never-ending study and dispute, marked by frequent revisions of ideas as well as by discoveries of new sources of information. No finality can be reached.

If Africa is the " youngest ", tropical Latin America is the " oldest ", region of European expansion overseas, and the psychological adjustments needed in western attitudes to the two areas differ considerably. Broadly speaking, the difficulties of adjustment seem to vary in some degree inversely with distance. Many British people found it difficult to adjust with reference to Egypt and the Suez Canal, particularly in regard to the withdrawal of the military bases which had never been willingly accepted by Egyptian Governments. The United States Governments took a more detached view and recommended British withdrawal. All this is now a thing of the past but the American people and Government cling to the Guantanamo base in Cuba as if they had a natural right to it. Similarly, while using their influence against Britain on the Suez affair of 1956, they assert right over Panama which, like their rights in Cuban territory, were obvious products of imperialism, much more so than western rights over the Suez Canal had been. Britain and France take a

[1] For an illuminating study of the post-war period up to 1956, see J. H. Brimmel, *Communism in South-East Asia*, Royal Institute of International Affairs, 1959. This work shows insight and calm political judgement, except in its dismissal in 1958 of the idea that Russia and China were likely to fall out with each other !

calmer and more correct view of these subjects of dispute, though they have shown timidity in public discussions of them.

But in all these cases the stirring of the emergent and reawakened peoples have been attributed widely to the influence of communism and the activities of communists. Sir Anthony Eden (now Lord Avon) struck this note over Suez in 1956 and President Kennedy over Cuba in 1961, each endeavouring to cover up flagrantly aggressive actions by representing them as defensive measures taken against " international communism ", which was alleged to be threatening the security of routes and areas of vital importance to the West. Yet in both cases this was an incorrect representation of the real issue, which, quite simply, was that of political independence,[1] and the real driving force, which was nationalism and not communism.

The repeated error of western policy, and most of all of the policy of the United States, has been to misconceive the nature of the problem of communism in Asia, tropical Latin America, and Africa, and overrate its importance. Since the first and foremost aim in these areas, supported with intense passion, is that of political independence, the influence and the prospects of Russian and Chinese communism are severely circumscribed, and communism under the direction of these powers, or one of them, can only prevail if direct military force, or an immediate threat of it, can be brought to bear. So long as the local communists merely support the nationalist causes, use nationalist slogans, and are able to create the impression that they are helping in a struggle for liberation and independence their help is likely to be appreciated if it is not too obtrusive. This is a role which local communist parties are often permitted to fulfil during a stage of what is supposed by communists to be a preliminary " bourgeois-nationalist " stage in the class struggle.

But this stage cannot last indefinitely. The orthodox communist parties, linked with the Soviet Union, which meet each year in Moscow at the congress of the parties from all over the world are constrained to follow policies that serve Russian interests. In some periods, these interests happen to coincide roughly with the interests of the emerging countries, especially in the earlier stages of decolonisation. To the peoples of some of these countries, in the first flush of independence, the coincidence appears closer than it really is : resentment against former colonial powers, fanned by demagogues,

---

[1] It should not be inferred from this or other references to the Suez affair in the present study, that I wish to endorse or even defend President Nasir's actions over the Suez Canal : on the contrary, I think they violated international engagements and were in themselves, in the form which they took, an unjustifiable type of riposte to the admittedly clumsy and humiliating blow struck by the U.S. Government in cancelling aid for the Aswan Dam project. But these things in no way justified the bilateral resort to armed force by Britain and France.

ends to cloud political judgement, keep alive grievances already
redressed, or on the way to being redressed, foment suspicions of the
West that are no longer justified, and for a time induce credulous
acceptance of Russian professions of disinterested benevolence. In
the longer run it would be a miracle if Russian national interests
always coincided with the interests of the emerging and reawakening
countries, especially since the interests of these countries themselves
do not always coincide.

When the inevitable clash comes, disillusionment sets in very
rapidly. In the more unstable societies of the Middle East, south-
eastern Asia, tropical Latin America, and Africa, it is impossible for
a great power to intervene actively in intra-regional differences and
controversies without incurring the resentment of some at least of
the countries concerned. Once an outside power is drawn into local
conflicts the prestige it formerly enjoyed at a distance soon evapor-
ates. Popular sentiment even in the countries which it favours may
turn against it when its support is seen to have aroused the hostility
of a large part of the people in neighbouring countries with which
ties of kinship exist. It was only in the mid nineteen-fifties when
Russia, seizing opportunities gratuitously offered by the blunders of
western imperialism, entered actively into Middle East politics. By
the early nineteen-sixties she had already lost much prestige, and
local communists linked with Moscow were far more widely hated
throughout the region than they had ever been in the days when
Russia was seen as a distant and disinterested power with a better
record than that of the western countries that had frequently inter-
fered in the area.

In some areas Russia has shown greater flexibility in recent years
in its dealings with the governments of the emerging and reawakening countries outside Europe. Those who resided in the Far East in
the nineteen-twenties will recollect the blunders of Mr. Borodin and
his group of advisers who attached themselves to the rising Chinese
nationalist movement of the day. Lately, the Russians have been
ready at times to accept rebuffs without discontinuing economic
help to the countries concerned. In such cases, however, as the
reports and resolutions at the Moscow meetings of the communist
parties and some of the radio broadcasts show, public diplomatic
restraint is accompanied by quiet activities of the parties in the background. The aims remain unchanged, but the means are modified
to avoid playing into the hands of the western powers.

But restraint, tactical astuteness, and propaganda devices cannot
long continue to cover up real divergencies of interest. The interests
of Russia as a state must predominate over doctrinal considerations,
and the further Russian influence extends, the greater are the
occasions for clashes of interests with the emerging countries. The

one thing that Russian communists cannot genuinely accept is the firm assertion of real independence in the emerging countries which it desires to maintain in alienation from the west. The Russian conception of neutrality is as little related to the accepted meaning of the word as their conception of democracy is ; only poor tactics prevented the West from taking advantage of this. A remarkable resemblance could be discerned in the nineteen-fifties between the Russian and United States attitudes towards genuine neutrality in Asia and tropical Latin America.

The tendency, which is most marked in the United States but is sometimes to be found on a smaller scale elsewhere in the western world, to treat as manifestations of communism, and communist influence and domination, the utterances and actions of a miscellaneous variety of left-wing movements in the emerging and reawakening countries, has created in the minds of the public a seriously distorted picture of the international scene. Those who have had any genuine practical experience of these peoples can hardly fail to realise that a substantial proportion of the active elements among them lean towards the political left, desiring fairly drastic social change. This would be so even if no communist movement existed. The clash of the generations, which is also evident in many of the more advanced countries, is found in the emerging and reawakening countries in a far more acute form than elsewhere. The western influences that have permeated the student and professional classes have opened a great gulf between the traditions of the older generation and the iconoclastic outlook of the younger generation that is conscious of the gap between development at home and development abroad. It is not surprising that this arouses in them an impatience to change the local world overnight. And, since the older generation and the more quiescent sections of the masses appear to them to be a drag on rapid change, they lean towards coercive measures to remove obstacles to progress. When, in addition, account is taken of the close resemblance between the slogans and battle cries of the radical nationalists and those of the communists, some western and most American observers are deceived into thinking, and are not slow in proclaiming, that this or that area is " going communist " I have heard slogans and political war cries from revolutionary nationalists in some of these countries, which were almost identical with those commonly used by communists ; yet independent evidence showed that those who uttered them would never have tolerated communist domination of their movement or Russian domination of their country.

This overlapping of political phraseology appears less surprising when it is realised that communists are adept in absorbing, and turning to their own purposes, popular phrases and slogans that came first from the non-communist left, and which at the onset had been used in their plain, generally accepted meaning. In the hands of the communists they were twisted to serve sectarian political ends.

The exaggeration in the West of Russian communist influence and alleged successes in Asia, in Latin America, and in Africa is useful to the communists themselves, giving them a greater feeling of importance and power than they really possess. If it merely represented genuine, though misguided, opinions and sentiment it would be much more limited in extent than it is. But, as we have seen elsewhere in this study, it is aggravated by the activities of a well-financed, thoroughly organised, semi-underground subversive movement of the right, linked with reactionary military circles, which stimulates the always latent fanaticism and plays on the genuine fears of substantial and politically important sections of the people in parts of North and South America. For these political manipulators of the extreme right, who, from a psychological point of view, have important characteristics in common with communists at the opposite pole, it may be said that if communism did not exist it would be necessary to invent it. They are a serious obstacle to the psychological adjustments which are imperatively needed as the political development of the emerging and reawakening countries proceeds.

II

Dangers of Anti-Communist Obsessions

Until the West completes its psychological readjustments to decolonisation, it will continue to provide openings for Russia and China to divert attention away from their own underlying aims, and direct it to the false steps which the West continues to make. Since the Suez affair, Britain and France have gone very far in the necessary psychological adjustments, but the actions of the United States in Latin America have been a major setback, adversely affecting the whole western world.

This raises a difficult issue of great importance to Britain and to France. The failure of the United States to readjust its attitude to tropical Latin America, and its out-dated clinging to a colonialist attitude towards its weaker neighbours to the south, are embarrassing to European allies which have accepted, after many vicissitudes, the necessity of full *de facto* as well as *de jure* recognition of the political independence of the emerging and reawakening countries, and whose only remaining problems are concerned with the stubborn resistance of a few minorities of European origin to decolonisation, together with the political immaturity and technical deficiencies of many of the emerging peoples. The continued appeal of the never effective and now long outworn and archaic Monroe Doctrine to political elements in the United States is a measure of the lag in the adjustment of the public in the United States to Latin American realities. It is axiomatic that Latin Americans, intent above all on the assertion of their political independence, will not acquiesce in the claim of their powerful northern neighbour to shape and exercise veto powers over their relations with other continents. Señor Castro, notwithstanding his extravagances and flambuoyancy, certainly reflected a spirit that permeates almost all the younger and many of the older generation in tropical Latin America when, in an earlier period, he denied that Cubans were communists but added that if they wanted to be, it would not be for the United States to interfere. The people of the United States cannot be said to have adjusted themselves to the revolution in international relations until they are ready to accept that position in a matter-of-fact way. And the main obstacle to the adjustment lies in the powerful influence still exercised by the anti-communist elements that have entrenched themselves in their country's political system. The ease with which these elements intimidated the majority of the people during the so-called Macarthy era, the weakness of the resistance to them, and the widespread lack of moral courage that revealed itself in that affluent society, are frightening reminders that, in Britain and in western Europe generally, it cannot be taken for granted that the United States, even with its machinery of democracy, can be relied on steadily to take the side of political liberty, freedom, and toleration when the communist scare is lashed up to a high pitch of fervour.

Thus there are two conditions to be fulfilled before a successful adjustment can be completed in the West to the rise and intensification of political consciousness in Asia, tropical Latin America, and Africa. The West must believe in and practise without lapses the principles of individual political freedom and representative government, reconciling the one with the other, and must be prepared to treat the emerging and reawakening countries on a basis of equality. This implies that intervention or connivance at intervention cannot be justified by the excuse that it is necessary in order to prevent communism from gaining control in the emerging or reawakening countries. The United States has fomented risings in a number of Latin American countries in the past for several reasons. Forcible interventions in open support of American commercial or other economic interests [1] would not now command wide support in the

---

[1] However, there is little doubt that U.S. economic interests supplied substantial funds to Cuban and other *emigrés* from liberal or left-wing Latin American régimes, and to professional anti-communist organisations.

United States, but the majority of Americans appear still to be ready to condone or support intervention to prevent real or supposed communists from gaining ground or from playing any part in the government of the smaller Latin American countries. The downfall of the legitimate government of President Arbenz in Guatemala was secured by intrigues conducted through the U.S. Embassy, which was used as a centre of conspiracy by subversive groups of the right.[1] The revolutionaries were supplied with U.S. materials. The motive here appears to have been that President Arbenz had appointed two ministers who were thought by U.S. agents to be communists. Following this, only governments of the right, bitterly opposed by the politically conscious younger generation, reigned in Guatemala for some years : they permitted U.S. " secret " agents to organise training of *emigrés* from Cuba and used Guatemala as a base for operations against Cuba. Nine years later the same attitude persisted when democratic elections were set aside by a military coup to exclude Señor Arevola !

The new U.S. Administration in 1960, however, became sensitive to criticism that the United States was associated with right-wing dictatorships among the reawakening countries, and its activities in some Latin American areas were turned against governments of the right, notably in the Dominican Republic and, later, briefly in Peru. In the former, Washington intervened actively to prevent some of those who were said to have been associated with the previous régime from being included in later governments. This corresponded with the contentions of domestic critics who, in pointing out that the former President Batista had received U.S. support, implied that the proper policy would have been not merely to refrain from the support, but actively to take part in the deposition, of Batista. One of the most dangerous aspects of U.S. policy in recent years has been a reluctance to stand aside and allow local forces to decide the outcome of local disputes. Yet the willingness to do this is essential if respect for the independence of small states is to become a reality. Interferences in Latin America after the middle of the twentieth century have usually been a result of anti-communist zeal, regardless of whether they supported the extreme right or opposed it. Support of dictatorships by the conservative régime of President Eisenhower for fear their collapse would let in communism was succeeded under the influence of the liberal imperialist advisers of President Kennedy by opposition to dictatorships whose régimes became a convenient target for effective communist propaganda. The attempt for a time to boycott a Peruvian régime resulting from a militarist coup, even when it was in firm control of the country, was based on the same

---

[1] This was again confirmed in 1963. See Hispanic-American Society, *Hispanic American Report*, XVI, April 1963, p. 118.

motive. But simultaneously the United States, as well as Russia, was bolstering up the military régime in Egypt and the authoritarian, inefficient, and demagogic régime in Indonesia

The pressure exerted on the Netherlands by the United States over New Guinea forced a settlement that, notwithstanding an insincere façade of United Nations consultation, in reality handed over the Papuans without their consent to a régime which, in the territory it already held, was insecure, corrupt, and inefficient. This was merely one example of the willingness of United States Governments since the Second World War, beginning with Formosa, to subordinate the interests of weaker peoples, and dispose of them without regard to their wishes, primarily out of concern for the supposed interests of the United States in the " cold war ". Other western peoples, by formal or tacit acquiescence, share the responsibility even though their fears of communism are not carried to the lengths which are commonly found in the United States.

These international insincerities are not confined to western statesmen. The motives behind them, and the tactics which they embody, are the outcome of the rivalries among the super-powers. They testify to the reality and strength of the forms of power other than armed power which have been augmented by the emergence of the new countries for whose favours the super-powers are competing. For Russia and the United States, from different points of view, have each calculated that its own interests were fostered best by seeking the favour of the politically stronger, and abandoning the cause of the politically weaker, Asian groups, out of fear that if it did not do so, its competitor would, and thus leave it to incur the hostility of the strong, while earning the gratitude only of the weak. The doctrinal trimmings which have enveloped the super-powers add a keener edge to their rivalries in respect to the balance of power. If these rivalries have worked in favour of the emerging peoples in some respects, the advantages have been mainly confined to the stronger groups among them and have been accompanied by injustices to the weaker groups.

The extreme fears of communism which characterise the attitude of the people of the United States towards the emerging and even more the reawakening countries reflect on the one hand the collective psychology of an abnormally conservative and conformist society, and on the other hand a remoteness from, and lack of comprehension of, the personal attitudes and the daily lives of the peoples of Asia, Africa, and Latin America, and the aspirations of their politically conscious classes. Unfortunately, the widespread circulation of well-advertised U.S. newspapers and magazines in Europe and Canada which reflect this psychology has its dangers. Although British people are unlikely to be attracted by these emotional extravagances there is some danger from the one-sided picture they received from such sources. The people of Britain and the people of the United States represent separate nations just as clearly as those of Britain and France do. But the similarity of language opens wider channels of communication in the former than in the latter case, often with unfortunate consequences.

To say that the influence and prospects of communism in the emerging and reawakening countries have been overestimated is not to say that they are unimportant. Let us turn to an examination of their real nature.

III

The Elements in Communism that attract " le tiers monde "

The elements in communism which attract many in the student and professional classes in the emerging countries are not the orthodox Marxian and neo-Marxian doctrines which depict the broad classes of society as engaged in perpetual struggle against one another, and create a sense of being borne on a fast-flowing historical current towards the haven where the toiling proletariat would be. Academic doctrines drawn up in the British Museum nearly a century ago, which attempted to interpret conditions in the most industrialised countries at the time, in terms of classes, some of which hardly exist in many of the emerging countries today, cannot be expected to arouse the passions of the crusader or establish cohesion among the masses in south-eastern Asia, the Middle East, and Africa.

On the other hand, the communist governments in power since the First World War have been forced to improvise methods of meeting conditions for which no prearranged guidance was provided by Marxian doctrine. As industrialisation was in an early stage they resorted to drastic measures of forced development under centralised control, with the object first of increasing the power of the communist state and later of raising standards of living. In agriculture they faced greater difficulties. Peasants had expected revolution to convert them from labourers or tenants to owners. But communist régimes are concerned first of all to establish dictatorial power by centralised control : to them a class of independent peasant owners appears incompatible with their political security and with the development of their economic plans. The rapid industrialisation which is the central economic aim can only be achieved by migration from agriculture to industry and by pressure on agricultural producers to part with a large part of their produce on terms favourable to urban consumers. In addition, as population grows and urban demand rises, greater efficiency is urgently needed in agricultural production.

Consequently the methods of regimentation which met with considerable success in industry are applied to agriculture. Collectivisation is arbitrarily imposed. The meaning of the term "co-operative" is inverted like that of democracy and many other terms, and compulsory " co-operation "—a contradiction in terms—is imposed. Forced development in agriculture is a very different task from forced development in industry, and no communist country has yet achieved real success in it. Yugoslavia and Poland have receded from it. But political conditions compel Russia and China to persist in the attempt. Governments whose rule is not based on consent have only a strictly limited range of alternatives from which to choose.

The economic resemblances between the starting points of the emerging and reawakening countries today and those of the communist countries in an earlier stage,[1] are an attraction to many in the younger, politically conscious classes in the former countries. Paradoxically, it is the very departures from the Marxian scheme, the unexpected beginnings of communism in comparatively undeveloped countries, that provide its most fruitful link with le tiers monde today. The politically conscious classes are above all in a hurry to turn their backs on the past and press on with the modernisation of their countries as rapidly as possible. The eastern countries seem to many of them to offer better models than western countries can supply to meet their special needs, particularly in centralised economic planning and industrial development. This presupposes close government control over economic activities and the nationalisation of certain industries—measures which are sometimes described as " socialism " and used to appeal to left-wing sentiment. But these measures are valued as supposed means to rapid modernisation rather than as the application of fixed doctrines standing on their abstract merits.

Consequently the elements in contemporary communist states that attract part of the rising politically conscious classes in the emerging countries are practical rather than doctrinal, related primarily to the real or supposed needs of the moment more than to any permanent faith or commitment. Doubtless a small minority goes beyond this and accepts communism as an article of faith to be adhered to in all conditions. But neither practical experience nor first-hand studies support the view that such tiny minorities can seize power

---

[1] This is not to imply that the cases are identical. Industrial development in Russia had begun several years before the revolution : the extent of progress was later obscured by Soviet writers for obvious reasons. Even the idea of the " Five Year Plan " preceded the revolution.

and sustain it unless Russian armies are available across their borders, or unless they are working in the aftermath of devastating wars which have shaken the foundations of society and undermined the morale of the armies. Communism in Cuba, which has been what Señor Castro, with his wide personal appeal, has permitted it to be, was partly the product of U.S. imperialism, and British and European fears of trying to uphold the rule of law against a super-power. Faced with an economic stranglehold, Cuba had no option but to appeal to the eastern countries for the help needed to survive. Even then Cuba was by no means a subservient communist country : independence was still the first article in its creed.

The attractions of some communist economic practices for part of the younger politically conscious classes in the emerging and reawak-ening countries are very different from, and far more limited than, the attractions of the creed of communism, and the political prac-tices of a fully fledged communist state. They may be allied to, or are compatible with, many different forms of the political state. It is true that some, though not all, economic practices in Russia require an authoritarian form of government. But there are many authoritarian forms of government besides the communist forms. As we have seen, some of the emerging and reawakening countries have shown strong tendencies towards authoritarian forms of govern-ment, but these have been either far removed from communism, springing from the right rather than the left, or they have pursued independent forms of Marxist-inspired doctrines joined with an uncompromising assertion of national independence in international affairs, or they have taken the form of a " régime militaire ", notably in Egypt.

It is possible, of course, that a few of the emerging and reawaken-ing countries may embrace a form of economic communism together with some features of the political communist state. But there is no sign yet, and it is difficult to conceive that any will appear in the near future, pointing to the full-fledged communism of a state voluntarily linked with Russia or China and taking instructions from Moscow as a satellite in the Russian orbit, or from Peking as a satellite in the Chinese orbit. Such a state would be accepting a new, just after emerging from an old, form of colonialism. It would be turning away from the central creed of the emerging and reawakening countries, the one thing they have in common more than anything else—political independence. There is no sign that communism can triumph over nationalism unless it can bring military force, or the imminent threat of it, to bear. If an opening is gratuitously presented to it, as it was by United States neo-colonialism over Cuba, it may derive considerable advantage from it, though even in such a case its hold would quickly diminish if the neutrals resolutely combined against the U.S. stranglehold. The U.S., whatever its military power, could no more afford to flout the vast majority of the powers in the United Nations than Britain and France could in the Suez aggression.

The dangers of dictatorship and authoritarian rule in the emerging countries today comes chiefly from the military classes, from demagogues, and from extreme nationalists of the right. These classes sometimes assume a radical economic guise for their own purposes, and may, indeed, use radical economic measures in some directions, but their bent is towards what has been loosely described as fascism rather than communism. Serious economic and social disharmonies in some of the emerging and reawakening countries give rise to widespread left-wing sentiment. Often this tends to be diverted by astute demagoguery into what in reality are reactionary channels disguised by a veneer of radicalism. But where attempts at this diversion fail, and the far left keeps control, the results, if they can be called communism at all—which is a matter of definition— are likely to be no more than national communism—which is a matter of domestic rather than international concern.

The interventions of Russia are sometimes more risky and more dangerous than the interventions of other Great Powers in domestic and intra-regional political issues : they have at their disposal local communist parties in the countries concerned which may be used either openly or clandestinely to further the aims of the intervention. Some types of intervention or attempted intervention consist solely in the instigation of local activities in support of or against particular governments. It should not be supposed that the Russians are alone in underground activities in *le tiers monde*. Startling revelations were made in the early nineteen-sixties of the conspiracies of U.S. agents seeking to instigate the overthrow of governments of comparatively weak countries which pursued policies that did not meet with the approval of influential members of the United States administration.[1] These are amateurish efforts, usually based only on *ad hoc* local support, while Russia has in effect a standing organisation in the communist parties. But this in itself carries greater risk of alienation of local opinion and sentiment as well as greater possibilities of effective intervention. An intervention which leads to a form of civil war, even if it is successful in its immediate aim, leaves a lasting resentment that in the longer run may bring more losses than gains to the intervening country.

---

[1] It was not always clear how widely these activities were known within the U.S. Government. For a popular account of some of these activities see Andrew Tully, *Central Intelligence Agency* (London 1962), which brings out the extraordinary nature of some of these activities, though they apparently meet with the author's approval in certain cases where they were successful.

But this is not the only difficulty of working through standing local parties. The control of such parties from a distant centre which has only a sketchy knowledge of the local conditions in which the parties act is a formidable task which can rarely be discharged successfully. Many decisions must be left to local discretion. The history of the relationships between Moscow and its parties abroad, especially in Asia and Africa, is full of blunders and failures : it is hardly necessary to take up space here to recount them. Sometimes the parties have been less active, at other times more active, than Moscow has desired them to be. Frequently the instructions sent from Moscow have seemed absurd and impracticable to those on the spot. No-one who reflects on the extreme difficulty which an outsider experiences in understanding the personal elements in the political life of a country can feel optimistic about the possibilities of wholesale appraisals of over one hundred countries made at a distance. Nor can this always be overcome by calling in local communist leaders from the areas concerned : most of them have their own ends to serve and rivalries to pursue within the parties. The history of communist parties in south-eastern Asia, for example, records many rifts and conflicts which have greatly reduced the effectiveness of the parties at critical moments.

It is sometimes supposed that communist doctrines and communist links with Russia ensure rigorous discipline and high efficiency of organisation within communist parties in the emerging countries. It is, of course, in the interests of fanatical anti-communists to create such an impression when they are pressing for suppression of such parties. But the reality is usually far from this seductive image. Often, it is true, communist parties are more efficiently organised for purposes of political agitation than any other parties in the emerging countries. But they cannot escape from the *milieu* in which they operate. Among politically inexperienced people they show political inexperience and fall into political misjudgements. Less sophisticated than communists in the countries where communism has been long established, they sometimes display fanaticism and commit excesses that destroy or indefinitely postpone their chances of acceptance in their own countries.[1] It should not be supposed that these excesses are necessarily instigated or endorsed by the Russians. Moscow's control in detail of the doings of local communist parties appears exaggerated in the light of what is known of the history of

---

[1] A notable example was the conduct of the Iraqi Communist party in the winter of 1958–9, when, during a period of considerable freedom for them during which the Government was using them as a counterweight to extreme Arab nationalists, they were responsible for outrages in Mosul and Kirkuk which made them the most hated political group in the country and disillusioned most of their former supporters outside the party. What years of repression, imprison-

communist parties in Asia. The interest of the Russian rulers in these parties has fluctuated widely. Stalin appears often to have been indifferent to them and little concerned over their fate, but he was ready to use them to further Russian national interests by instigating militant tactics in many countries, including Asian countries, from 1948 to 1952. Since they were called off in 1952, no militant tactics on a comparable scale have been used. Frequently Russia has aided countries in which local communists spend much of their time in prison.

When left to themselves, or left with only vague, general instructions, communist parties sometimes fall into internal differences over the most appropriate policies to pursue, rival would-be leaders sponsoring different approaches to applied communism. After the rise of China another source of division appeared. Since the national interests of Russia and China often diverge and cannot always be harmonised by doctrinal ingenuity, it was almost certain from the beginning that fissures would appear in the communist camp, and that they would create embarrassing problems for the leadership of communist parties outside Russia and China. Even in parties which unhesitatingly cling to one side in the controversy, much time and energy are consumed in the preparation of supporting documents, and in the activities of conferences concerned with the internal affairs of the communist, rather than with those of the non-communist, world.

Thus it is not surprising that at times communist parties, far from being models of political efficiency, advancing steadily towards local and individual political power, " using " other political parties for their own purposes, are themselves " used " successfully by non-communist rulers and parties engaged in domestic and international conflicts of their own. This aim was successfully accomplished in some of the western European countries in the period of reconstruction after the Second World War, and in the Middle East in the late nineteen-fifties and early nineteen-sixties, when communists played a limited role among those groups and in support of those rulers who frustrated President Nasir's expansionist ambitions. Paradoxically, during much of this time the Soviet Union and the United States were giving substantial aid to Egypt, the former with a view to keeping her out of the western fold, and the latter with a view to keeping

---

ment and the execution of some of their leaders had failed to do, a few months of freedom accomplished. It does not appear that Moscow either instigated or could control these actions, though it was able later to make the party confess its " errors ". Nearly four years later the Ba'ath, on seizing power, carried out a massacre of communists and other opponents on a scale that made the communist outrages of 1959 appear more modest. By the end of the year the Ba'ath were " confessing their errors ".

her out of the eastern fold.   Future historians who look back on our times will have many ironies of history to write about !

Thus the naïve idea that communist views and communist actions are universally evil, in their intent and in their results, is an *a priori* assumption rather than a statement of verified fact.   Even when, as usually happens, the motive of communist actions in the emerging and reawakening countries is simply to serve the narrow interests of Russia rather than the interests of the community of nations, the results may be as favourable to the latter as to the former.   There are a number of spheres in which the two sets of interests coincide. If a universe of crude rewards and punishments based on results is postulated, it may be said not only that hell is paved with good intentions but also that heaven is paved with bad intentions !

We may, however, go further than this.   It has never been valid, and is even less likely to be valid in the future, to regard Russian communism as a wholly malign influence in the international community.   This follows logically from the fact that the interests of the Russian communist state and the interests of the international community sometimes coincide.[1]   But it may be confirmed from other angles.   The great contribution of Russia to the defeat of Hitler is an obvious case in point.   The communist state was clearly more effective in this sense than the Tsarist state had been.   There is no space to enumerate other cases but it may be hoped that the desired coincidence of interests will become more frequent as the evangelistic spirit of the original revolutionaries gives way to a more experienced and informed understanding on the part of their successors.

In any case, one of the main strands of my argument in this study is that the effectiveness and danger of communist evangelism in the emerging and reawakening world has been grossly overestimated by honest fears and deliberately exaggerated by anti-communist vested interests, and that the rising new world is no more likely than the politically sophisticated older world to be willing to barter its independence and place itself in a satellite position in exchange for a political doctrine alleged to have been the subject of a nineteenth revelation into the nature of the universe and human society.

---

[1] In the Middle East one hears communist arguments cautioning against hasty attempts at unification of Arab states without consultation with the peoples. This was the argument at the time when the U.A.R. was formed, as well as at many other times.   Doubtless the motive was the familiar Russian antipathy to the unification of small states into large and potentially more powerful ones near its borders—an antipathy that long preceded communism.   Nevertheless the argument and advice was perfectly sound on much more tenable grounds in this case, as the outcome showed.

Similarly Russia correctly opposed British and French aggression over Suez, and communist parties in the Middle East worked against intra-regional imperialism for a time.

Part III

NATIONALISM, FUSION, AND SEPARATION

CHAPTER VIII

NATIONALISM, SELF-GOVERNMENT, AND POLITICAL FREEDOM

I

Nationalism and Independence

THE great upsurge of nationalism in Asia, Africa, and Latin America has coincided with a questioning of the foundations of nationalism in the western world. In the first flush of enthusiasm in the nineteenth century nationalism in Europe was hailed by liberal-minded people as the ideal end towards which the whole international creation moved. Today, many look on it as parochial and out-dated, overtaken by the modern requirements of technology and economic development, and by the administrative needs of the modern state. These critics also deprecate the idea of independence and would substitute for it that of inter-dependence. They assail even more strongly the idea of national sovereignty, regarding it as incompatible with international peace.

To one who lives part of the time in Britain and part in Asia, the contrast is striking. During part of the year one lives in an atmosphere of fervid nationalism in which independence is the keynote, and dependence a mark of ignominy, nationalism a religion, and cosmopolitanism a camouflage for imperialism. In another part of the year one may listen to discussions on the Third Programme by eminent university scholars who dismiss nationalism as outmoded, and political independence as incompatible with economic interdependence, and who deplore the adherence of the emerging peoples to notions allegedly discredited in the western world. The contrast is all the more striking when both the British scholars and the spokesmen of the emerging countries are of the left or left-centre in political outlook. It exposes the deep chasm that often separates supposedly similar doctrinal orientations in the West and in the emerging countries.

To add to the confusion, on further examination these contrasting attitudes show an overlapping in detail. In Europe differences have arisen between those who desire the existing states to remain independent, and those who desire to merge them into larger unions. And among the latter there are differences over the nature of the larger unions and the extent of local independence that should be

retained. At the other end of the scale, both in Europe and among
the African and Asian countries, examples can be found of minorities
in existing states that desire either to form independent states or to
obtain much larger autonomy in domestic affairs and be recognised
in effect, as nations within multi-national states.

Thus the dissatisfaction which exists is dissatisfaction with the size
of some of the existing states, and not with the division of the world
into separate states.   In itself it seeks no fundamental change in
principle. Ever since states came into being they have been enlarged
through imperialistic expansions or voluntary coalescence, and
diminished through aggression from without or disintegration
within. These processes of fusion and separation, of integration and
disintegration, have gone on simultaneously in different parts of the
world, and analogous processes may have taken place among tribes
from the time when human societies were first formed. The ends of
freedom, national and individual, and of political, social, and
economic advance have been served sometimes by the one, sometimes by the other, of these opposite processes in the international
organisation of peoples.

The distribution of states has never coincided exactly with the
distribution of nations. A state may be defined in terms of law and
jurisdiction, government, and administrative organs, territorial
boundaries and participation in international treaties and organisations. A nation is above all a group conscious of binding ties of
sentiment and culture and ways of life which create a supreme
desire to live together under institutions giving adequate expression
to them, and protecting them from threats of external interference
which are incompatible with their survival. The growth of such
group ties and group consciousness is often aided by geographical
conditions, language, historical experiences, and traditions in common, ethnic origin, and religion. But the comparative importance
of these contributory influences varies widely and some of them are
not found in all nations. Nationalism is a sentiment, a state of mind,
indefinable in physical terms, though physical conditions occasionally contribute to its development.

So far as the divergencies between the distribution of states and
that of nations are accounted for by genuine multi-national states,
in which the national aspirations of each group are met satisfactorily
through cultural autonomy and various degrees of regional or local
autonomy, it is not a source of instability. There is indeed some
unrest in the existing multi-national states, arising out of the desire
of the more ardent nationalists for a greater degree of local autonomy than they possess, but in all cases a balance has to be struck
between the degree of local autonomy on the one hand, and
economic efficiency on the other, the former being maintained at a

high enough level to prevent the development of a separatist movement. The tensions in a multi-national state are of international
significance when, as in parts of the New World, the national groups
derive their cultures from different sources overseas. The impracticability of military conscription in Canada in the World War
illustrated this.

The main effects of nationalism lie elsewhere. First, nationalism
has sometimes intensified the rivalry among states by giving a more
popular and self-conscious complexion to patriotic sentiment towards
the state. The popular enthusiasm for the Crimean War in
the eighteen-fifties, the popular pressure that forced President
MacKinley against his better judgement into an aggressive and
unnecessary war with Spain, are two examples out of many in which
" mob " interests have forced the substitution of generals and
admirals for foreign ministers, and military for diplomatic solutions,
in disputes between states. Democracy is not a panacea ensuring
international peace.

The second effect of nationalism on international relations comes
from the emergence and rising strength of new nationalisms, and the
re-emergence of hitherto suppressed national sentiment. In the
twentieth century these have appeared on a large scale in three
continents. They have been the mainspring in the revolution in
international relations which has been advancing since the Second
World War. Although, as we have seen, self-conscious nationalism
began among small minorities of educated people, it spread among
the masses much more rapidly than ever before through the new
means of communications. Mass support gave it such strength that
policies of " gradualism " were no longer practicable. With the
great majority of the people on the side of the nationalists it was no
longer possible to suppress the movements except at high cost and
by methods that would have alienated the outside world.

It would be an oversimplification to represent all movements
against external rule as simple cases of nationalism. A single movement for independence, or close co-operation among two or more
movements within a territory subject to a single external rule, may
cover more than one strand of nationalism. To this subject I shall
return later.

Other qualifications are necessary. Academic discussions of the
idea of nationalism are based on a high degree of abstraction. The
mind and the sentiments of the individual are not partitioned into
neat categories of ideas and feelings. The motives for supporting or
opposing any political movement are often varied and even confused. Different individuals often support the same movement for
widely different reasons and out of widely different feelings and
expectations. The academic student who has had no direct contact

with revolutionary nationalism is in danger of creating artificial worlds on paper which give all too clear-cut and neatly arranged pictures of what, in the light of his categories, is supposed to be taking place in parts of the world with which he has no direct acquaintance. Perhaps the greatest danger is that of failing to allow for the rapidity of change, and for the fluctuating and sometimes fickle states of feeling and categories of ideas in areas of unrest in the course of transformation from pre-modern to modern societies.[1]

It does not follow that academic categories should be summarily discarded, but rather that they should be used with understanding— derived as far as possible from personal experience—of their limitations and with an acute sense of the ceaseless flux and change in national life, and their bearing on international events.

The lack of precise correspondence between independence movements and unified nationalist movements has greatly confused the pattern of decolonisation.   In some of the colonial and former colonial territories pronounced regional differences exist among the indigenous peoples.   While the great majority desire independence they do not feel themselves to be a single community and the choice is between the establishment of a multi-national state, or the separation of the area into more than one national state, or the imposition of a unitary state in which the strongest group uses authoritarian forms of government to suppress the political aspirations of the smaller national groups.   In other territories which have been or are to be decolonised, the sense of community extends not only over the whole native population but beyond it to populations under other jurisdictions.   Just as, in the first case, decolonisation creates unrest within the liberated territory, so, in the second case, it creates unrest within and between neighbouring countries whose peoples are in important respects similar in outlook and social heritage to the peoples of the newly independent state.

Additional complications arise when the newly independent country is inhabited by peoples of radically different social heritage who are so widely intermingled that they cannot be segregated into separate regions without destroying the economic structure of the area.   This is merely one variety of the problem of minorities which has beset the Old World as much as the New.   It constitutes one of the most important limitations on the possibilities of applying the principle of national self-determination in the establishment of independent states.

But the limits to the application of the principle of nationality are

[1] In one such area I have heard the same individual acquaintances professing vehement right-wing nationalism in the first year, left-wing ideas not far from communism in the second, and total disillusionment with all political movements in the third.

only a matter of degree and cannot be invoked to discredit the principle itself. The fashion among some eminent western scholars to disparage nationalism in itself is singularly ill-timed and merely arouses suspicions in the emerging countries that western " imperialists ", who have enjoyed the benefits of nationalism themselves, wish to discourage Africans, Asians, and Latin Americans from following suit, out of a fear that they could no longer be exploited in the interests of imperialism. Today, nationalism is to the emerging countries what it was to European countries during the nineteenth century—virtually a synonym for political independence.[1] Do the critics who assert or imply that the emerging peoples are mistaken in espousing nationalism consider that they should have remained in their colonial state ? If not, do they wish to imply that they should enter into a world state ? There is none for them to enter, nor have the Great Powers shown any inclination towards the establishment of one, nor would it be possible for them to do while present radical divergencies on the nature and forms of government remian. Do they suggest that the peoples should combine into larger regional units ? What would that be but the substitution of larger nations for smaller nations or large multi-national states for smaller nation-states.

In short, the world state is impracticable, and the large state which ignores nationalism is a source of internal strife and instability. The principle of nationalism has the outstanding advantage of corresponding to the desires of peoples to be governed by persons of their own groups who share their distinctive social heritages from the past. Like all sound principles it should be applied within reason and not pushed to extremes of fragmentation.

If the critics of nationalism had in mind only " narrow nationalism " their strictures might be accepted within limits. Those perversities of nationalism which overlook the interdependence of states in many fields of activity, which vainly strive, at great cost to themselves and others, for self-sufficiency, and which refuse to play their part in the comity of nations, are a legitimate object of criticism. The national state has duties as well as rights with respect to the rest of the world.

But the attempt to identify nationalism with narrow nationalism, and thus attach a pejorative sense to the term itself, merely adds to the widespread confusion of political thought and political terminology. Nor do arguments in general terms over the question whether, and if so, when, nationalism is associated with liberalism or with

---

[1] Strictly speaking the terms are not precisely identical : some groups in a combined struggle for independence of a single foreign government which rules them as a unit may be unwilling to live under a single government of their own after independence has been achieved.

chauvinism serve useful purposes. It is true that young nations, if
they are powerful enough, tend to develop imperialist tendencies.
The conditions which account for this will be discussed later, but
meantime it may be said that the imposition of a nation's rule on an
outside territory is the antithesis of the principle of nationalism, not
an application of it.

Far from being outmoded, therefore, nationalism is a more potent
force in the world today than ever before.[1] The next step to the
nation state is the multi-national state, which is the most appropriate
means of removing the difficulties created by the fragmentation of
some areas into nation states too small for economic and administrative efficiency. But, as a rule, if the multi-national state is to
endure harmoniously, the separate national elements in them, often
based on deep-seated and long-enduring traditions, must remain,
and find means of expression in the lives of the people and the institutions of the country. In time, large-scale economic organisation
may reduce national differences and make for uniformity, but that
is not necessarily a consummation devoutly to be wished. In the
nineteen-sixties uniformity, and the conformity that goes with it,
have reached disturbing levels in the United States and symptoms of
the same tendency are emerging elsewhere. Individual liberty tends
to be more insecure in big democracies than in small ones, as the
history of the United States since the outbreak of the Korean War
and the growth of rivalry with Russia has demonstrated. The
multi-national state preserves diversities that enrich individual lives
and relieve that drabness and monotony resulting from the undivided
pursuit of technical efficiency. It extends the scope of government
by consent of the governed. Whether or not, in the longer run, the
tendency to increasing centralisation of government, largely under
economic pressures, will weaken the co-existence of nations in multi-
national states cannot yet be forseen. But if it does, the outcome will
be to replace small nations by big nations, the area of the nation
coinciding with the area of the state. Nationalism will not be
eliminated but extended, though at the expense of diversity.

Thus the serious student of international affairs would do well to
refrain from joining in fashionable disparagement of nationalism in
itself. The principle of nationalism is not an all-sufficient guide to
international harmony and development. If misdirected it may lead
to disaster, but the same may be said of any alternative single
principle or aim. Nor should the term independence be dismissed

[1] As Dr. Benjamin has said in a valuable short study, *State and Nation* (London
1964) :
"For the present century, and probably for a good many centuries to come,
nations are here to stay. Rather than dream about their disappearance, it is
better to learn how to live with them."

as archaic. In the world today independence coexists with interdependence. If the former is allowed to encroach too far on the latter, disaster will follow. But independence is real within its limits : the Great Powers are continually demonstrating it, and if the term is belittled by their nationals when it is used by the spokesmen of the emerging and reawakening countries, it is not surprising that the suspicions of the latter are aroused. The term independence, like the term nationalism, has its uses as well as its abuses. Let us preserve both terms in the language of international relations, and refrain from destroying their uses by fastening a pejorative sense on them and turning them into mere instruments of emotional propaganda.

In later chapters I shall attempt to show the vital constructive roles which both of the ideas in question should play in a more peaceful world of the future.

II

Unification and Tyranny

The history of Europe is a great repository of experience of the problems of reconciling political freedom with political unification. Today, under the shadow of the mighty armaments of Russia and the United States, it is fashionable to decry the division of Europe into many nations and states. Yet in range, in diversity, and in variety, the contribution of Europe to human advance has been unmatched in the modern age. North American and Russian achievements have been dependent on it, not only in respect to historical origins but also through the recent and contemporary migrations of highly skilled specialists, and through the fundamental ideas of pure science that lie behind modern technical advances. Moreover, the awakened peoples of Asia, Latin America, and Africa are striving to modernise their countries on European lines.

Yet Europe, after the dissolution of the Roman Empire, which itself fell short of covering all Europe, was not unified. The development of the modern state did not come first in the largest countries. Attempts at empire-building either by expansion into contiguous territories or by absorption under a single rule of territories separated by an intervening state, as in the Habsburg effort to unite by marriage, broke down before external resistance from more compact states and internal resistance from diverse groups which felt no sense of kinship with one another. Even in the nineteenth century a number of small countries resolutely refused to yield their identity, while others were only united by unscrupulous statecraft which

created future conflict.   The attempt at the end of the Napoleonic
Wars to unite Belgium and Holland broke down a decade and a half
later.   Norway and Sweden were separated in 1905.   The separated
peoples remained on friendly terms with each other, and sentiments
of kinship, less than nationalism but distinct from sentiments towards
the peoples of other regions, remained.   It was not out of enmity but
out of a desire to live under governments representing different
public sentiments and traditions, that they went their separate ways,
each of them still within the vanguard of twentieth-century
civilisation.

Variety, diversity, liberty, and toleration stand among the greatest
characteristics of civilised life, and so far they have been nurtured
more successfully in comparatively small than in large states.   But the
small state, simply becauae it is small, is usually at a disadvantage in
defence against external foes.   In earlier times, geographical
obstacles sometimes enabled favourably situated small states to
defend themselves against larger states.   But this never applied to
small states situated in plains, and in modern times changes in the
technology of warfare have reduced its importance.   The old and
cruel divergence between the conditions that favour freedom and
diversity and the conditions that provide successful defence has
reappeared in a more acute form.   The fundamental issues have not
changed since the time of the Italian Renaissance, during which
many of our modern international problems were strikingly foreshadowed in the Italian peninsula, where the failure of feudalism to
take hold led to the early development of small competing states.
The Machiavelli of the *Discourses* appreciated them, for in his day
the civic freedom of Florence was threatened by the expansion of
the Duchy of Milan.   As Dr. Hans Baron has pointed out :

> The heart of the challenge presented to the neighbour regions
> by the emergence of the Duchy of Milan was that tyranny was
> by its nature a dynamic, expansionist, and potentially unifying
> factor in inter-state relations on the Peninsula.   Ever since the
> emergence of the first tyrannies in the thirteenth century, the
> despot's independence of historical tradition and democratic
> procedure had given him a better chance than the republics had
> had to crush rival neighbours definitely, and to unite victor and
> vanquished in a provincial state where all citizens of the former
> city-states were levelled down to mere subjects under a bureau-
> cratic administration.   Tyranny, therefore, was from the outset
> a natural champion of the advantage brought about by political
> and economic integration on a broad territorial basis.[1]

[1] Hans Baron, *The Crisis of the Early Italian Renaissance*, Princeton, 1955,
pp. 12–13.

Civic freedom in small states, or unification under despotic rule —this was the choice in several areas in Renaissance and post-Renaissance Europe. The present study is written in the belief that it is better to be a citizen of a small state ruled by consent than of a large state ruled by a despot, and that it is preferable that an area should remain parcelled into small states in some of which at least substantial freedom exists, than that it should be united under a single authoritarian rule. This belief is not shared by all the political leaders in the emerging and reawakening countries, some of whom consider that modernisation should come first and that it can be accomplished more rapidly under authoritarian rule than under representative government. They are willing to sacrifice individual freedom for national freedom, at least in the earlier stages.

Much of the debate during the Quattrocento and part of the debate during the Trecento are of interest in our twentieth-century predicament. Notwithstanding Marx, the history of political thought and practice are not closely analogous to the history of technology. The fundamental political issues reappear in spite of radically changed economic environments. Is enlightened despotism superior to rule through processes of consultation in which even the ignorant citizen may play a part? Should despotism be endured simply on the ground that to shake authority might bring a return of anarchy and close the door to enlightened as well as to evil rulers? How can the disputes and discord between contending parties in the state be resolved except by a single ruler at the head? Such issues were as alive and real in Shakespeare's day as in our own : in his lifetime he saw the transition from the most outstanding to the most foolish monarch in British history.[1] The rejection of the Stuarts settled the question for Britain, and the French Revolution and experiences of two Napoleons settled it for France in spite of subsequent temporary deviations during emergencies. But in much of the world the example of western Europe and its offshoots has not been followed, and political development has hardly gone beyond that of the late mediaeval or early modern period in Europe. India and Japan are outstanding exceptions.

Yet there is a great difference. The *milieu* in which political change takes place today is far removed from that in which European changes took place in the late mediaeval and early modern periods. It is hardly necessary to elaborate the differences in detail. The economic and technological settings have radically changed, but so also have the ideas in the minds of the peoples. These two changes are interconnected at many points. In the period of the Renaissance

---

[1] Recent scholarship seems to place more emphasis than ever on the delinquencies of James I, even to the point of partially excusing the failures of Charles I because of the pitiful inheritance from which he started.

the printing press had begun a revolution in the means of transmitting ideas which has become increasingly important ever since. But, as the preceding chapter showed, in our own time the radio, and to a much lesser extent television, have created new means of spreading ideas, among the illiterate as well as the literate, much more effectively than street oratory, which governments could easily suppress. The effectiveness of a modern Mark Antony would depend on his ability to seize the broadcasting station long enough to make himself heard all over the large centres of population. From one point of view the improvement of the means of communication is simply an adaptation to the increased density of population. But it also supplies a powerful new instrument which may be monopolised to serve the purposes of autocratic rulers, submerging its victims in an unreal world.[1]

Since the time of the Italian Renaissance it has been possible to establish representative government in some comparatively large states. But those states already possessed stronger political traditions than many of the emerging countries have yet developed. Moreover, they are not yet among the freest of the democratic states, and new difficulties have arisen through the growth in the functions of government.

The problems of unification are wider in some respects than the problems of individual freedom, and will be discussed in different contexts later. But the problems of individual freedom are wider in other respects than the problems of unification. All the emerging and reawakening countries face the problem of maintaining orderly development in face of elements making for disorder or revolution.

Today the attenuation or suppression of individual liberties in parts of *le tiers monde* is more often than not excused on the ground that it is necessary to prevent disorder or " subversion ". The forces of order and disorder are commonly symbolised by the army and the mob. The mob is conceived of as an instrument of chaos, the embodiment of unreason. And so, at times, it may be. But even when it is, its actions are not without significance.

What seems reasonable and wise to a student of international relations and of economic development often appears in a different light to the masses of people in the emerging countries. Actions appear rational or irrational according to the knowledge and aims of the individual who chooses between them. Frequently, actions

---

1 This is written with a vivid recollection after nearly a quarter of a century of how, during a short stay in a Rhineland town, for illegal purposes, the world outside appeared when the sole available knowledge was derived from the channels supplied by Goebbels. Since no-one believed in their veracity, a total scepticism, hardly lighted by a single ray of hope, settled over those classes who knew they were the potential, as some of their members had already been the actual, victims of the system.

that offend the judgement of a western critic are denounced as " irrational ", or " emotional ", or perhaps as an example of the old adage about " cutting off your nose to spite your face ". In reality, however, the attitudes and actions complained of may appear reasonable in the light of the information available to the persons concerned ; the western critic drops into the fallacy of assuming, perhaps unconsciously, that the information and the viewpoints open to him are also open to those of whose behaviour he complains. Frequently, western critics neglect even to make an effort to enter into the outlook of the peoples of Asian, Latin American, and African countries, to study their historical experience and their interpretation of it, and to consider what sources of information are open to them. If allowance is made for these fundamental differences in starting points, the actions of the emerging peoples will less often appear " irrational " and more often appear misinformed. Even some of the actions that appear misinformed to the western critic are seen in a different light in the emerging countries : for example the western critic assumes in certain situations that western countries are acting in good faith, and he may be correct in doing so, but he is wrong in supposing that Asians, Africans, and Latin Americans are necessarily " irrational " or perverse when they take the opposite view. They may be reasoning from precedents derived from the past : in this they may be wrong because of faulty analogies, but they are not necessarily " irrational " ! [1]

Thus the generalisations so often heard from liberals and humanists regarding the alleged " flight from reason " in our age shed no more than a fitful and sometimes deceptive light on international affairs. When one observes at close quarters a mass political demonstration in an Asian, Latin American, or African country, there is an obvious temptation to characterise the excited crowd, shouting and chanting slogans and gesticulating defiantly against alleged enemies at home and abroad, as a convincing example of the dethronement of reason by wild emotions. But this is a superficial interpretation. The study of " the mob " and its manifestations should be taken more seriously.[2] A spontaneous mob uprising appears to be the exception and not the rule today. The use of the mob as a political instrument has been thoroughly exploited in the Middle East and in parts of

[1] When Mr. Neville Chamberlain and his Cabinet gave the guarantee to Poland in 1939 it was not surprising, nor " irrational " that in many parts of the world it was believed that they would back down rather than go to war. Some British people who had denounced the previous surrenders to aggression, were unable to convince non-British friends of this. The issue depended, not on abstract reasoning, but on a psychological appraisal. See C. A. Macartney and A. W. Palmer, *Independent Eastern Europe* Macmillan & Co., 1962.

[2] The interesting recent studies on the Paris mobs during the French Revolution might well stimulate contemporary students of international relations to study the

Latin America and North Africa, and is now generally the result of careful organisation in detail.   What might appear to an unsophisti-cated onlooker to be spontaneous may be the outcome of careful planning and regimentation.   And if the mob is often, in the first instance, an instrument in the hands of revolutionaries, it is subse-quently used to consolidate their power.   Political demonstrations may be made into a sort of festive occasion, serving as a substitute for the " circuses " of Roman times which, along with free distribution of bread, was calculated to keep the mob out of mischief.

If this appears to any reader as a cynical interpretation, it should be remembered that the mob would not lend itself so readily to political exploitation if the revolutionary leaders whom it is so often used to support, both before and after their attainment of power, were not popular with the masses, and did not express deeply rooted popular beliefs and feelings, and if the pre-revolutionary govern-ments had not lost the confidence of the people and become an object of attack by the student and younger members of the professional classes who set the tone of politics.   It is only when the political seed is sown on fertile political ground that it yields fruit to the sowers.

This, in turn, raises the important question, why is the ground fertile ?   The popular answer is generally an economic one : the poverty of the masses, it is said, predisposes them to revolution, especially when it exists alongside the wealth of a privileged minor-ity.   For long this type of theory was the basis of attempts to explain the French Revolution.

But poverty is an ambiguous term.   It may be used in an absolute sense, as it is when it denotes an inability to satisfy the bare element-ary needs of food, shelter and, in the temperate and frigid zones, clothing.   More often it is used in a comparative sense, referring to wide gaps between the economic positions of different groups within a society, or between one society and another.   But irregularities in both these senses have been found in western as well as other countries, though poverty in the former sense has now virtually disappeared from the western world.   They were not necessarily accompanied by revolutionary feelings or activities.   The conditions are more favourable to revolution when poverty in both the absolute and comparative senses thus defined are found simultaneously.   But even this statement must be qualified.   Extreme poverty in an absolute sense may unfit the masses to engage in any organised political activity.   Living from hand to mouth leaves as little oppor-tunity to take thought for the morrow in a political sense as in any

---

" mobs " of our own day at first hand.   There can be no assurance that prefectures of police will compile written records comparable to those of the Paris police during the Revolution.   See especially George Rude, *The Crowd in the French Revolution.*

other sense, which leads, finally, to the question whether poverty is increasing or decreasing. Even this question is ambiguous, and the ambiguity is particularly troublesome in its implications for the student of politics. First, the idea that poverty is increasing creates no difficulty if it simply means that all, or at least the great majority of people, command less goods and services than before. But let us suppose that their command of goods and services is gradually increasing on the average but the population is also increasing rapidly. This appears to be happening in most of the emerging countries. Then the masses may be said to be slowly improving their lot, but, as the population is rising rather rapidly, the total number of " poor " people is greater than ever. This is not " the Malthusian situation ", as some writers misleadingly state, but it is of special concern to the student of politics, since even the very slow improvement of economic conditions and the still greater improvement in health, together with the substantial increase of numbers, are accompanied today by a rise in the number of educated people and a growth of political self-consciousness, which make the masses less resigned to their lot than they were in the past. " The increasing misery of the proletariat " is a Marxian fiction that never had much substance except temporarily in highly specialised areas whose industries were on the decline, or in even shorter periods during the downswing of the trade cycle. But the increasing numbers of comparatively poor people whose economic position is improving very slowly, but whose political consciousness is rising very rapidly, may provide a more fruitful opening for the political agitator than a half-starving proletariat would ever have done.

Finally, it would be unsafe to consider only long-run changes : violent fluctuations, such as may occur in countries dependent largely on export of a few raw materials, may lead to political disturbances, even when the long-run tendency appears to be upwards. Such fluctuations are unevenly spread over different areas and the chances of political disturbances based on economic discontent depend partly on local conditions. During the period of the French revolutionary governments the Paris mob was the power that overturned successive revolutionary groups, and politicians could turn it to their purposes by street oratory. But it now appears that the scarcity of bread in Paris was the underlying source of discontent that enabled politicians to make such effective use of the mob until Napoleon, under the Directory, changed the whole picture by his " whiff of grapeshot ". Today it is the guns of the tanks that, in the last resort, can clear the streets.

Yet, in principle, things have changed less than might appear on the surface. The problem of getting enough food out of the hands of the cultivators to allay urban discontent became more important than ever in countries which adopted totalitarian political and economic controls, and even under humane political régimes which are in an early stage of industrialisation it remains a leading preoccupation of economic planners.   In the mature industrial countries under German occupation and exploitation during the Second World War it became, and remained during the earlier years of reconstruction, the chief economic problem.   It is at once a problem of production and of distribution and will continue to vex politicians and administrators in many of the emerging countries for a long time to come, as well as in the communist countries whose agriculture is subject to bureaucratic regimentation.

III

Mobs, Armies and Political Liberty

Nor has the situation with respect to the control or suppression of mobs changed in principle.   A small armed and disciplined force with fire power immeasurably superior to that in the hands of any mob has a decisive advantage.   The cannon at Napoleon's disposal have been superseded by the much superior tank and armoured car ; this is a difference in degree rather than in kind.   The same under-lying problems remain, for the effective use of arms depends on the attitudes and morale of those who are called on to use them.   Since the early stages of the French Revolution, modern armies have increasingly tended to become fairly representative cross-sections of the people—never more so than today.   Hence they are open to the influences that shape public opinion.   It is, therefore, difficult to screen the army from the winds of change that blow over societies. This was shown in dramatic fashion in Japan in a period in which the " young officer " class, drawn largely from distressed rural areas, became a leading source of unrest and a threat to the established order, restrained only with difficulty and not without serious lapses from time to time, by the senior officers and civilian leaders.   Here was a curious combination of radicalism and reaction [1] which revealed a type of political force elsewhere unfamiliar at the time but which has since established itself in widely separated parts of the world.   " Militarists " are often conceived of in political analysis as constituting a self-contained entity which stands outside the market-place of political ideas, ready to take the reins of government out of the hands of all contending political factions if internal political

---

[1] Described in some detail in the final chapter of my *Population Theories and their Application, with special Reference to Japan*, 1934.

strife seems to the armed forces to threaten the safety of the state by creating civil disorder and political impasse that may paralyse the nominal government. This picture has limited relevance occasionally to political developments in a few of the emerging countries, but it is often misleading. The wide acceptance it sometimes receives in the West is influenced by the fact that it is the explanation or apologia issued by the military themselves when they take power, and holds the field mainly because, at the time, censorships suppress the alternative explanations from other political groups concerned. This has been particularly so in the Sudan and Pakistan. In Turkey the censorship seems to have been less rigid and the reasons for intervention were stronger than elsewhere.

It cannot be assumed that the armed forces will stand aloof from ordinary political issues that tend to split the political world. Signs of a rift between the " young officers " and the senior officers became apparent in several countries. As in Japan in the later nineteen-twenties and in the thirties, the division does not fit well into the older political categories. The " young officers " are commonly regarded as " left-wing " and the senior officers as " right wing ". But the split has to do with the speed and scope of both economic and political reforms, and the economic radical, because he is in a great hurry, tends in practice to drift into reactionary political practices, while the older and more experienced officers are sometimes less ready to upset the constitutions of the past too drastically, and more ready to see the future as a development towards genuine representative government. There are of course individual exceptions to this alignment, but the case of Japan fitted it well, and the methods by which Colonel Nasir removed and imprisoned General Neguib, and suppressed his student supporters, revealed an aspect of it in Egypt.

Militarism has become a particularly complicated political influence in the emerging and reawakening countries. But this represents little change *in principle* from the time of the French Revolution. In his own far smaller world, Colonel Nasir and his fellow officers, using military force to suppress the mob, went on to impose authoritarian rule. Just as Napoleon nullified the Convention in practice, while continuing it in name, and turned himself into a much more efficient despotic ruler than Louis XVI and his predecessors had been, so Colonel Nasir became a more efficient and conscientious despot than King Farouk had been. The " President " became a more thorough-going dictator than the " King " had been : he planted military officers in many key civilian positions. Probably, if the fashions of the Napoleonic age had invested the title President with a more potent political appeal than the title Emperor, Napoleon would have chosen it. But in both cases the new despots succeeded

11

in capturing some of the *élan*, and maintaining some lip service to the doctrines, of the political *avant-garde* of the day, while perverting much of their content and substance.[1]

As the military authorities do not have all the administrative and technical resources within army circles to carry on the duties of government, so they are a more effective instrument for seizing power than for maintaining it, and they can only continue to hold office by diluting the military with an increasing civilian element in the work of administration and even in the formation of policy. As a rule they are notably wanting in economic knowledge and ability —a deficiency that has sometimes brought down their rule or forced them to restore civilians to their posts. But the ablest civilians are not always ready to serve régimes dominated by the military, and even when they are, their help is sometimes conditional.[2] As we have seen, divisions are apt to appear in the ranks of the army, some of whose officers are generally much less zealous for revolutionary ends than others. Similarly, in the ranks of civilian experts and administrators, differences arise both on the desirability of co-operating with a régime dominated by the military, and on the policies to recommend the latter to adopt. Hence a revolutionary *coup d'état* carried out by the army soon leads to a complicated inter-action between military and civilian elements that make it difficult to determine how the real power and influence are distributed.

If, however, the military head of government can still rely on the support of the army in any threat to internal security, he can over-ride civilian opposition so long as the economic situation does not deteriorate too far or too long. But army staffs are as much subject to rivalry as most institutions, and it is obvious that when splits appear in them the stability of the régimes concerned is doubtful. The difficulty about a military *coup d'état* is that it tends to under-mine the sense of loyalty of the armed forces to the government of the country—no matter who the ministers in the government may be— on which representative government is based. Loyalty is directed to a head of government whose title to power rests on a *coup d'état*. Officers cannot rely on the rule of law in the state : the loyalty of today may become the treason of tomorrow.

Finally, in some of the countries in question the danger arises of a cleavage between officers and the rank and file, who are sometimes drawn from less well-to-do classes. When the danger of this cleavage arises, the army loses much of its power and influence : officers can-not be confident that, in the event of civil strife, their orders will be obeyed.

---

[1] It is uncertain whether or not Colonel Nasir would have succeeded without the unintended help of the British and the U.S. governments in 1956 !

[2] Events in Syria in the early months of 1962 illustrated this point.

An unusually complicated case occurred during the civil strife in the Lebanon in 1958. Here the position was complicated by the considerable regional concentrations of ethnic and religious groupings. All the groups were represented in the army, and General Chehab, a remarkable soldier who possessed unusual political sense, diplomatic skill, and high integrity, confined military measures within the limits consistent with the preservation of unity among the rank and file of the army. The Government of the day, devoid of political tact and understanding, would have desired stronger military measures, but the General's standing in the country, unlike the Prime Minister's, transcended the divisions of party, of group origin, and of creed, and, by setting limits to the scope of military action, but at the same time acting firmly within those limits, Chehab was able to confine civil strife within manageable bounds, until the contending parties wearied of political deadlock and economic stagnation, and in the end recognised the necessity of compromise.

This case holds a model in one respect for emerging countries composed of groups of different ethnic origins and social heritage. Under such conditions, restraint and compromise are necessities for survival. When a deadlock has been reached among contending groups and resort is made to compromise, the first and most critical steps in political education have been taken. And political education is the first and foremost need in Asian, Latin American, and African societies today.

The western attitudes towards the role of the military in the emerging and reawakening countries have fluctuated widely. Too often, a military *coup d'état* has been looked on with approval if it seemed likely to benefit foreign economic interests. It is not in the long-run interest of the western countries to judge events by such narrow criteria. Great harm has been done to the reputations of states that profess and practise democratic principles at home, when, out of supposed self-interest, they go out of their way to approve of the establishment of military dictatorships among the countries of Asia and Latin America.

If the western world loses faith in the applicability of representative government to the emerging and reawakening countries ; if it shows approbation and particular favour to those militarist régimes that serve or appear to serve the economic interests of those of its nationals and business firms that have connections with them ; if it prefers to see order, regimentation, and quiescence under authoritarian rule to the greater turbulence, the more discordant voices, and the frequent changes of personnel and policies of governments, that characterise the earlier stages of ascent towards stable representative government, then it is unfaithful to its own heritage. It has no message of hope for the emerging countries. It is tacitly turning away from the principle of the equal potential capacities of groups of different races or different social heritage to a belief in the inherent incapacity of the peoples of most of Asia, Latin America, and Africa to reach the levels of civilisation attained in western Europe, North America, Australasia, and India and Japan. The flimsy evasion that they are not yet ready for representative government and must pass through preliminary periods of autocracy or despotism will hardly serve in the second half of the twentieth century. As we have seen, autocracy in western history was part of a world-wide condition, and our ancestors had to pioneer the way that led out of it. Today this is no longer the case and, indeed, the leaders in the struggles for independence have assailed autocracy as a product of colonial rule !

Looked at objectively, the strongest case against colonial rule is that, because it finds its ultimate seat of authority outside the colonial area, held by peoples of different social heritage, who are felt by natives to be foreigners, it cannot go beyond the preliminary stages of transition to self-government, and must remain authoritarian at the highest levels of government. But this objection loses its force if the argument is accepted that the peoples concerned are incapable of making representative government work. In this case the continuation of colonial rule, if it could be continued under the conditions of the past, would be preferable, since it would leave open important areas of self-government at lower levels. As I have already explained, my only reason for not applying the conclusions from this argument to a certain number of colonies and former colonies today is that the changing social psychology of the areas in question would make it impossible to continue colonial rule on the mild and liberal lines of the recent past.

The psychological adjustments in the West to decolonisation ought to include a greater sense of responsibility regarding the course of self-government in the emerging countries. It is not a matter of indifference to Britain whether representative government continues to exist or is replaced by various forms of militarist autocracy in the emerging countries. There are still opportunities for influencing, though none for coercing, the peoples concerned, not only by indirect forms of assistance which create a better material basis on which to build the new societies, but also by maintaining a high level of constructive criticism. Nor should we shrink from unofficially expressing conclusions, when they are well founded, which are unpalatable in the ruling circles in some of the emerging countries. It is of the utmost importance in the West to establish the best possible relations with the emerging and reawakening countries, but this will not be accomplished by publicly approving whatever uses they make of their newly asserted independence. In politics, as in law, there is an inescapable moral element, however misconceived its nature may be in popular discussion.

But the preservation of a critical attitude towards the uses made of the liberties gained by decolonisation must be carefully dissociated from any desire or attempt to interfere with the political independence of the countries of *le tiers monde*. Nothing could be more damaging to the international relations of the future than the adoption, tacitly if not explicitly, of double standards in the treatment of long-established and more advanced states on the one hand, and the emerging and reawakening states on the other. To this no exceptions are justifiable. However strongly we may hope and desire that the countries that have recently won national liberty shall respect individual liberty, we must continue to recognise that it is for the peoples of those countries themselves to decide under what forms of government they shall live and who shall fill the leading ministerial positions. Nor can we permit this principle to be limited to democratic forms of government, and justify interference when the peoples concerned have fallen under dictatorships which give the majority no voice in the choice of government. The principle enshrined in the " Platt Amendment " of 1904 with respect to U.S. rights in Cuba created nothing but resentment and friction. Although, of all forms of government, representative government is the least objectionable, the attempt to impose it on any people by outside interference is an act of imperialism encroaching on political independence. This is obvious when, as in the case of the United States with respect to Cuba, the forcible interference is a unilateral act. The suggestion that it would be otherwise if the interference were a collective act, under the auspices of an international organisation, is no more tenable in practice, even if it appears, at first sight, more plausible in theory. Outside western Europe, North America, and Australasia genuine representative government is not so commonplace as to enable a widely representative group of states to impose it upon an authoritarian state without hypocrisy, even if, for political reasons of their own, some authoritarian states were ready to join in the act of imposing it. Moreover, it is inconceivable that a collective attempt would be made to impose a particular form of government on a Great Power at the risk of general war : consequently efforts at collective interference would necessarily be confined to powers too weak to resist by force, and lacking in powerful allies to come to its aid. Nothing retards the growth of the rule of law in international relations more decisively than discriminatory treatment of this kind —one law for the well-to-do and another for the poorer nations.

The attempts of the United States to persuade or coerce the members of the Organisation of American States to join in measures aimed at encompassing the downfall of Señor Castro and a change

in the form of government in Cuba illustrate the dangers of interference in the internal affairs of the emerging and reawakening
countries.   It would be credulous, indeed, to suppose that these
arbitrary actions were designed to further the noble cause of representative government.   The real distinction made by U.S. adminis-
trations was not that between representative and authoritarian
government, but that between right-wing and left-wing governments.   But as Señor Castro had adopted authoritarian methods of
government, the issue could be superficially represented as one
between democracy and dictatorship, and public memories of past
support of right-wing dictatorships were notoriously short.   As we
have seen, however, the United States was spending large sums to
sustain dictatorial rulers elsewhere whose activities threatened neighbouring countries where a greater degree of political freedom was to
be found.

CHAPTER IX

THE INTEGRATION AND DISINTEGRATION
OF STATES

I

Arab and African " Nationalism "

IN LARGE areas of the world ideas have developed, sentiments have been formed, and slogans concocted, which are not easily classifiable in the customary language of international relations or political philosophy. They represent special affinities between the peoples of different states which, however, are vaguer, less intense, and more wide-ranging than nationalism proper, though in some cases they are misleadingly described as nationalism. There is a variety of such ideas and sentiments, ranging from the tenuous " special relationship" between Britain and the United States to the politically much more significant ideas of " Arab nationalism " and " African nationalism ". Discriminations are made between outside powers, not simply on objective grounds of common interests, but out of a sense of deep psychological ties which cause a particular power or powers to be regarded with a sense of kinship resting on an historical, or racial, or ethnic, or religious and cultural basis, or some or all of these affinities combined. This reads like a partial description of nationalism, but an essential characteristic of nationalism is lacking, namely, a general readiness to live under one government and to intermingle with complete freedom. Lip service is indeed sometimes given vaguely to this ideal, but unless and until lip service to it is followed by concrete steps, voluntarily accepted on all sides, to achieve it, attempts to equate the sentiment with nationalism are unsound and merely confuse discourse.

In actual practice it cannot be said that Arab or African nationalism yet exists in the accepted meaning or any useful meaning of the term nationalism. For the number of people in the Middle East who, in practice, would welcome a single government over the whole Middle East is very small.[1] Similarly with Africa. The terms pan-Africanism and pan-Arabism are perhaps appropriate though less used. The reality that lies behind the outward manifestation o

---

[1] I refer, of course, to a concrete single government drawn from available alternatives, and not to a remote abstract ideal to which people would assent in principle while knowing that it was beyond realisation in the near future.

these sentiments is not that the Arab peoples and the African peoples at present feel an urge to unite under a single government, but that each of the various groups within them feels a sense of kinship to the others which it does not feel towards outside peoples. It is difficult to estimate the strength of that feeling. Like nationalism, it is stronger among a small, politically conscious section of the more educated classes than among the masses, but the former are able, when they desire, to evoke a considerable response from the latter.

Until the second half of the nineteenth century, and in some areas later still, it seems unlikely that national consciousness had penetrated to the masses of people in many areas of Asia or Africa. Even now, while unmistakable nationalism is to be found in a considerable part of Asia and has developed in an increasingly intense form in tropical Latin America, there remain parts of western Asia and most of tropical Africa in which strong but only vaguely defined mass-sentiment predominates which, as we have seen, is difficult to classify as " nationalism " in the more carefully defined meanings of the term, and which comes closer to a group feeling of kinship based on certain common features of social heritage, as for example, in the ideas of " Arab nationalism " and " African nationalism ", or the still vaguer idea of " Africa for the Africans ", which in turn may be little more than mere " anti-foreignism " but is capable of arousing intense political passions. In " African nationalism " there may be an element of " racialism " in the true sense, as defined in physical anthropology. But in other cases the term racialism would be entirely incorrect. The Arabs are not a race, and in fact belong to the same race as those western peoples whose imperialistic activities in the past they resent. " Arab nationalism ", broadly speaking, seems intended to cover groups with a common Islamic tradition *and* a common language. This perhaps leaves doubtful borders in some areas but serves a useful purpose. As to Asia, rather fortunately, perhaps, we do not hear of " Asian nationalism ", but, as we have seen, Indonesia bases wide claims partly on vaguely conceived traditions and perhaps still more doubtful ethnic grounds.

All these wide-ranging sentiments, claims, and slogans far transcend the territorial scope of nationalism as it has been defined in any definite sense. The facts show that in each case the peoples concerned are not now ready to sink the separate identities of the states in which they live, for a single, all-embracing, unitary government of the area as a whole. Not only are they not ready to do so now, but it is by no means clear that they will be in the foreseeable future. Nor, in some of the areas, can the presence be overlooked of important minorities which do not share the sentiment in question and which fear that their rights would not be maintained in a larger unit embracing all the groups which do feel and respond to it. The alignments of those countries which have important economic ties outside the group may also turn in different directions in the future.

Pan-Arabism and pan-Africanism create complications for the governments and peoples of the states within these groups. They tend to set in motion a competition between two objects of loyalty. They hinder the growth of a sense of loyalty to emerging states, particularly when the boundaries of the state were laid down in a colonial period, and political agitators can lay claims to their extension, blaming " imperialism " for fragmentation of former allegedly larger units.[1] The more fervent supporters of these movements regard them as a constructive force that will ultimately lead to the creation of large and powerful units capable of holding their own among the Great Powers which they distrust, following the subordinate relations in which they stood to them in the past. But this is a long-run possibility rather than a force to be reckoned with in the near future, and in the meantime Arab nationalism and African nationalism are as often a source of friction as of solidarity. They are slogans that no politician dares to question, however aware he may be of their dangers and their impracticability as a guide to immediate policy.

These ideas, and the mass sentiment based on them, have sometimes been used as a screen to cover the adoption, and excuse the maintenance, of autocratic methods of government. By calling for unity over very wide areas, such as the Arab world or a large part of the continent of Africa, they meet with much local resistance in practice, even when lip service is given to them in theory by all parties. A common religion, like Islam, and a common language, like Arabic, certainly give rise among the states concerned to a strong sense of kinship and to a special identity in face of the outside world. But they are accompanied by substantial differences in origin and heritage, in the types of relations with the rest of the world, and in local political and economic interests. To some of these are added, in much of tropical Africa and in certain parts of the Middle East, tribal divisions. If such differences, deviations, and divisions are to be overridden in a short time, as some impatient politicians would wish, an autocratic form of government appears to many to be the only means of doing so. The real issue, then, is concerned with the

---

[1] When living in the Middle East I have frequently met nationals of Middle Eastern states who would acknowledge no nationalism but " Arab nationalism " and denied the existence of any nationalism centred on the states of which they were citizens. But when asked whether they wished to see one Arab state, where its capital should be, and what sort of government it should have, all but a small minority answered only with generalities so vague as to commit them to nothing definite. The very small minority wanted the extension of Nasir's dictatorship over the whole Middle East, with Cairo as the capital. It seems likely that an attempt to accomplish this would plunge the Middle East into war.

respective values given to political unity on the one hand, and human liberties on the other.

Broadly speaking, some of the more ardent " nationalists ", who are in a sense empire builders as well as nationalists, place national independence above the liberties of the individual. Questioning an exuberant Arab nationalist not long ago in the Middle East, I was met with the frank reply, " What we have to think of first is national liberty from foreign domination. Every Arab must accept this and we must unite behind a leader to get it. We do not want opposition. Those liberties that you value so much in Britain may come later among us but we have something more important first. We must win our independence and freedom from the imperialists." Actually, his country was politically independent and a member of the United Nations. But to most Arabs, at least those in the Fertile Crescent and in Egypt, the idea that sinister " imperialists " are ceaselessly plotting against the Middle East countries is so firmly ingrained, and fulfils such a leading role in the propaganda armoury of Arab politicians, that it lies beyond the scope of critical analysis. It was immensely strengthened by the blunders of the British and French Governments over Suez. The warlike atmosphere that it engenders, and on which its continued appeal depends, has hindered the establishment of stable relations between Europe and south-western Asia, though by the mid-twentieth century the intra-regional and domestic party animosities were overshadowing external animosities.

It would be an error to dismiss the wearisomely reiterated allegations of imperialist plots against some of the Arab and tropical African countries as merely the product of nationalist and communist propaganda based on exaggeration of charges which have had some substance in the past but have now ceased to be relevant. In the Middle East the charges are natural enough when applied to past history, which records a number of far from happy interventions by Britain and France, from the bombardment of Alexandria to the Suez aggression. But now that these unhappy incidents have receded into the past, it would be naïve to take these charges simply at their face value : the fact is, that a strong vested interest has grown up in them. They provide a convenient external object to which attention can be diverted away from internal divisions. They serve as an instrument of internal rivalry, each political leader trying to outdo the other in denunciations of imperialism and of Zionism. Again, as with imperialism, so with Zionism, there is much substance in Arab charges, but dangerous accretions have accumulated around a sound core.

Unification under what government ? [1]   This immensely difficult

---

[1] Limited analogies may be found in the ancient as in the Renaissance world. Claude Mossé remarks : " *L'impérialisme athénien avait ainsi jeté les bases d'une*

question opens up such possibilities of internal strife, of one *coup d'état* after another, of Napoleonic methods, that those leaders who have been ambitious to assume the mantle do not dare to avow their ambitions openly. Hence, they have rivalled one another in attributing difficulties within the Arab world to machinations outside it. If western powers have usually been the chief object of attacks and insinuations, the tables have sometimes been turned unexpectedly when Russia, or the local communists, have tried to press their activities too far. President Nasir has at times turned his anti-imperialist batteries on Russia.

Naturally the West has been attacked more often than Russia : its interventions in the Middle East go back further and have been far more frequent than Russia's, which only began in the nineteen-fifties. But the Russian advantage is quickly lost as soon as communist intervention clashes with Arab nationalism. The Soviet leaders must walk warily : every false step plays into the hands of the West. Their position is much weaker in the Middle East, Africa, and Latin America than is commonly imagined. The rivalry for the leadership of the Arab or the African world, half-concealed behind vague slogans projected on the outside world, is as likely to impinge on the communist as on the non-communist world if the Russian or Chinese leaders interfere too obviously or too effectively, or if it is convenient for Arab or African politics to represent them as doing so.

Just because such sentiments as those misleadingly called Arab nationalism and African nationalism are vague, loose, and difficult to apply concretely in domestic affairs, but at the same time appeal to deep-seated emotions that are stronger for their vagueness and their inaccessibility to sceptical criticism, and are founded on a genuine sense of kinship, they are all the more explosive and dangerous in some of their practical manifestations. What comes in them from the heart is often not balanced and given reasonable direction by what comes from the head. So long as the chief political issue is that of emancipation from foreign control, as it was for a time in the Middle East and North and central Africa, and still is in parts of southern Africa, unity can be attained behind the slogans of Arab nationalism and African nationalism, unity for a negative purpose. But when external control has been withdrawn or is on the verge of being withdrawn, the full dangers of these slogans, when used uncritically and as propaganda, appear. As, in reality, they stand for something less than nationalism, the rivalries to which they lead among the aspiring political leaders in the various parts of the Arab

---

futurè commonauté hellénique réalisée sans l'egide d'Athènes". But unlike some classical scholars Professor Mossé recognises explicitly the limitations of the evidence as to how far into the population these sentiments of leaders went. We must beware of projecting the idea of nationalism into pre-modern times. *La fin de la démocratie athénienne*, Paris, 1962, pp. 400–25.

and African worlds overlap the two worlds at certain points. Since
democracy has few roots in the Arab world, and an uncertain hold
in Africa, there is insufficient political machinery through which a
voluntary unification, establishing a parliamentary government,
open to opposition parties, and subject from time to time to elections
and changes of ministries, can be proposed and calmly considered.
The question of unification thus becomes a subject of under-cover
intrigue and of the pull and thrust of rival authoritarian or would-be
authoritarian leaders. This creates friction and antagonism, the
real sources of which cannot be acknowledged publicly. The
political leaders are thus obliged to invent artificial public issues
to serve as a screen for the real issues. These forms of political
" shadow-boxing " degrade political discussion to the level of demagoguery, and retard the much needed political education of the
masses of the newly independent peoples. A certain minimum of
insincerity in political utterances in public is inescapable, but a price
has always to be paid for it, and when insincerity reaches the scale it
has reached in some of the emerging countries the price is high.

The vagueness of Arab and African " nationalism " also opens it
to the danger of degenerating into a *Volk* sentiment such as that
cultivated by the Nazi and other German movements in the past.
The demand that all peoples of supposed German ethnic origin, and
who spoke the German language, should be brought under German
political control contributed to one of the two greatest disasters in
international history. The Arab and African countries do not
wield power comparable to that of pre-war Germany, and the
danger is less than it was when Germany advanced her *Volk* claims.
But it is not negligible : the more aggressive Arab and African
leaders sometimes talk as if any of their own or related peoples who
do not share their attitude to the outside world were " traitors " or
" lackeys of imperialism ". Such language, up to now more often
heard in the Arab world than in Africa south of the Sahara, is
deliberately aimed at arousing mob passions which leave no room for
reason, toleration, and rational discussion in political life. And the
flight from reason in the public discussion of politics is in danger of
ending in the slough of despotism, thinly disguised by a verbal
screen woven out of the corrupt use of words.

Again, this does not imply that these broad sentiments, already a
dynamic force in international politics, can be neglected or frontally
opposed in the West. As we have seen, the essence of the matter is
that the majority of the peoples who entertain them in the Middle
East and in Africa, and, perhaps, in a somewhat different form in
tropical Latin America, do feel towards one another a special relationship which they do not share with the outside world, and, in a
loose sense we may look on it as a feeling of kinship. Even in the

midst of internal discord in the Arab and African worlds an all per-
vading tendency prevails to adopt common or at least outwardly
similar attitudes to the rest of the world.

II

Unification and Disintegration

But before turning to the question how these " nationalisms " may
be directed into a constructive channel, we must examine the opposite tendency, that towards disintegration, which has been discern-
able in some emerging countries in Asia and Africa since the Second
World War, as it was in Latin America well over a century earlier.
Just as, in some directions, there are movements to form larger states
out of unions of smaller states, so, in other directions, there are
movements on the part of minority groups within certain states to
secede or obtain regional autonomy from the state in which they
were included at the time of decolonisation. At certain points there
is even an overlapping between the forces aiming at fusion and those
aiming at autonomy or separation : certain states with discontented
minorities have not hesitated to join in the movements for enlarging
themselves by merger or " take-over ".

Some of the newly formed states as well as the previous states in
Asia and Africa contain groups of different social heritage and
regional interests, which were brought together generally under
colonial or other rule based on external sources of power. In some
cases decolonisation has made it more difficult to hold the parts
together. Rule based on external sources, though it may be opposed
on other grounds, has the advantage of appearing impartial in respect to differing regional interests and desires. When independence
comes, it is difficult to constitute an indigenous government which
will not appear to be unduly weighted on the side of this or that
region. A peaceful solution can only be reached under a representative government in which the majority show restraint and forbearance in the use of their power. But restraint is not a common
characteristic of political life in the emerging states : too often, heads
of state have merely tried to bludgeon the opposition into silence by
conniving privately at threats of personal violence and by scrapping
constitutional guarantees of the rights of minorities.

While some of these actions may be regarded as defensive, aimed
at preserving a pre-existing unity under dependency, they may,
paradoxically, be accompanied by a simultaneous drive to expand
abroad, partly through the desire of the leaders to promote unity at
home by diverting the attention of the people abroad, and partly

through a widespread tendency among newly established states, if they have the power, to expand their boundaries, even at the expense of their neighbours.[1]

But expansion abroad fails to solve the problems of minorities at home. It tends to engulf the minorities still further and increase their discontent. If in time it erases their identity and special characteristics through coercive measures and sheer weight of numbers, that represents a net loss of human variety and individuality which is not compensated for by simplifying the task of the administration and strengthening the centralisation of government controls. Governments were made for man and not man for governments.

Thus the tendencies towards the fusion of states and those towards the disintegration of states, though moving in opposite directions, raise the same or similar issues, which are concerned with the form and structure of government and administration. These in turn are affected by the state of political development of the communities concerned under imperial or colonial rule and only emerge in acute form after liberation. The disappointment and embarrassment felt when they arise has sometimes led to allegations that they are intrinsically a product of colonial or imperial rule.

The boundaries established between different colonies and mandated territories did not necessarily correspond to any " natural " geographical characteristics, nor were all of them convenient for administrative or efficient for economic purposes.[2] Owing, partly, to rivalries among the colonising powers they sometimes cut through territories inhabited by peoples whose social heritage, habits of life,

---

[1] The United States is a result of this process.

[2] The idea of " natural " boundaries is, in any case, a slippery conception, particularly since the advances in modern technology have reduced the importance of physical obstacles to movement and communication. The significance of physical obstacles is popularly related to their defensive potentialities and these change with changing techniques of warfare. The founding of the Netherlands in the sixteenth century as an independent state was partly a result of skilful use of terrain broken up by water and the ability to obtain external supplies by sea. Although the Spanish troops of the Dukes of Alva and Parma were perhaps the best in Europe in their day they were unable to prevail in this terrain although they had overrun Flanders where probably as many of the people wished for independence as in Holland. In the last decade of the eighteenth century the French revolutionary armies soon overran the whole area. Although this was partly due to dissatisfaction within Holland, military techniques had also changed and the natural obstacles were a less formidable barrier. But the question is not one simply of defensive obstacles ; physical characteristics of the earth's surface have also affected the groupings of mankind and the growth of separate nationalisms in some areas. It would require too much space to treat the subject in the present study, but enough has perhaps been said to call attention to the dangers of superficial, popular use of the idea of " natural boundaries " supposedly violated by colonialism. Under different techniques of warfare the state of Holland would probably never have been founded.

and sense of community had much in common. In such areas it has been argued that coalescence should be one of the first aims of emerging states. But however close the ties may have been in pre-colonial times, developments in the colonial period have created new obstacles to coalescence—for example, the different languages and administrative systems in adjoining former British and French colonies. In addition, the struggles for independence in adjoining former colonies were necessarily waged by separate movements each with its own leaders, and few, if any, are willing to relinquish their positions to place combined territories under outside leaders. This formidable problem is easiest to solve under representative government with freedom of political parties, and most difficult when a " cult of personality " has been built around individual leaders.

But, as we have already seen, it is misleading to suppose that colonisation was generally a disintegrating influence. Not only has the extent of pre-existing unity been widely exaggerated for propaganda purposes, but in fact imperial and colonial ventures have sometimes established unity where none previously existed, and established it so firmly that it has survived, or appears likely to survive, the relinquishment of imperial rule. Probably the phrase " unite and rule " is more often applicable than the phrase " divide and rule "—so often repeated in routine fashion by propagandists.

In the circumstances it is not surprising that in areas where the smaller states have gained independence, tentative moves have been made towards closer association or even unification. The wisdom or unwisdom of these attempts depends on so many influences that the student of international affairs must examine each case separately in the light of its special circumstances, holding himself free from, though taking account of, the emotional involvements of the politicians and masses of people in the areas concerned. He must balance the advantages of moving quickly, before new vested interests have become entrenched, against the disadvantages of locking up a large part of an inadequate administrative organisation in the detailed planning for unification, at a time when pressing economic problems threaten the stability of the new state. Above all, if the criteria adopted in the present study are accepted, the decisive influence should be the attitudes of the peoples concerned. Ambitious politicians in the stronger of two territories which it is proposed to amalgamate sometimes gloss over the objections of groups in the weaker area, and are ready to override them by intimidation. The statement that " a volunteer is worth three pressed men " is nowhere more applicable than here. Forced unification, or unification achieved or maintained by the intimidation of substantial minorities, tends to inhibit the growth of stable representative government.

It tends to weaken, and not strengthen, the state in its relations with other states.

In Syria, without preliminary preparation or consultation with the electorate, a minority, fearful of being dismissed from power at home, organised a *coup d'état* which " unified " it with a country of much larger population. The gift was received ; the bearers of it in due course, as Machiavelli would have seen in advance, were removed from power in the U.A.R. more completely and irrevocably than they would have been if they had remained in the hands of their own electorate in Syria ; and representative government in Syria gave way to rigid autocracy controlled from outside and reinforced with the machinery of the police state. This merger cut across the aspirations towards a unification of the " Fertile Crescent ", and provoked a counter-move to unite Iraq and Jordan, also without consulting the peoples. Both " unions " collapsed. Such arbitrary acts, far from creating a true spirit of unity in the minds of the peoples, foster competitive rivalries which keep alive a spirit of intrigue among rulers ambitious to enlarge and perpetuate their powers, without scrupulous attention to the wishes of the peoples who are drawn into unifications on which they have had no chance to express themselves.

Nothing in these pages is intended to discredit the unification of territories by voluntary means, or to disparage the obvious economic benefits of merging very small territories deficient in natural resources but which supplement one another's resources. The merging of Gambia and Senegal and of part of the former U.K. mandated territory in the Cameroons with part of the adjoining former French territory would seem natural.[1] In time the advantages of wider unification will doubtless come to be realised in areas where representative government takes root.

This, after all, is the essence of the whole issue. The preoccupation of President Nasir with centralised military power, the efforts of a number of other heads of states to establish a permanent lease of power by suppressing opposition parties, have associated unification with empire-building under authoritarian rule. Such a conjunction endangers the whole movement towards unification, threatening to turn it into a series of clashes between rival intraregional empire-builders ; thus contributing to the chronic instability and unrest which, more than anything else, tend to undermine the fair promise of decolonisation and to open the menacing prospect that the later state for some time to come might be worse than the earlier.

The problem of unification requires patience in an impatient age, restraint in an age of aggression, peaceful methods in a warlike

---

[1] Even here there are practical difficulties to be overcome.

international atmosphere. In African societies that have moved suddenly from tribalism to nationalism, time and tact are needed to offset the disintegrating tendencies of a tribal particularism which hinders advance from the formal structure to the realities of a modern state. But government and politics are arts to be acquired by experience and education. If decolonisation is to be followed by a decline in the number of those who share in responsible decisions and in freely conducted political activities ; if press, radio, and " information " services are to be controlled in the interests and for the glorification of a one-party system headed by a president determined to hold on to power indefinitely ; then the political education of the people, which had made considerable progress in the later years of British and French colonial rule, will come to a standstill. The achievement of greater genuine cohesion among disparate groups within a state requires a supreme effort in the art of negotiation, in the development of the habit of deliberation and discussion, in the spread, through voluntary as well as government channels, of an understanding of the advantages of wider unity, both in home and external affairs, achieved by the arts of persuasion, not of coercion.

III

Persuasion, Coercion and Unification

The size and composition of states, and changes in their boundaries arising out of changing internal and external conditions will occupy the minds of statesmen for many centuries. The conflicting approaches among the emerging and reawakening countries are the result, partly of divergent aims and ideals, partly of ambition and opportunism. Here, as elsewhere in international affairs, power and liberty are often in conflict. The large state is looked on, not always correctly, as the strong state, and the enlargement of an existing state as adding to its strength. But at times the process of enlargement can only be obtained by overriding small nations ; union is then achieved by coercion, and the population no longer comprises a single nation united in a voluntary desire to live under one government. Authoritarian methods are then used to suppress dissent, and dissenters are labelled as " stooges of the imperialists ". Since the mass of the people just brought into the enlarged state have not been consulted, free representative bodies cannot be allowed to continue, and authoritarian rule is substituted, as happened in Syria when the U.A.R. was formed, for whatever elements of democracy existed in the area taken over. The hasty pursuit of the ideal of unification, running ahead of the wishes of the people

and of the capacity for rapid administrative and economic readjust
ment, ends in the same way as the hasty pursuit of other ideals—in
the assumption of totalitarian powers. Those who place unification
and power as the foremost ends to be pursued at all costs will accept
this as a price to be paid.

But history is sprinkled with the records of disintegration as well
as with those of unification, and it is the unifications achieved by
coercion and maintained by authoritarian rule that are most likely
to crumble under internal dissension and external pressure.

Thus, in approaching these issues at the present time, the first
step, and one which is too often evaded by the leading politicians in
the newly emerging countries, is to choose between coercive and
persuasive methods of approach to both domestic and wider unification. In our impatient age the method of persuasion finds least
favour among those who feel themselves to be trailing in the race
for modernisation. The communism and " fascism " of the twentieth century have aggravated the propensity to violence which
most nationalist movements have shown, particularly in their earlier
stages. The obstacles to wider and closer unification arise out of
local differences within and between many of the newly independent
countries. When different ethnic or tribal groups, marked by differences in social heritage and social consciousness, are distributed
among separate regions in a single state, as in Ghana, Nigeria, and
the ex-Belgian Congo, mutual suspicions are likely to arise, which
may be allayed by political tact and by leaving considerable regional
autonomy. Alternatively, an attempt may be made, as in Ghana,
to ride roughshod over the politically weaker groups, suppressing
effective opposition through the establishment of one-party government, the abrogation of constitutional guarantees, and the " cult of
personality ".

Some western observers today are inclined to excuse the substitution of authoritarian for parliamentary rule in newly independent
countries, on the ground that the methods of constitutional representative government adopted in western countries are unsuitable for
export. It has even been suggested that a phase analogous to that
of Tudor government in Britain would meet the needs of the newly
emerging countries better than the parliamentary systems of democracy adopted in part of the western world. But the analogy is
dangerous.[1] In the fifteenth and sixteenth centuries, the art of
government was still in an early stage of development. The signifi-

---

[1] A more useful analogy may be made between early Tudor governments,
especially that of Henry VII, and new governments in some of the emerging
countries today in respect to the difficulties of establishing a sense of " legitimacy ".
This is particularly marked when the central government tends to be overweighted
in respect to one of the varied groups in its territory.

cance of the Tudor Period for our age lies, not in the merits of
arbitrary rule, but in the development of curbs on it, and in the
organisation of legislative and executive powers.   These developments, crude as they may appear in retrospect, and interrupted from
time to time by the reassertion of arbitrary power, were in the van
of progress in their day.   There were no advanced models to draw
upon.   At present, even making allowance for the early stage of
modern development in some parts of Africa, Latin America, and
Asia, it would be a form of atavism to ignore centuries of experience
in the western world and to emulate models from pre-modern times.
Such atavisms have indeed occurred in the West : the Second World
War was a consequence of the worst of them.   But they only reinforce
the case for seeking, in the emerging states, to profit from experience
in the outside world, and to avoid as far as possible the centuries of
painful travail which the pioneers of the modern world, groping
forward with little precedent to guide them, were obliged to pass
through before they could replace despotism by stable forms of
representative government by consent.   The objection sometimes
made that the masses in some of the areas concerned are no more
advanced in a political sense than the masses in England were in the
times of Henry VIII will not hold.   The appropriate form of government depends, not simply on the level of advancement of the people,
but also on the knowledge and resources available to those who
govern.   Even if the first has remained stationary at a primitive
level, which in many of the areas at least is not the case, the second
has not, and the imposition or reimposition of despotic forms of
government by ambitious native politicians could only lead to
political retrogression.   In some cases decolonisation has already been
followed by a decline rather than an increase in human liberties.

This is an anomalous state of affairs : the chief gain of decolonisation ought to consist in an extension of the freedom of the individual.
As we have seen, colonial rule, whatever benefits it may have
brought, in the nature of the case could only be temporary : no
people will accept indefinitely an external seat of authority maintained by another group of different ethnic origin or social heritage.
This set limits to the extent of self-government, which extended the
liberties of the people, both individually and collectively.   Once a
colonial power, preparing the way for ultimate independence,
embarked on this path, it set minimum standards in the light of
which individual liberties could be measured after independence
began.   When independent governments, seeking to perpetuate
themselves in power, drop below those standards, or fail to rise substantially above them, it is difficult to maintain that human welfare
has undergone any advance through the replacement of colonial
status by independence.

It is sometimes maintained that *any* form of self-rule is better than even good external rule ; but this claim is usually made by politicians who feel assured that they will be among the ruling classes, and there is no convincing evidence that the " common man " who suffers under native rule as much as, if not more than, under foreign rule, would always acquiesce in it if he could express himself freely without intimidation. Since it is impracticable to carry out tests to settle this question, the realities behind the widespread nationalist and communist propaganda remain uncertain.

But when nationalist fervour, backed by modern means of communication, is raised to a high pitch, even the most benevolent colonial rule is impossible. The time has passed for imposing external rule on the ground that local rule is incompetent. The day of tutelage under external dominion has gone for those territories formerly controlled by western countries ; it will probably be on the way out for the eastern world before the end of the century.

The problem of the future is how to create and maintain political freedom within the emerging states. That western institutions cannot always be taken over indiscriminately in areas of widely different conditions, and that political resources are sometimes inadequate to construct more than one well-organised party immediately after independence, may be readily agreed, but it does not follow that the grant of political monopoly to a *parti unique*, prohibiting the formation of opposition parties, is justifiable. Of course, even in the most democratic western countries coalition governments, embracing all or most parties, are sometimes formed to meet emergencies, and for a time this approximates in practice to a *parti unique*. These arrangements, however, are voluntary and consistent with the maintenance of representative government. We cannot say the same of the *parti unique* when it is accompanied either by a statutory prohibition of opposition parties or by intimidation of those who seek to form such parties. The argument that opposition can be expressed within the party before decisions are reached—a paraphrase of the communist doctrine of " democratic centralism "—is a specious evasion of the issue. When a régime in power is given a monopoly of the right to organise, it has an overwhelming advantage over individual dissenters. The heart of the matter lies in the right to organise.

The preceding discussion has shown that the same or similar fundamental issues have arisen over the efforts of some governments in the emerging countries to consolidate regionally diverse groups, and the efforts of others to enlarge their inherited boundaries by unifications with other states in the regions in question. In both cases the issues are concerned with the methods of achieving unification, and with the forms of government adopted with a view to maintaining it.

The term unification, as popularly used, conceals important differences of meaning. At one extreme it is sometimes taken to cover the results of annexation by conquest ; at the other to denote a voluntary coalescence, entered into by each party without coercion and in the belief that its self-interest will be served. Between these forms of unification various intermediate types occur in which pressure on some groups brings them in line with the self-interest of others.

Unification by annexation and coercion has a sad and tragic history of bloodshed and suppression, sometimes of the decline and virtual extinction of weaker and less advanced peoples, sometimes of the creation of a spirit of irredentism culminating in later wars of revenge and liberation. Of these results, the former has occurred most frequently in the New World, and the latter in the Old. In the course of time the memory of the circumstances surrounding unification fades, and even historians are all too ready to extenuate the crimes committed in its name, after opposition has passed away among new generations in a changed environment, facing new types of problems. But it does not follow that, because unification is accepted today without resistance, high-handed, coercive methods of obtaining it yesterday are now justified by results. Thus, one might attack uncompromisingly the proposals of the British Prime Minister and the President of the United States at one time during the Second World War to dismember Germany, without in any way extenuating the unscrupulous measures and the bloodshed by which Bismarck originally achieved the unification of Germany. In this case, it might be argued that the methods by which German unity was achieved helped to bring on the First and Second World Wars, and were therefore not justified by their consequences. Even so, however, it would not follow that forced dismemberment, against the wishes of the present generation of German, would repair past damage or prevent future strife. If we consider other cases, in which unification by coercion and bloodshed has been followed after many years by the development of a state in which new generations are living in harmony at home and abroad, it is no less fallacious and dangerous to excuse or gloss over the methods by which the state was established within its present boundaries. Such methods affected individual lives, and the moral responsibilities of individual personalities apply to the actions of those who devised and used them in public affairs. The idea that a satisfactory political unity could only be achieved after an initial stage of bloodshed and coercion cannot be accepted, but even if it did appear probable, the aim of political unity over a given area cannot be given such overriding pre-eminence over other aims as to justify violence and duplicity. The centenary of Cavour in 1961 evoked the customary eulogies of his services in unifying Italy, but the less creditable aspects of those services cannot be extenuated by the unwarranted assumption that haste in unification was so all important as to provide a special dispensation from moral restraints that readily command a consensus in personal dealings among individuals.

CHAPTER X

APPROACHES TO UNITY IN DIVERSITY

I

Contrasting Lines of Approach

BROADLY speaking, there are two approaches to the enlargement of political units. The first begins with political union, with centralisation of powers. It may be expressed in the statement inscribed in Accra, to the effect that if " the political kingdom " is placed first, all other things will be added. Indonesia and Ghana have tried to follow this path, so far without conspicuous political or economic success. The second approach is the reverse of the first, and is being followed in Europe and parts of Africa. It seeks to establish economic and technical links, freer migration, and an approach to unified transport, in the belief that co-operation in practical, day-to-day matters will gradually spread a sense of common interests and open the way to closer political relationships.

The differences between these approaches cannot easily be bridged. The attempt suddenly to force a union on states which were set up as independent units following the colonial period runs counter to the interests of political groups some of which would fall into a subordinate position or suffer proscription after a union. It clashes with the economic interests of important groups, when one of the states brings comparatively greater economic resources but less political power and influence than the other. Under genuine representative government, these conflicts of interests may be reconciled ultimately, if a spirit of compromise prevails, and if, as in Canada, the politically stronger unit refrains from taking full advantage of its greater numbers and political power. But newly born states are not noted for political restraint, nor the stronger among them for deliberately refraining from taking advantage of the weaker.

It is therefore no accident or mere coincidence that the pan-Arab and pan-African movements are sponsored most aggressively by authoritarian political leaders, intolerant of political opposition. The creation of a single unitary state with centralised powers over such wide areas and among people who, notwithstanding racial or ethnic affinities, exhibit much regional diversity of characteristics and social heritage, could only be achieved in the short run by aggressive, dictatorial measures, and maintained by the methods of the police state. In practice, the local attachments of the peoples, and, as we have seen, the ambitions of the leaders, whenever more than one leader appears, greatly hinder the tendency towards complete coalescence : yet at the same time self-interest is served by keeping down economic barriers and facilitating trade. In some cases free migration may benefit all countries concerned, but in others it would create serious antagonism, particularly if workers moved suddenly in large numbers from densely populated areas where incomes are low to less populated areas where agriculture is expanding with the aid of considerable capital investment. Equally, friction tends to arise from influxes of small merchants and town labourers, especially where they show more skill and tenacity than the native peoples in the same occupations.

Economic adjustments take considerable time and cannot be hastened unduly without risk of serious conflicts. Consequently, resounding declarations of political union tend often, as in the case of Mali–Guinea–Ghana, to be followed by a rapid anticlimax and a striking contrast between what is stated on paper and what is operating in practice. Soon the differences between the two approaches towards unity, while remaining as sharp as before in theory, are narrowed appreciably in practice.

The second approach, through economic and cultural co-operation, appears slow to impatient would-be empire builders. But the European Common Market shows that it can be effective on the economic side and at the same time serve as a prelude to progress on the political side. It has the supreme merit of harnessing voluntary effort towards common action instead of forcing reluctant participants to accept an imposed unity. This, I suggest, is the crux of the matter.

Britain has already attempted to hand over power to states which will be as large as seems practicable when account is taken of group differences. Some of the countries which have been given independence by Britain and France contain heterogeneous groups whose interests are not always easy to harmonise. This has greatly complicated the making of constitutions, and still more their working in practice.

Among politically immature peoples, who lack a spirit of toleration, a complicated constitution designed to avoid inter-regional conflict or conflict among groups scattered through all regions, or both, makes great demands on political skill and forbearance. The personalities and insights of political leaders become all-important. Some of the necessary qualities may be seen in the career of the Prime Minister of an advanced country, the late Mr. Mackenzie King. But the difficulties are greater when illiteracy and sometimes primitive traits are widespread among the peoples : an additional quality to those possessed by Mr. Mackenzie King, that of political oratory with emotional appeal, is then required. Unfortunately, skill in political oratory and emotional appeal are not necessarily accompanied by personal integrity, administrative ability, and statesmanship. The long political life of President Sukarno and the meteoric career of M. Lumumba are, in very different ways, examples of the political consequences which sometimes follow from an inharmonious blend of qualities which creates leadership without statesmanship.

II

Forms of Intra-Regional Association

The problems of unification, integration, and association are so varied and intricate that each case embodies much that is unique. This raises great difficulties for the formulation and development of political constitutions. A large literature exists on the subject but space limits the present discussion to a few of the broader issues.

Among peoples with only a short experience and little tradition of modern government, and with few politicians and civil servants familiar with the practical problems of administration and legislation, there is an understandable tendency towards centralised control in the new governments, often to the neglect of differing regional conditions, especially differences in the social heritage and the feelings of the regional groups which modern developments have brought into the same state.

But federations and confederations are clearly preferable in a number of areas to unitary states, and unifications based on representative government can only be attained, in many cases, by one or other of these forms of organisation. Nigeria is an instructive example. Space will not permit capitulation of the main steps taken to achieve the present form of unification of diverse groups and regions under a federal constitution. Immense labour and much ingenuity were necessary to reach consent on the form of the state of Nigeria. The danger of dictatorship, which would inevitably override minorities by coercion, was always present in the minds of the architects of the new state. As Mr. Ezera has pointed out :

" . . . there are certain peculiar, hard and stubborn features in Nigeria's federal system which make the emergence of dictatorship less likely. These features can be seen in the nature of federal government by itself, the balanced state of the parties, the deep-seated sectional and tribal parochialism and, not the least, in the entrenched fundamental human rights in the Constitution."[1]

Mere constitutions in themselves cannot ensure true representative government. In the early stages they are as vulnerable as all untried institutions are. Once they are established and working without undue conflict, they gather the strength of tradition and can no longer be spoken of contemptuously as " mere paper constitutions ". If Nigeria can pass successfully through the early stages of her existence as an independent state, she will be a healthy check on the restless empire-building ambitions of the leaders of some of the other African states. A federation by consent of some thirty millions of people, firmly attached to government by representative institutions, would fill a most significant role in the balance of power on the African continent.

Federation in itself provides no simple, ready-made formula for dealing with all the problems of the new states. The precise forms which are best adapted to each new set of circumstances have often to be determined by experiment, and the possibilities of special adaptations to conditions not previously encountered are by no means exhausted : there is still room for inventiveness and ingenuity. " Federation " and " confederation " are not to be treated as " blue prints " but as embodying general principles which must be applied differently according to the circumstances of each case.

Yet some of the popular objections to federations in the new states are highly questionable. It is sometimes said that a country where poverty is rife, and where skilled administrators and technicians are scarce, is unsuited to a federal form of government in which a larger number of experienced civil servants and ministers are needed than in a unitary state. But this should not, I think, weigh heavily in the circumstances of the emerging and reawakening states. The Colombo plan, the United Nations Technical Assistance, and other schemes can be used to assist the training of civil servants. As to the politicians, it is doubtful how far economic criteria can be used to predict the probable quality of political representatives. In some cases lucrative economic opportunities tend to divert the abler and more intelligent part of the population away from politics. The United States, in spite of its wealth, is notorious for the poor quality, and in some areas the doubtful integrity, of the representatives and some of the officials in state and local government ; [2] yet this would

---

[1] *Kalu Ezera, Constitutional Developments in Nigeria* Cambridge, 1960, p. 260. Though these circumstances have not prevented serious strains and stresses since independence, there is still hope for Nigeria.

[2] I once asked an American business man whose home was in an Atlantic coast state, what sort of representatives his state legislature attracted. " Why,"

not be a good reason for abandoning its federal form of government. Nothing is more important to the emerging and reawakening countries than the development of political, including parliamentary, ability and experience. Large unitary states give a minimum of opportunities for such experience. The rapid growth of population in the countries in question will bring larger and larger numbers of people under each of the existing governments, even if unifications do not exceed disintegrations, and this will continue to reduce the proportions of people in each country who have opportunities to gain political experience of any kind. The resulting dangers ought not to be increased by undue centralisation in states inhabited by peoples of diverse origins and customs.

"Confederation" is a still more wide-ranging term than federation, but, like federation, it stands for an important conception which some of the emerging countries would do well to make use of. Here the central organ expressing the common will of the groups of peoples is without the direct coercive powers of a federal government, and must act generally by consent, at least in domestic matters. It is tempting to describe it as acting only under the rule of unanimity. But in practice a single dissenter may be placed in an untenable position at times if the rest of the members act in their own spheres to put a disputed measure into force. However, in a formal sense confederation requires unanimity and has no limited sphere in which it can act by majority on matters affecting the member states, and for this reason, and perhaps most of all because the confederation of the North American states and that of the Swiss cantons ended in federation, it tends to be regarded with suspicion as a weak device perpetuating divisions rather than advancing unification, and incapable of supplying sufficient strength to enable the group concerned to hold its own in international affairs.

But these criticisms are unsound in detail. The confederations of the American colonists and of the Swiss cantons, though they gave way in time to closer forms of political association, were as close a move towards unification as could be obtained without disrupting the association at the time when they were made. They served a most useful purpose while they lasted. Even if they are regarded merely as stepping stones to federation, the first step in a series of stepping stones is indispensable and the rest of the steps could not be laid without it. But in any case contemporary problems should be met by whatever measure seems to fit each case best, and even if

---

he replied, "many of them are the sort who might be able to get temporary jobs in a circus in summer if they had to make their own living. The rest of the year they would be on relief." It is to the immeasurable credit of the people of the United States that, notwithstanding a clumsy constitution and much corruption and inefficiency in local government in many areas, the specious attractions of authoritarian rule have been successfully resisted.

precedents concerning confederation had been more discouraging or less encouraging than they are, it would still be worthwhile to begin with some form of confederation in a number of areas where diversification is so great, and agreement on unifying measures so difficult to obtain, that an attempt to establish anything closer than confederation would exacerbate frictions and divergencies, and compel a " show-down " in which either coercion would have to be used by the physically stronger over the weaker, or the split would be accentuated and the last state would be worse than the first. Almost certainly, confederation in some form or other, probably differing in detail from those of the past, will find a place among some of the emerging and reawakening countries, although the term itself may be replaced by others. Again, precedents should not be overstressed : it may be that some forms of confederation will be not so much a stepping stone as a firm platform which will serve long as a foundation for concerted action in external policy while retaining as large a scope as is practicable under modern technical conditions for independent internal policies—larger than in practice is likely to be maintained under federation.[1]

Some form of confederation seems clearly to be the most appropriate aim for those groups of states whose peoples are related by a sense of kinship falling short of nationalism, particularly the Arab and African peoples. To attempt anything more at present is to invite frictions and clashes that accentuate present divisions : in the quest for unity a false move is worse than no move at all. Confederation, then, may be taken as the aim in the near future, but even confederation will be difficult and may be long delayed by attempts at intra-Arab and intra-African imperialism sponsored by a few authoritarian rulers.[2] The quest for confederation and, in some cases, federation will, to a considerable extent, go hand in hand with the quest for stable representative government throughout the areas : each setback for the latter is apt, on the whole, to be a setback for the former. The relationship is not wholly straightforward. In the quest for better understanding with India, General Ayub gave the impression of being more restrained and accommodating than the political leaders of the former parties were, though this may have been due partly to a desire on the part of the latter to exploit popular prejudices to their advantage in their struggle with the Generals, in which case it would have been toned down if they had reached positions of responsibility. But, looking back, we perceive

---

[1] The chief difficulties in the way of this are in economic matters, where concerted currency and credit, as well as balance-of-payment, policies are necessary.

[2] In this matter African states have the advantage over Arab states that no one state among them is large and powerful enough in a comparative sense to dominate the others. Among the states the majority of whose peoples are Arab, Egypt is comparatively strong enough to attempt intra-regional imperialism single-handed.

that if Indian independence could have been put off until after Mr. Jinnah's death, there would have been, almost certainly, no division of the sub-continent.

Here again the pursuit of the substance should take precedence over the pursuit of the form. The most appropriate first step towards a confederation would be the adoption of a common foreign policy. This in turn would be preceded and heralded by frequent consultations on foreign policy, preferably through a regional body of the countries concerned.

In this connection the history of the Arab League serves both for instruction and as a warning. In many of the Middle Eastern countries authoritarian régimes have been the rule rather than the exception. Moreover, most of the countries are divided sharply by contending factions within : these may be suppressed for a time but their underground existence is a constant threat to stability. In such circumstances the time is not yet ripe for voluntary unification, and attempts at the creation of larger units too often tend to take the form of intra-Arab imperialism aided by aggressive propaganda and incitements against rulers who stand in the way. It is as yet impossible to foresee whether or not the Maghreb will be an exception. It may be hoped that, in spite of frequent setbacks, efforts will be directed towards the co-operation of independent Arab and Arab-Kurdish states through an Arab League or association, through Arab cultural organisations, and through freer movement within the Arab world. Intrigues against neighbouring Arab countries, attempts to undermine their governments by incitements to revolt, and even by underground attempts at assassination as practised by U.A.R. agents in Jordan, and unsuccessfully by Egyptians in Tunisia, hindered instead of advancing a genuine *rapprochement* among the Arab peoples.

At the formation of the Arab League the member countries were insistent that the constitution should unequivocally affirm the obligation of each member to respect the independence of other members. Yet the organisation has not flourished. The main reason has been the failure of some of its stronger members to keep their obligations, and the unavowed but unmistakable tendencies of certain members towards imperialist aggression at the expense of other members. As we have seen, Egypt has been foremost in these breaches of the charter : her much larger population, her greater armed strength, and her hold on the finances of the League, have placed her in a dominating position in the organisation. When her will was frustrated she threatened to boycott, and sometimes boycotted the League.

These questions have been important also in Latin America over an even longer period. The end of Spanish rule created even greater problems of the demarcation of new states and their subsequent association than the end or impending end of British and French rule has created in Africa and south-eastern Asia. Fragmentation without general over-all control followed. It is doubtful whether this was really as disastrous as it appeared to be to Bolivar, who, in the end, seems to have regretted the revolution he did so much to sponsor, on the ground that it ended in less rather than more unity than existed under Spain. But here, as in other areas of the world, it may well be asked whether the lack of political and economic capacity needed to sustain well-ordered small states is not evidence of a still greater incapacity at the time to create and sustain large states.[1] Today the problems of association and co-operation between long-established states subject to external pressures seem more important than problems of unification. They have not yet been satisfactorily solved.

The Organisation of American States includes, not only the Latin American states, which have important elements of common heritage, including language and culture, but also the United States, which has a radically different heritage and culture, language and outlook, and a much greater comparative preponderance of power than Egypt has in the Middle East. Moreover, Latin Americans have encountered the imperialism of the United States on a much larger scale than Arabs have encountered Egyptian imperialism. Meetings of the O.A.S., like meetings of the Arab League, have therefore been dominated by one power, whose delegates endeavour to control the floor and carry on far from unobstrusive " lobbying " to press their views, sometimes with free use of blandishments and veiled threats, on issues which they regard as vital to their interests. The work of the O.A.S. has often been dominated by the U.S. fears of communism, which find a ready response among the extreme conservative forces that govern some of the Latin American states and form a dangerous opposition in others. The Organisation has been pressed continuously by the United States to boycott Cuba against the overwhelming sentiment of the student and other politically conscious classes among the rising generation, by whom it has been regarded as an instrument of imperialistic designs. However excessive this hostility may sometimes seem to be, it is not without cause, and it must be reckoned with as the significant single fact in the politics of the American continent.

After the Cuban crisis near the end of 1962 the United States

---

[1] *A priori*, the answer is not necessarily in the affirmative. If a small state is grossly deficient in the natural resources in demand under the technical conditions of the time, if it is badly situated in relation to transport routes, and if there is little scope for complementary trade with neighbouring countries, economic advance will be difficult and the sort of political unrest that goes with poverty will be fostered. But these conditions do not apply to all areas where political instability has been the rule rather than the exception.

appeared to be riding high. Señor Castro had shown political mis-judgement in departing from neutrality, even though in the abstract he was justified in doing so. For the introduction of additional nuclear weapons into Latin America entangled the Latin American states in the " cold war ", and this, more than anything else, is what *le tiers monde* wishes to avoid, regardless of which side introduces it.

A major change is needed in the regional organisation of Latin America. The Organisation cannot flourish while the United States dominates it, and it will be long before Latin American states become powerful enough to meet the United States on equal terms. The remedy would be, either that the United States should leave the Organisation and negotiate with it from outside on matters of common concern, or that the Latin American states should form an additional organisation of their own. As the United States is unlikely to agree to the first alternative, the second is the only practicable one in the near future. It would doubtless be opposed by certain states dominated by extreme right-wing governments which, for internal reasons, prefer to maintain the closest connection with the United States. But at least a beginning might be made by extending and speeding up the process of consultation and exchange of information among " like-minded " Latin American states. The methods by which these processes are carried out in the Common-wealth would be worthy study by those governments which appreciate the importance of developing genuine Latin American cohesion, free from the over-zealous solicitations and pressures of the imperial giant in the north.

Whatever the methods adopted, all moves towards closer relations and a more or less common front to the outside world among the Latin American states are to be welcomed. They would rest upon a large degree of common interests and heritage. Since important regional differences exist within Latin America, the move towards a common foreign policy and wide cultural interchange will probably succeed first among small groups. But each local success will be an impetus to further advances in other areas. The Latin American states embrace such wide differences in local and regional conditions that even confederation may appear only as a distant ideal. But the sense of kinship is real and important and common interests will inevitably draw the countries together in foreign policy. They already desire the extension of their relations with Europe. Britain's response has been inadequate, both in the economic and in the political sense. Unduly exclusive concentration on Anglo-United States relations has hindered the development of Anglo-American relations.[1]

---

[1] It is regrettable that the tendency to use the term " America " as a synonym or " United States " seems to be spreading. The B.B.C. is a persistent offender. This naturally offends Latin Americans. It creates inevitable confusion to

III

Problems of Unity in Diversity

The new African statesmen are justified in discouraging tribal particularism, and in seeking agreement to fusions between, or closer working relations among, contiguous territories in some parts of the continent ; but if, under cover of doing so, they suppress legitimate [1] opposition and set aside guarantees of minority rights, if they seek to extend their personal rule without the free consent and at the expense of regional and neighbouring political leaders, and to establish permanent " single party " states, then they will retard or reverse the all-important processes of political education and training in the responsible uses of individual freedom which, in some areas, had already begun in the later years of colonial rule.

The new African world is so young in a political sense that we cannot yet discern the political groupings of the future.[2] The influence of " African nationalism " or " pan-Africanism " has been shown particularly in the African political parties, some of which have not confined themselves to single states. This has led to a cleavage between the aims of parties formed to serve domestic aims within single states, and parties formed to serve aims which extend abroad as well as at home.[3]

The outlook of the new states in Africa changes in the light of their early experience. Any statement concerning the lines of future grouping would soon need amendment. It is not easy to choose among the criteria for grouping—political doctrines, geographical propinquity, racial affinity, economic interdependence, religious affiliations, colonial heritage. For example, race and colonial heritage seem both to have influenced the *rapprochement* in 1962 between Côte d'Ivoire, Guinea, and Mali after political doctrines had tended

---

transfer the name of a continent to one state within the continent. Perhaps there is a psychological explanation of this tendency ; it is not, however, flattering to Latin Americans !

[1] Account must of course be taken of the violent and unscrupulous tactics of some groups in opposition in some of the African and Middle Eastern countries, and full account must be taken of them before judging acts of suppression, especially in Ghana and in countries where President Nasir connives with the opposition groups.

[2] Philippe Descraene conveniently summarises " Les Regroupements Regionaux " up to 1959 in his *Le Panafricanisme*, Paris, 1959, Ch. VI.

[3] See Thomas Hodgkin, *African Political Parties*, London, 1961, pp. 151–3 and Fernand Van Langenhove, *Consciences Tribales et Nationales en Afrique Noire*, La haye, 1960, pp. 274–83.

to hinder relations between Côte d'Ivoire and the other two states. This prompts an observer to remark : " *L'unité Africaine suppose d'abord celle des peuples noirs d'expression française.*" [1]

The distinction between the indigenous peoples south and those north of the Sahara is important in any assessment of future lines of unification in Africa. It is more than a racial distinction : the social and political heritage of the two peoples differs considerably. But the racial distinction is associated with such obvious differences in outward physical appearance that it attracts the notice of the masses. In the Congo the sight of the U.N. Tunisian force brought home to many central Africans the close racial affinity between North Africans and Europeans, and the wide difference between the Africa they knew and the Africa that had lain previously beyond their ken. The peoples of North Africa and, for that matter, the peoples of the Sudan are geographically in Africa, but in a political sense they have attachments divided between Africa and a " Middle East " which includes south-western Asia. Some of their political leaders have ambitions to extend their influence in both areas but there have already been signs, and they are likely to become more pronounced in the future, that the political leaders to the south of the Sahara will not welcome any attempts to encroach on their own sphere of influence.

The colonial heritage will probably leave a permanent influence in part of the continent, first, and most obviously, because it started the process of modernisation in Africa, and, second, because it introduced two different forms of culture and two different modern languages. No-one today can hope to study African conditions, either on the spot or through the literature of the subject, without a good knowledge of both French and English. As we have seen, the different methods of government, administration, and education in the two systems have introduced complications in the way of unification between former French and former British colonies. But he who regretted that one uniform culture only had not impinged on the indigenous culture or cultures in Africa would be taking a very narrow view of human development. In the end, African culture or cultures will predominate, but they will be all the richer for having absorbed elements of more than one western European culture. Dull uniformity and regimentation are more to be feared than variety and fragmentation. To repeat : government was made for man, not man for government.

If these two elements in African heritage derived from Europe are to be a source of cultural enrichment and not of division, positive steps are needed to build bridges between them. Encouraging steps have already been taken in some of the countries concerned. It

[1] *Europe Outre-Mer, 1962*

seems obvious that in the English-speaking areas French, and in the French-speaking areas English, should be the second language in school studies, and moves have already been made in these directions. In higher African studies a basis for co-operation and exchange was laid at the International Conference of Africanists at Accra in December, 1962, and the decision to hold the next conference at Dakar removed the danger of separate and isolated development of research carried on in the French and English languages. British and French scholars have an opportunity, in unobtrusive ways, to assist in the *rapprochement*.

In the earlier stages of decolonisation it seemed that doctrinal differences might bring clear-cut rifts among the newly independent countries. The communist scare was raised in some circles, particularly outside Africa. Agents of the United States were at work, particularly in the Congo, scheming against political leaders whom they suspected of " going communist ". M. Lumumba was a foremost object of their attention for a time, and after his death M. Gizenga was the object of similarly unflattering attentions. Naïve agents of the U.S. Central Intelligence Agency and equally naïve officials at the " Africa desk " of the State Department in Washington, directed the policy of the United States towards unreal issues, and its operations into illegitimate channels, confusing still further an already confused situation. Similarly the Soviet Union for a time placed an unreal doctrinal interpretation on Congo politics and tried to interfere, with equally unhappy results. M. Lumumba was neither a hero nor a villain : he was a supporter neither of communism nor of capitalism. Rather he was, in his later stages, a study in abnormal psychology. His career, if it demonstrates anything, demonstrates what can happen to a man elevated into positions beyond his psycho-physical capacity to fill. Rarely has a name been enshrined in institutions and handed on to posterity with less justification. The legends of the twentieth century sometimes far surpass those of ancient times in their travesty of the persons and events they are supposed to enshrine. The legend of Lumumba is a witness to the desperate craving to interpret events in terms of doctrinal symbols.

Doctrinal elements will continue to play a part in the relationships of the African states, but lines of doctrinal cleavage are likely to be blurred and indistinct. Economic needs, economic resources, and the varying opportunities to obtain external help, all combine to shape the economic order according to practical necessities rather than doctrinal blueprints, and in such contingencies distinctions of " right " and " left " cannot find clear-cut practical counterparts in administration, even when attempts are made to dress up actual practices in doctrinal garb.

All acceptable political doctrines will have to be reconciled with the idea of African independence of powers outside the continent. The disputes which continue will concern the shape and extent of states within Africa, but there will be no compromise over the independence of these states in their relations with the outside world. This precludes Russian or Chinese communism or any other form of communism that recognises the authoritarian political position of any other state, or its right to determine the standards of doctrinal orthodoxy.

African states may use some of the economic methods used by communist states, but they will do so incompletely and only as part of a structure that, taken as a whole, is incompatible with Russian and Chinese communism. Marxian ideas will affect the structures of African states unevenly : this may hinder economic integration in a few cases but should not preclude close political co-operation with reference to the world outside Africa. I suggest that attempts to represent Africa as predominantly the scene of a doctrinal struggle over allegiance to communism and allegiance to the " free world ", which will divide the African states, is a fiction. Communists will continue their efforts to win over the younger Africans, but they have already recognised how far Africans are from the ideals they would map out for them, and they have nothing but disillusion awaiting them if they believe that Africans who have emerged from one form of dependency will ever be seduced into submitting themselves to another.

Finally, we may reasonably conjecture that small groupings, particularly of neighbouring states of similar race and heritage are likely to make the greatest progress in the near future. Various criteria may determine the nature of groupings in the longer run. Platform oratory about unity is easy : but how many of the orators, and those who have applauded them, have studied the processes by which, for example, Benelux came into being, or have yet realised that wider unions, highly desirable though they are in several parts of Africa and the Middle East, can only be achieved through immense labour, much trial and error, and a readiness for inevitable self-effacement in some quarters. Disintegration may have run its course in Africa but the road towards fusion is a long and arduous one.

In south-eastern Asia there remain a number of difficult problems of fusion and separation and of inter-regional disharmonies in the same state. Independence in Ceylon has been followed by a political intolerance towards minorities which is reminiscent of practices in central and eastern Europe in the nineteenth and early twentieth centuries. Unfortunately, this kind of persistent intolerance to minorities, particularly minorities composed of comparatively recent immigrants, is all too characteristic of some of the

emerging and reawakening countries. It is true that similar intolerance with respect to minorities speaking a different language has
been shown in Europe and the United States, but the dismal record
of that discrimination should be an example of what to avoid rather
than to emulate in new independent states. One might hope that
the great example of Switzerland would take precedence over the
deplorable examples of the Tyrol and parts of central and eastern
Europe. After all, the political leaders of Ceylon have been educated
in western learning and cannot plead ignorance of the experience of
mankind. Notwithstanding their tone of virtuousity towards the
West in respect to colonialism, they have failed themselves to practice
toleration within their own boundaries.

Other examples can only be touched on briefly here. The blunders
and cross purposes of both Dutch and inter-Allied policies and operations in south-eastern Asia during and immediately after the War led
to the worst of all settlements short of war—a settlement to which
some of the Indonesian leaders never intended to adhere. The
wiser among them failed to make headway against Dr. Sukarno, the
clever crowd orator. From the start, the problem of unification was
the most important of all problems facing the new state-builders.
Unfortunately, Dr. Sukarno's idea of a solution was that of almost
complete centralisation, under cover of which the Sukarno Government exploited Sumatra's substantial export earnings mainly for the
benefit of Java. In a sense Sumatra, and what used to be called the
" Outer Islands ", merely passed from one form of colonialism to
another. The chronic unrest and sporadic risings, alleged by the
extreme nationalists and the communists to be due to " imperialistic
conspiracies ", to a considerable extent were the outcome of genuine
economic grievances, and, most of all, of the grievances which arises
when the size of the political unit is too great for equitable and efficient administration by a centralised government with extremely
limited resources. The muddle and confusion in Indonesia under
the Sukarno régime would probably have resulted in total collapse
in an area less richly endowed with natural resources than Java,
with its volcanic soils, and part of Sumatra, are.

The tension and conflict between Java and Sumatra have been, of
course, a resumption of a long history of differences in economic
interests, and of struggles for supremacy, interrupted only by the
period of Dutch rule. The whole history of the area is one of over-
ambitious attempts at conquest or integration, followed by disintegration. No doubt the decline and fall of Majapahit were
hastened by the inroads of Moslem traders and the establishment of
Moslem sultanates around their colonies ; but grave internal weaknesses would seem to have been present in all the larger mediaeval
kingdoms in south-eastern Asia. The idea of a genuinely unified

state comprising islands spread over a distance as great as that from the Atlantic coast of Portugal to the Black Sea was chimerical in mediaeval times, and today could only have been accomplished harmoniously by consent after trial and error with various forms of decentralised government. Attempts to accomplish it by coercion lead to the exploitation of the politically weaker outlying areas for the advantage of the area in which the central government is established. Federation between some areas and confederation between others would have more appropriate political relationships than those which now co-exist uneasily.

Summarising, it may be said that all avenues of approach to problems of unification among peoples of diverse heritage and outlook are sooner or later confronted with the question, whether government is to be imposed by political leaders who, though they may have been chosen by popular acclaim at the outset, shrink later from submitting their continuance in office to the free choice of an electorate and try to perpetuate themselves in power by intimidating the opposition, or whether government by consent will be accepted by the political leaders as well as their followers, in spite of its difficulties and complications. As we have seen, federation can only become a reality and confederation can only be placed on a workable basis, if they rest on representative government by consent. There may be mere nominal federations, like that expressed in the high-sounding title, The Union of Soviet Socialist Republics, but these do not solve the problems of unity in diversity ; they are the despotic unitary state in disguise, using local rulers whose " election " is manipulated from the centre. Whether despotism can ultimately produce unity by long-continued intimidation, until new generations arise without direct experience of the sources of older divisions, is an arguable question, the answer to which may depend partly on the nature of changes in technological conditions, and their effects on communication and movement. The outcome cannot be known in advance and, even if it were known that the end would be achieved, the means would not, according to the premises adhered to in this study, be justifiable. The losses in the intervening generations through overriding diversities, some of which improve the quality of civilisation and break the monotony of standardised ways of living, are once for all losses, and cannot be atoned for or made good by future generations. They are analogous to economic losses from prolonged unemployment : the goods and services that might have been produced in the period are lost for ever. And if we regard as of equal importance the well-being of individuals belonging to different generations we cannot justify the engineered losses of one generation by the hypothetical gains of another.

The well-being of peoples in the different countries of the world, and the power and influence which they exert in international affairs, are related very unevenly to their numbers and the extent of their territories.   A large, sprawling state beset with widespread regional unrest and general political instability is no advance on, but a retrogression from, a group of compact small states animated by a harmony of wills on external matters.   Fusion or closer association is a desirable aim in many areas of the world, and it would be a misunderstanding of the present study to interpret it as lukewarm to the needs of the future.   But the manner in which and the methods by which it is obtained are all-important and determine whether it will ultimately be an enduring blessing or a mere phase in a recurring cycle of integration and disintegration.

PART IV

TOWARDS A NEW STRUCTURE OF INTERNATIONAL RELATIONS

CHAPTER XI

THE BALANCE OF POWER, THE INTERNATIONAL ORGANISATIONS, THE RULES OF THE GAME, AND PUBLIC OPINION

I

Misconceptions Concerning Balance of Power

SO FAR, so good. The first step in any attempt to analyse the under-lying realities in contemporary international relations is to dispel the confusions, the sentimentalism, the self-righteousness, and the fanaticism resulting from excessive stress on doctrinal, or, in the current infelicitous jargon, ideological, differences among peoples, and to reaffirm, and restate in the contemporary context, the central role of balance of power among independent states.

But, while balance of power is essential to harmony between, even to the survival of, independent states, there is no assurance, or even likelihood, that any particular balance, once attained, will continue indefinitely without danger of breakdown and conflict. The primary ingredient out of which a balance of power is composed consists in the pursuit by each state of what it considers to be its own interests. But undiluted and uninhibited pursuit by each state of what its government believes to be its own interests within the balance of power existing at the time will not necessarily ensure international political harmony, any more than a system of *laissez-faire*, in which each individual and each economic unit pursues his or its self-interest, will necessarily ensure international economic harmony. As we have noted, some states have sought from time to time to upset a given balance of power at the expense of other states, and ambitious leaders in large states have dreamed of world hegemony.

These dangers can only be met by the defensive pursuit of a balance of power which will hold the aggressive state or states in check. It was the neglect of a defensive balance of power that brought on the Second World War.

Professor George Kennan, Professor Hans Morgenthau, and a number of other writers of the " realist " school of international thought in the United States, have tried since the last war to dispel illusions on this subject among the people of the United States, and to make the idea of balance of power respectable to public opinion.

It is all to the good that they have recommended their listeners and readers to eschew " moralistic " and " holier than thou " attitudes towards international affairs, to grasp the realities of the politics of " balance of power ", and to have faith in the ordinary processes of confidential diplomatic negotiation which, since the Second World War, have too often been superseded by rancourous public debate directed to the purposes of propaganda rather than to the reduction of differences and the pursuit of a *modus vivendi*. These recommendations represent the beginning of wisdom in international affairs.

But they are not the end. Although they point to old and well-tried approaches and instruments which have lost none of their value, they are not enough in themselves in the mid-twentieth century, if, indeed, they ever were. If the neglect of balance of power produced the Second World War, the uninhibited, or insufficiently inhibited, pursuit of ideas of self-interest within a system of fluctuating balance of power helped to produce the First World War, and to rely on the old and tried aims and methods of diplomacy alone would be to leave the way open for the ultimate repetition, on a vaster scale, and in an infinitely more dangerous setting, or processes similar to those which preceded the catastrophe of 1914–18,

The century from 1815 to 1914 gave ample opportunities to observe the system of balance of power in European practice. The final collapse in 1815 of the attempt of a single state to establish a hegemony over Europe was followed by the restoration of a balance of power ; or, perhaps it would be more accurate to say, the establishment of a new one,[1] and an important attempt to reinforce it by the so-called Concert of Europe, which, in practice, consisted in a series of *ad hoc* collective consultations as well as diplomatic exchanges to avert dangers to the peace by agreed action among the Great Powers. But this raised difficulties and worked spasmodically and imperfectly. In the light of the conceptual scheme of the present study, it may be said that the troubles of the Concert of Europe arose over the failure to recognise the relations between internal and external policies and to agree on the attitude to adopt towards internal political changes. Doctrinal differences created divergent attitudes towards the *status quo* and political and social change. Broadly speaking, the eastern members of the Concert, especially in the early period, resisted liberalising changes and strove to maintain the principle of " legitimacy ", while the western members were

---

[1] But in the eighteenth and nineteenth centuries, the aims of "unconditional surrender" and of eliminating the defeated powers as far as possible from occupying any role in the balance of power after their defeat had not become fashionable and the new balances formed after war were not so radically different from the pre-war balances as they became in the twentieth century.

ready to encourage aspirations to limited forms of representative government where there seemed to be a prospect that these could be satisfied in part, if not wholly, without unduly disturbing the balance among the Great Powers. Such clashes were usually conceived of in doctrinal terms, but they can perhaps be more profitably regarded as clashes between a static and a dynamic approach to the balance of power and to international affairs in general. The strongest argument for maintaining " legitimacy " and the *status quo* was not that it was the best form of domestic government, but that it held out the best prospects of maintaining a stable system of balance of international power. After twenty-two years of almost continuous European wars, external peace might well seem preferable to internal reform. Rapid and uneven internal changes among states tend frequently to disturb the existing balance of power, and to require readjustments which threaten international peace.

But in the longer run the decisive objection to this view is that social and political change at home cannot be held back indefinitely in the alleged interests of stability abroad. It is illusory to interpret the idea of stability itself in a static sense : the underlying dynamic influences in society cannot be ignored or stifled or, as it were, put into cold storage. This is the fundamental objection to the approach to international affairs commonly associated with Metternich. The issue is not primarily one of doctrine or party ; it is one of change and adjustment. The problem of stability is not concerned with the maintenance of the same fixed weights on both sides of the scale, but with the frequent addition of new and subtraction of older weights, and with the maintenance of a balance among the changing components in each scale.

Nevertheless the efforts to maintain a Concert of Europe were not wholly unsuccessful during the first half, and occasionally in the second half, of the nineteenth century. Fluctuating and uneven gains were made in the practice of international consultation, and concerted action was taken to achieve peaceful settlements of disputes without disrupting the balance of power. Unfortunately the attempt to establish regular meetings gave way to *ad hoc* consultations to deal with conditions that had already reached a state of emergency. Nor was there any assurance that organised multilateral consultations would be held whenever an emergency arose, and after the middle of the century the Great Powers failed to hold them on some critical occasions, when the existing balance of power was threatened.

In 1870–1 the older balance of power was radically changed, and for this the way had been prepared by the inaction of the powers over the seizure of Schleswig-Holstein and over the Prussian-Austrian war. As Mr. Hinsley puts it :

The Franco-Prussian War of 1870–71 . . . was the last blow
to the old balance of European power. Based for centuries on
a weak German centre and strong French, Austrian, and
Russian wings, European politics were to rest in future on the
dominance of the new Germany.[1]

Although some notable *ad hoc* meetings and conferences and
occasional skilful diplomacy kept the Great Powers at peace for
nearly half a century under the new balance of power, the underlying conditions were changing ominously, and war among the Great
Powers, when it came, was bound to be far more destructive than the
Napoleonic Wars had been. The *milieu* in which diplomacy was
carried on changed, and some of the changes increased the difficulties
of diplomats. The new methods of warfare practised after the
Crimean War made effective use of mechanical transport : not only
could troops be moved faster during campaigns, but also mobilisation at the outset was much more rapid. Consequently surprise
attacks, sometimes without previous declaration of war, became
practicable as well as advantageous against inadequately prepared
opponents. General staffs in the leading armies prepared plans for
war during times of peace. The rising political power of the heads of
general staffs and the privileged positions of the ministers of the army
and the navy in Germany and Japan, created new obstacles for the
customary channels of diplomacy.[2]

The breakdown of international diplomacy in 1914 has led since
to intensive studies of the activities of the ministers and diplomats
concerned in the negotiations that preceded the war. As late as
April-May 1962, forty-eight years after the event, a controversial
discussion took place in *The Times* on the role of Sir Edward Grey's
diplomacy. And, in the minute examination of the diplomacy of
the European statesmen of the same period by Signor Albertini,[3]
searching criticisms were made of the conduct and capacities of
almost all the diplomats and statesmen who took part in the negotiation. His study leaves in the mind of the reader an impression of
ineptitude among all the chief actors concerned.

From such an estimate it is only a step to the viewpoint that sees
the main cause of disaster in a decline in the quality of statesmanship
and diplomacy. If only, the critics say or imply, there had been a
Palmerston, or a Salisbury, or perhaps even a Bismarck, some means

---

[1] F. H. Hinsley, op. cit.
[2] It appears that the Kaiser, who was long made the chief scapegoat, in the
search for the source of the war, was satisfied with the Serbian reply to the Austrian
ultimatum, but the general staff had already ordered mobilisation and could not
be countermanded.
[3] Luigi Albertini, *Le Origini della guerra del 1914*, 3 Vols., Milan, 1942–3

would have been found to avert a war that brought disaster to all Europe, weakening it in relation to other continents.

It cannot be denied that breakdowns in a defensive balance of power have sometimes been mostly due to the fault of individual statesmen who, at critical times, departed from the methods, and fell short of the standards, of predecessors who had successfully maintained the balance of power. This may be said of western statesmen of the nineteen-thirties who, in practice, abandoned the aim of maintaining the balance of power in Europe and the Far East. But it can hardly be said of the statesmen in office on the eve of the First World War, many of whom were even more alive to the dangers of a disruption of the balance of power than their predecessors had been in 1866 and 1870,[1] but who failed to control the new forces in international affairs. Thus we must seek explanations in a changed international environment at least as much as in different qualities of statesmanship.

But if the causes of the Second World War differ sharply from those of the First, there is nevertheless a relationship between the two sets of causes. In attempting to explain the simultaneous departure of several countries, in the interwar period, from the time-honoured aim of seeking first the preservation of a balance of power, any inquiry has to start from the fact that the aim itself was widely discredited after the First World War. As we have seen, it was roundly denounced by President Wilson and held up as the antithesis of the principles on which the League of Nations was to be founded after the First World War. It was similarly attacked by President Franklin Roosevelt and held up as the antithesis of the principles on which the United Nations was to be founded after the Second World War. And President Wilson, in particular, was speaking not only for himself but was reflecting a widespread public reaction which, after the war, permeated nearly all circles concerned with the problem of preventing further wars. The pursuit of a balance of power, it was held, caused the formation of hostile armed alliances which were bound sooner or later to clash. The only remedy was to set up an international organisation to deal with all international differences in the light of principles to be laid down in a charter.

These identical responses of President Wilson to the First World War—which was the outcome of an undiluted, *laissez-faire* pursuit of a balance of power, and of President Roosevelt to the Second, which

---

[1] The sudden death of Lord Clarendon, who was bent on preventing the war of 1870, may well have turned the scale, for though his successor attempted to follow a similar policy he had immensely less prestige in European diplomatic circles. " Bismarck . . . told Lord Clarendon's daughter in 1871 that he was never in his life more glad to hear of anything than of her father's death, because if he had lived he would have prevented the war." Camb. Hist. of For. Pol. III, 27.

was the result of wholesale neglect of balance of power, show how difficult it is to obtain an appreciation of the true role of balance of power, either from politicians or from the public. As I have already shown, the pursuit of an international balance of power is neither a menace nor a panacea, neither a cause of war nor an assurance of peace. But it is an indispensable element in international institutions designed to preserve peace and to advance international co-operation.

Thus the cardinal error, shared by Presidents Wilson and Roosevelt, lay in their assumption that the creation of an organised society of nations with appropriate deliberative and executive bodies would be a substitute for, and a displacement of, the pursuit of balance of power ; that the one was righteous, and the other sinister, that the one would bring peace, and the other war. Unfortunately, this superficially simple, clear-cut view appealed to that widespread evangelical spirit, which conceives of human issues in straightforward categories of right and wrong, and of human beings as divided into the children of light and the children of darkness.

Such simple approaches to international affairs can only lead to disillusionment. If the society of nations—or states, as it would be more accurate to describe it—was to assume the responsibility for keeping the peace, from what sources would it derive the means of preventing conflict among states which failed to solve their disputes by diplomatic exchanges or through the international organs which provide instruments for conciliation and arbitration ? And, since the international political body or bodies were controlled by representatives of states, was it to be supposed that within those bodies states would act in complete independence of one another, and never concert their actions in groups which conceived themselves to possess common interests or ties ? These questions were not faced by those who thought of the international organisations as a substitute for a system of balance of power. Expectations were raised that could not be fulfilled, and disillusionment inevitably set in. The last state was worse than the first.

Actually, the international organisations, far from being a substitute for the pursuit of a balance of power, have been and are themselves the scene of such a pursuit, conducted on an even wider scale than that which found expression only through bilateral diplomatic channels and infrequent international conferences limited to Great Powers. It was not the countries which pursued, but the countries which rejected, the aim of balance of power, that defied the League of Nations and took themselves out of it with the deliberate aim of upsetting the balance.

But the naïve elements in the " idealistic " approach to international affairs, which ignore the realities of human nature and

nternational relationships, must not be allowed to obscure the shortcomings of systems of balance of power, pursued through *ad hoc*
diplomatic means. The criticisms directed against the workings and
the fruits of this system before the First World War were not all misplaced, and the restoration of a similar system after the War would
have given no guarantee, and in the long run held out little prospect,
of prolonged international peace. The " realist " school of thought
in the United States, correctly reacting against the crudely " moralistic " and sentimental attitudes of the United States public on international affairs, has tended to overestimate the efficacy of a simple
pursuit of balance of power, and to underestimate the role and
importance of international organisations. We must penetrate
beyond both " realism " and " idealism ", admitting that balance of
power is inseparable from peace, that the pursuit of balance of power
will continue as long as the world is divided into separate states, and
that, even if the latter, in a distant future, found it possible to
coalesce into a single world state, it could only be through the establishment and maintenance of a balance of power among regions,
which itself would have to be adjusted from time to time in the light
of changes affecting the comparative positions of the regions.
Balance of power remains inseparable from world peace, and its
antithesis is a state of anarchy and war. This is realism, if realism is
defined as a recognition of realities. But it is only an incomplete
recognition of realities if we stop there and ignore the instability of
any particular balance of power in an ever changing world ; the
temptation of the stronger powers to mix diplomacy with war, as
Bismarck did, in order to subvert one balance for another more to
their advantage ; and the likelihood that particular balances, originally established at the expense of comparatively weaker powers,
will be forcibly overturned as the latter grow comparatively stronger.

Again, as in economics, so in politics ; both conceptions of self-
interest and decisions to act are based on expectations of the future
which, in a changing world, are subject to error and miscalculation.
The changed balance of power in Europe after 1870, to which
Mr. Hinsley refers, was partly the result of a lack of foresight. The
fear of France, based partly on remembrance of Napoleon I and
partly on judgements of Napoleon III, tended to inhibit Britain and
Russia from restraining Prussia at critical turning points. Napoleon
III, who found European support in the fifties against Russia, failed
in the sixties to appreciate that changing conditions had harmonised
French and Russian interests on a number of leading international
issues. Moreover, he allowed doctrinal considerations with respect
to Polish aspirations to hinder co-operation with Russia to meet the
dangers of a Germany united under Prussia.

It is easier to detect such errors of judgement in retrospect than it

was to foresee their consequences at the time when they were made
The unification of Germany was not widely regarded as a danger in
the eighteen-fifties and the earlier part of the sixties. There had ever
been hopes in the West and fears in the East that a unified Germany
would be a liberalising force in Europe.[1] For a time Napoleon III'
ambitions on the Rhine had aroused more apprehension than
Bismarck's ambitions in Europe.

In the present study it is impossible to analyse in detail the shifts
and turns, the hopes and fears, the expectations and disappoint-
ments, the ambitions and frustrations, the sins of omission as wel.
as those of commission, that characterised the fluctuations in the
European balance of power from 1870 to 1914. If we accept the
view that a substantial change in the composition of the balance of
power came from the rise and unification of Germany under Prussia,
and that this change tended to increase the instability of the balance,
it does not follow that a world war was an inevitable result. The
more we study the international events of the period since the middle
of the nineteenth century and the outbreak of the First World War,
the more impressed we are likely to be both with the dangers avoided
on some critical occasions and the opportunities lost on others. In
times of crisis the role of the individual was sometimes decisive, but
in the circumstances that led to the crises, the comparative growths
of populations, resources, and technology, and the awakening and
intensification of political consciousness among minorities and
among the hitherto less advanced peoples of Europe and the Mediterranean and Middle East, all played a part in shaping the changing
conditions in which diplomacy had to be carried on. It follows that,
if the instruments of international diplomacy are not developed and
adjusted to keep pace with the changes in the conditions of international life, the chances of war will increase.

II

Rules of the Game and the International Organisations

Among the instruments of international diplomacy through which,
in the future, a balance of power may be maintained and adopted to
a changing world, the international organisations will almost certainly play a role of increasing importance, differing, indeed, from

[1] The assumption has often been made uncritically that liberal or socialist
policies at home are a reliable safeguard against aggressive policies abroad.
Actually, the Frankfurt liberals in the mid-nineteenth century, and the German
Social Democrats during the First World War, were markedly imperialistic in
their outlooks on external policy.

that desired by the idealists, and that expected by many who claim to be realists, but constituting an irreplaceable part of the whole body of organised measures designed to save the world from suicidal armed strife. Bilateral diplomatic exchanges will continue to play an indispensable role, particularly when they are conducted without publicity, but they are obviously insufficient in themselves to meet modern needs. The " realist " writers in the United States who tend to be sceptical of the value of the United Nations are more interested and experienced in Great Power politics than in the politics of Asia, Latin America, and Africa, which some of them tend to regard mainly as mere complicating factors in the relations of the Great Powers. Their historical studies of international diplomacy are largely concentrated on the affairs of the Great Powers. The Concert of Europe, when it was in fitful operation, was a concert of the Great Powers. The great congresses and conferences of the seventeenth, eighteenth, and nineteenth centuries, were confined to the Great Powers of the times, and weaker powers could make their voices heard only on sufferance. That era of Great Power domination is passing, and, with self-government replacing dependency among Asian and African powers, and with intensified political consciousness among the rising generation in the Latin American countries, international business—diplomatic, economic, and political—could no longer be carried on without standing, permanent machinery, representative of small as well as Great Powers.

International relations between governments today are carried on through a variety of means—bilateral diplomacy, regional alliances with their organisations, associations of states with special regional or historical or economic links, and the permanent international organisations. The range of international communication through all these channels is far wider than that which the limited channels of the years before the First World War ever carried. This development is an indispensable preliminary to the creation of an international community.

The international organisations are not a guarantee against failure, but they are a condition of success. For, as we have seen, the balance of power, if it is to be maintained, must be adjusted to changes from time to time. If the processes of adjustment are to be accomplished without armed conflict they must be conducted and regulated according to " rules of the game ". But rules can be established, and adherence to them secured, through organisations in which the states affected are adequately represented : otherwise partiality in the rules, and injustice in their application, will create new sources of instability, and a wide gap between the rules of the game in international affairs and the rule of law as it is conceived in the domestic affairs of states under representative government. In

14

the mid-twentieth century such a gap exists even though, with the glaring and indefensible exceptions of China and Germany, the international organisations are widely representative of both great and small powers.

In short, the international organisations, properly conceived, are organisations to facilitate adherence to the older rules of the game and to establish new ones, in a system of balanced power. The establishment of a true international community requires that the rules of the game should approximate closer and closer to the rule of law among states. But this is bound to be a slow and difficult process, which is as yet in its infancy, for the international organisations reflect a series of struggles for power, both in regions and in the world as a whole, and the compromises and expedients which are the outcome of these struggles are often dictated by comparative strength more than by a sense of impartial justice. The relationship between the rules of the game and the rule of law is an uneasy one. The former often results in inconsistencies, occasionally in contradictions, arising from unequal treatment of similar or analogous acts of different states. Breaches of treaties and lesser engagements, as well as a variety of other arbitrary acts, are ignored when committed by some states, and penalised when committed by others. Interventions take place here but not there, when in both places the issues are identical in principle. Nor are the rules of the game laid down as rules of law by legislative bodies : on many political issues the rules of the game in international politics tend to emerge gradually and tentatively as informal understandings, sometimes accepted only fitfully at first. Actually, to a large extent, the emergence of law was confirmation and generalisation of customs which were widely accepted and practised already and resembled rules of the game. In international affairs the rules of the game are still in a primitive state, and fall short of the rule of law. This may be said without overlooking the recognised body of international law, much of which existed before the United Nations and even before the League of Nations were established. Far from minimising this, I would accept the view that international law is not fundamentally different from municipal law, and that the mere fact that there is no single central authority to enforce the observance of the body of international law everywhere does not destroy its legal status and significance.

But it is on political matters which are not covered by existing international law, and which contain dangers of conflict and injustice that additional rules of the game are urgently needed. A collective desire for the extension of rules of the game is more likely to arise through the international organisations than through bilateral diplomatic exchanges. The increased channels of communication among the nations, and the special interest of the smaller countries in using them to make their power felt and their will known, represent an important advance on the conditions of the last century, in which bilateral diplomacy was supplemented only by irregular conferences of a few Great Powers which made and remade the political map of the world in the light of their interests. The history of the League of Nations, far from supporting a pessimistic view of the usefulness of international organisations, shows a remarkable contrast between the course of international relations during the decade in which the League was widely supported, and that during the decade in which it was abandoned by some of its leading members and thrust into the background by others.

The revolution in international relations makes it inconceivable that the world could revert to reliance on bilateral diplomacy and irregular *ad hoc* conferences alone in the future. Such limited means of conducting international relations belonged to an age when Great Powers occupied a dominating influence over the rest of the world and the small countries were obliged to fall into line. With more than one hundred independent states, inspired by a heightening political consciousness, the hegemony of the Great Powers is on the decline. To the smaller powers the international organisations serve as a channel through which the power that they exert in groups can be focused and supplemented by international assistance of various kinds. The great Secretary-General of the United Nations during several critical years, Mr. Dag Hammarskold, perceived this clearly and gave effect to it whenever he could. There can be no going back.

If the international organisations are indispensable instruments for the conduct of international relations, they are no more than instruments, and great harm was done by the exaggerated expectations created by enthusiastic idealists who represented them as substitutes displacing the older and allegedly discredited aims and methods of diplomacy. Instruments are useful only as far as their potential use is transformed into actual use. Both the League of Nations and the United Nations proved their practical value in a series of cases where conflicts were averted or shortened and settlements facilitated. But there have also been inconsistencies and omissions, and unresolved differences. The development of an international community and the growth of the rule of law in international affairs are still at a primitive stage. Many of the crudities in international life under the older, traditional instruments of diplomacy can be found today within the international organisations, which are themselves the scene of struggles for power accompanied by compromises and expedients often resulting in inconsistencies, occasionally in contradictions, leading to unequal treatment of similar or analogous acts of different states. As in domestic affairs, so in international affairs, the consistent recognition of the rule of law, based on principles, precedents, and practical expediency, will appear gradually, with frequent set-backs, and, until it is firmly established, gross inequities will continue in the treatment of the same issues in respect to different countries. In domestic affairs centuries passed before all persons were treated equally before the law, and practice still falls short of principle in many countries. Kinship, influence, feuds, the fear of alienating friends of an offender, animosities originating in a distant past, stood in the way in internal affairs, as they now stand in the way in inter-national affairs.

Actually, in seeking an explanation of the comparatively primitive state of international relations, it is impossible to dissociate sharply the external from the internal affairs of nations, and one of the greatest obstacles to the development of the rules of the game and the rule of law in international affairs both within and outside the inter-national organisations, lies in the frequent subordination of inter-national to domestic policy. As I have argued elsewhere in this study, the statesmen responsible for the execution of foreign policy are often narrowly limited in the choice of measures and the scope of their actions by pressures from domestic interests and from rivals for office. These constraints affect foreign policies under all forms of government, though under some more than under others. They have been aggravated by the tendency in recent years to reduce the status of foreign ministers and to bring heads of state into personal negotiations on all important issues. The reduction in status tends to bring a decline in the quality of those who are willing to serve in the posts. Heads of state are necessarily preoccupied with domestic affairs and with maintaining their personal power and political posi-tion. In democratic states they tend to shun external policies that clash strongly with the interests or prejudices of organised groups that can influence the electorate. In totalitarian states they often have an interest in maintaining a certain measure of international tension in order to divert the people from domestic discontents to alleged external threats, or to outflank rival aspirants for power who might otherwise insinuate that they were too complaisant to foreigners.

Thus the disharmony between internal and external policies arises both in democratic and in authoritarian societies. In the former, the principle of Cabinet responsibility is the least imperfect among the various forms of government yet devised : it tends to minimise the danger of irresponsibility in international affairs. But it does not eliminate them : for example, it failed to prevent the disastrous decision of the British Government in 1947 to withdraw from Palestine without provision for a successor government. On the same issue, almost equally irresponsible attitudes prevailed in the United States, where policies were determined by the individual sentiments of the President and by the rivalries of the parties for the Jewish vote in New York state. The outcome has been to corrupt international relations in the Middle East for at least a generation. In this case the United Nations, which had only just come into operation when the crisis arose, failed also. Since then its observers have been able to keep down frontier clashes.

But the greatest obstacle to the establishment of a rule of law and the most outstanding danger to international peace arising out of domestic political exigencies in a democratic state may be found in the Far Eastern policies of the United States after the collapse of the Kuomintang. More than a decade passed ; Republicans replaced Democrats and Democrats Republicans, and still the responsible executive authorities of the United States Government feared to change what by all odds must be rated as the most indefensible policy towards China that it is possible to conceive of, short of actual war— a policy which embarrasses the Allies and assist the enemies of the United States, a policy which was largely responsible for drawing China into the Korean War, a policy which makes a mockery of the representation of eastern Asia in the United Nations, and which flouts all rules of the game by victimising one country on grounds that apply equally to other countries accepted in the United Nations before and since the present Chinese Government came to power. Other states, such as Britain, France,[1] Canada, and Australia share in the discredit by an irresolute stand against this anomaly. Nothing prejudices the development of rules of the game in international affairs more than the arbitrary exclusion of countries from the international organisations on doctrinal grounds. Universal membership is the only principle appropriate to the United Nations.

The obstacles to the entry of China into the United Nations are part of the pathology of international relations. But in different settings the politicians of a number of democratic countries have often " used " international issues in home politics with a view to gaining or retaining power in domestic affairs, without regard or with only secondary regard to the international consequences of their acts. For example, the manoeuvring of Belgian party leaders seeking advantages over each other had much to do with the ill-timed and inadequately prepared grant of independence to the Congo.

The dangers in international affairs arising out of domestic political exigencies hardly need detailed illustration where authoritarian régimes are concerned. They are conspicuous in almost every political discussion that takes place in the public session of the Assembly. They are a chief source of the insincerity which characterises so much of the discussion in the international organisations

---

[1] Since this was written France has recognised China.

and poisons the tone of so many national and international broad-casts. Political exigencies at home lead the heads of authoritarian states to maintain fashionable antagonisms abroad long after any occasion for them remains. They lead to a refusal to co-operate in measures that serve the general international interest, merely out of fear that apparent co-operation on any issue among countries regarded, with or without good reason, as foes or exploiters or oppressors, would be interpreted at home as political backsliding, and would supply an effective battle-cry to political rivals and opponents.

Nor are these tendencies confined to outright authoritarian rulers. Even in a democracy like India, and still more in régimes like Ghana, which tend to pass from democracy to authoritarian rule, they may be found. Some of the leading Asian and African politicians are caught up in this confused tangle of internal and external interests that do not coincide. Finally, there is the temptation which besets all authoritarian rulers—a very old temptation appearing in new forms—to exploit external antagonisms in order to draw attention away from internal deficiencies and discontents. If I have repeated this point in the present study in different contexts, it is because it plays, and will probably continue to play, an outstanding part in an age in which rapidly increasing populations create chronic economic difficulties.

But the line between pathological and healthy political life, between political fanaticism and make-believe and political integ-rity, is blurred. The dilemmas which face those who have been given or have assumed for themselves responsibility for foreign policy should not be underestimated. Even the most conscientious foreign ministers and heads of state, when faced with an emotional and intractable public sentiment and opinion on international affairs, may be forced to choose between forfeiting political support at home and adopting what they know or believe to be a policy abroad which is not in the best interests of their countries or of the world. If, on such occasions, they defy public sentiment, then, under representa-tive government, they will be defeated, unless an overshadowing domestic issue arises on which they espouse the popular cause. Under various degrees of authoritarian rule they may prop up their positions by methods of the police state, but revolution and assas-sination remain as a constant threat. The downfall of Nuri as Said in Iraq appears to have been largely due to his external policy of close collaboration with the western Great Powers.

In such circumstances, the wisest political course appears to be to follow a policy of restraint, in which the heads of state take positions deliberately falling short of the policies they believe to be best, but also decline to be led into the opposite extremes which alone would satisfy the most intransigent critics. Under representative government, efforts may be made at the same time to educate the public and moderate its point of view. The way out is not to " give the people what they want ", for that might bring the country into international conflict, but to try to guide them gradually into the way of peace, as far as it is possible to do so in the temper of the times, meanwhile deliberately maintaining a position that, in the estimation of those who follow it, is only second-best.

Among the emerging and reawakening countries now represented in the United Nations these issues are of leading importance at the present time. The increase in the votes of the Afro-Asian group has given it much greater power to determine the outcome of the political discussions in the United Nations, and the future of the organisation will depend partly on the degree of responsibility with which this power is exercised. It raises questions that affect the whole structure of the international organisations. To these we must now turn.

III

The Problem of Bloc Voting

The geographical distribution of votes cast on many issues in the Assembly of the United Nations has aroused widespread criticism and acrimonious controversy, which began at the San Francisco Conference, where the Charter of the United Nations was adopted. The mobilisation of Latin American votes behind the United States on all controversial issues disturbed the Russians, and confirmed them in their suspicions that the United Nations would be merely an instrument to serve the purposes of the western powers. The Latin American solidarity behind the United States was shortlived, but the lesson was not lost to view. The Russians stiffened their attitude on the " veto " and dominated the votes of such neighbouring countries as they could control, but their bloc was numerically inferior, even when the U.S.S.R. was represented by a trinity of votes. Ever since, many countries in the international organisations have cast their votes, not so much on the merits of the issues on which they voted, as on the company they have wished or have been obliged to keep.

The mainsprings of group or bloc voting lie in a number of widely different influences, which must be analysed and differentiated carefully before remedies can be found for abuses. At one end of the scale it is a by-product of the struggle to maintain a balance of armed power. One country fears to vote on the opposite side to another country with which it has a defensive alliance designed to maintain the existing balance of power. For example, Britain, after setting an example at the outset by recognising the new Government of China, supported the immediate admission of China to the United Nations in the first half of 1950. Then in July she turned against it but in September voted for it. Subsequently both the Labour and later the Conservative Governments maintained that the question should be postponed until the end of the Korean War.[1] But when that came, other flimsy excuses were made for doing nothing. Sir Winston Churchill, on returning from a visit to Washington in 1954, declared that the matter " was not of immediate importance ", and Mr. Selwyn Lloyd said that it would be " foolish " for Britain " to seek to force this through against the wishes of their American Allies ". It would be difficult to find among the Asian and African countries a more blatant defence of bloc voting in its worst form, or of the reduction of British policy to that of a timid satellite state. So the matter drifted on year after year. The records of France, Canada, and Australia are no better. Foreign policy without courage leaves a sorry record to posterity. The western countries are in no position to assume white mantles in respect to " bloc voting " in the international organisations.

In defence of bloc voting it is sometimes argued that it sacrifices a principle on a secondary issue in order to preserve a principle on a primary issue. If, it is added, the balance of power among the Great Powers is disrupted, the benefits from voting on the merits of secondary issues will be quickly dissipated.

But this argument presupposes, first that the member of the alliance for whom the sacrifice was made would have broken up the alliance if its partners had voted against it on issues other than those which brought the alliance into being. In the case of British and French weakness on Far Eastern policy, it is difficult to believe that the United States would have broken up the North Atlantic Alliance, or seceded from the United Nations, if China had been admitted to the United Nations.[2] It is true that the less instructed sections of public opinion, including the truculent extremist groups of the right, would have called for such a step, but it seems unlikely that the responsible authorities in either political camp would have been forced to take steps so flatly against the country's international interests. Russia's temporary withdrawal from the Security Council between

[1] See above, p. 38, where it is maintained that if China had been brought into the U.N. in 1950 she would probably not have entered the Korean War, since her position concerning General MacArthur's ill-advised approach to the Chinese frontier would have been made convincingly clear directly to U.S. representatives. The Korean war made it more and not less urgent that she should have been brought speedily into the United Nations.

[2] The " veto " power of the *emigré* " government " of China in Formosa was, of course, a complicating issue.

January and June, 1950, and the consequences in respect to intervention in Korea, demonstrated that the United Nations is a force to be reckoned with ; that, if it has its dull, unprofitable periods, they are punctuated by bursts of activities, some of which create new precedents and enlarge the scope of collective international action ; and that even a super-power which boycotts or leaves it injures its own interests more than those of its rivals.

The second assumption behind the apologia for bloc voting was that the effects of excluding China were less important than the effects of offending the United States through admitting her would have been. This assumption became less and less tenable every year. Exclusion helped to drive China into more intransigent attitudes and to intensify her isolation. It made it impossible to bring the concerted opinion of other countries to bear on her when she became involved in serious conflicts and disputes with other countries. To treat all this as a secondary issue year after year showed a singularly one-sided preoccupation with the issue of Russian power alone, and an inadequate realisation of the strength of the new forces at work in the rest of the world.

But the practice of voting in accordance with the company in which the voter finds himself, instead of in accordance with the merits of the issue on which the vote is taken, is not confined to any particular group of powers. The illustrations just taken from western powers show the incongruity of the high moral tone in which rebukes over bloc voting are directed towards the Asian and African countries by western statesmen who seem not to recognise that they have indulged in the practice themselves for a number of years. But this fails to mitigate the dangerous consequences of a practice that does more than any other to retard the development of international law and rules of the game. As the late Mr. Hammerskold emphasised, the United Nations is needed above all to protect the interests of the small powers. It is in the interests of the emerging countries, therefore, to avoid actions which lower the prestige of the United Nations and weaken the incentives to use its machinery and accept its findings and recommendations.

The resolution passed at the General Assembly in September, 1960 illustrates the extreme lengths to which bloc voting at its worst can be carried :

> Le manque de preparation dans les domains politique, économique et social ou dans celui de l'enseignement ne doit jamais être pris comme prétexte pour retarder l'indépendence.

Well might *Le Monde* comment :

> Que personne n'ait osé voter contre un texte aussi éloigné du

bons sens est bien révélateur du climat actual des Nation Unies. L'anti-colonialisme est devenu un article du " credo ", et l'on ne saurait faire la moindre reservé a son sujet sans s'attirer les pires approbes.[1]

When we consider that, at the time, in a number of territories on the road to independence, the delicate process of reconciling tribal and racial groups was far from complete, and the groups in the majority were greatly lacking in political experience and technical skills, such resolutions can only be described as irresponsible.

Yet self-defeating acts require explanations : they cannot be dismissed as simply " irrational " or " emotional ". They are the outcome of a complicated mingling of emotions and reasoning. The motives behind Asian and African bloc voting differ in important respects from those of western bloc voting. At one extreme, herd instinct plays a much larger part, particularly among Arab and African countries, in each of which, in spite of frequent internal quarrels, a strong feeling of kinship exists in face of the outside world. Though it falls short of real nationalism, it creates reluctance in members of each group to be found voting against other members of the group, and arouses resentment among the majority against any minority which does so. These proclivities are strengthened in some areas by old grievances against outside powers, even when the occasion for them has passed away, and by feelings of inferiority, even after the equality of the inherent capacities of all peoples has been recognised. But these emotional influences often tend to weaken among the more educated political leaders with experience of the outside world, and their direct effects are seen mainly in the student classes, some of the younger members of professional classes, and certain sections of the more skilled workers, who try, with varying results, to communicate their emotions to wider and even less instructed circles. The leading politicians cannot afford to ignore, and have only a limited power to modify, these sentiments among the politically conscious classes.

Hence a large part of the explanation of the political behaviour of the emerging countries in the United Nations Assembly is to be found in the relations between internal and external policy. The politicians in these countries are sharply circumscribed by the passions of the politically conscious elements among the masses, and although many of their leaders are aware that the more extravagant

---

[1] *Le Monde*, 16 December, 1960, p. 1. As the reader will have seen, I have argued that decolonisation is necessary for reasons of group psychology, and that long periods of further tutelage are impracticable. But this is far from saying that " no account " should be taken of the readiness of any peoples to take over government at once.

charges against the West are often unfounded, and the less extravagant charges often exaggerated, they cannot afford to alienate their
followers by saying so in public, and, more often than not, they swim
or float with the tide of popular sentiment among the masses. The
statesmen in some of the emerging countries recognise the wisdom of
maintaining good relations with the western powers, and are aware
of the absurdity of supposing that the latter are continually plotting
to take away the independence they have given them recently ; but
the prevailing anti-foreign attitude among the uninstructed masses,
and the vulnerability of the countries to outside propaganda, forces
them to take account of the sentiment of the left-wing and the
extreme nationalist groups, and avoid being made the target of
propaganda alleging them to be " stooges of imperialism ".

Even in the dictatorships and in the somewhat autocratic régimes
based on the " one-party " system, it would be an error of judgement
to suppose that individual leaders, however powerful they may
appear from the outside, are free to adopt whatever policies they
wish. As we have seen, even the dictator must " keep his ears close to
the ground " if he wishes to survive. But beyond this lies another
factor. The authoritarian ruler of today may differ in many respects
from the monarchs of the late mediaeval and the early modern
periods of European history. But he resembles them in having his
favourite ministers and cliques around him, and in being susceptible
to their influence. In the political climate of Asia and Africa after
the Second World War a number of the younger men from whom
advisors and civil servants were drawn were often uncritically left-
wing or extreme nationalist in outlook.

In this connection it is misleading to suggest that a *parti unique* can
give free play to criticism and dissent. The " machine " within the
party has an immense advantage over isolated critics who are unable
to form a counter-organisation. The free play of criticism can only
be achieved when the right to voluntary political organisation is
recognised.

The final and the most decisive ground for disapproval of mechanical " bloc voting " is that it impedes progress towards the true goal of
the international organisations, which is that of serving at once as
guardians, and as instruments for the extension, of the rule of law and
the rules of the game. The practice under which the statesman votes
according to the principle, " my group of countries, right or wrong ",
inevitably leads to unlike treatment of countries in like situations—
the direct antithesis of the rule of law. The same consideration
applies to those looser understandings which I have designated as
" rules of the game ". Countries which refused to support the admission of China to the U.N., while raising no question about others of
the same political persuasion ; countries which joined in condemn-

ing aggression against Egypt and Hungary, but refused to condemn
aggression against Cuba and Goa ; countries which joined in con-
demning the Soviet Union for interference in the internal affairs of
other countries, but refused to support Mexico at a critical time in
calling for non-interference in the internal affairs of Latin American
countries—all contributed by such actions or inaction to retard the
growth of international justice and to create in the United Nations
those very deficiencies which they are among the first to complain
of when the results affect their interests adversely.

CHAPTER XII

THE EQUALITY OF STATES AND THE INTERNATIONAL ORGANISATIONS

I

Tensions between Great and Small Powers

THE process of decolonisation, together with the acceptance of certain states whose foreign policy is constrained to follow that of the Soviet Union or the United States, has brought the number of states in the United Nations to more than one hundred. The unwieldy size of the Assembly and the tendency at times of some representatives of the emerging countries to vote in blocs without careful regard for the intrinsic merits of the issues on which they vote, has disconcerted many western observers as well as governments.

The charters of the League of Nations and the United Nations were prepared in the late stages of two large-scale wars. On those occasions the Great Powers, armed to the limits of their capacity, and with colossal forces in the field, were in an abnormally dominating position. They controlled the high seas and, directly or indirectly, were in command of most of the economic resources of the world. Without their consent the smaller countries could neither obtain essential materials from abroad nor question decisions that affected them but were made without consulting them. The political climate of the times inevitably influenced those who drafted the charters, which were adopted before the psychology of wartime had given way to a new post-war mood.

From the spring of 1945 there were clear signs that the lesser powers were not prepared to accept a continuation of the wartime dominance of the Great Powers. Stalin, indeed, desired to maintain that position of dominance in peace-time, but Britain and the United States quickly realised the strength of the objections to it in economic matters. The Anglo-U.S.-Canadian Combined Boards were reorganised with wider representation during the period in which allocation of scarce resources was necessary for the activities of reconstruction. In political matters small powers began to reassert their independence. Russia continued to hold that important international affairs should be controlled by the Great Powers, which, it held, had been reduced to three.

Since that time three great changes have taken place. A new category of " super-power " has been informally established, following the invention of atomic weapons. This category, however, signifies only armed power, and in respect to power other than armed power the two super-powers have experienced a comparative decline : their influence in this sense is less today than it was at the conclusion of the war. Second, the remarkable recovery and growth of Europe, assisted in the early stages by indispensable financial aid from the United States in restocking Europe with raw materials, has rendered obsolete the wartime habit of limiting the category of Great Powers to three. Third, the lesser powers have continued to reassert themselves on a much greater scale, as well as to increase in numbers. The drive towards independence in Asia, Africa, and Latin America has accelerated the movement away from Great Power domination which began as soon as the war against Germany ended. Recent developments in the United Nations which reflect this movement represent the continuation of a trend which had begun outside the United Nations and would have been increasingly felt in any case.

The rapid increase in the membership of the Assembly of the United Nations has thrown into sharper relief the long debated questions concerning the comparative powers of the Assembly and the Security Council, and, more generally, the position of the Great Powers in relation to the smaller powers. The privileged positions which the Great Powers established for themselves in the charters of the League of Nations and the United Nations has been under challenge, directly or indirectly, ever since the San Francisco conference opened on the 25th of April, 1945. At that conference the challenge, although it was vigorously pressed, was met by the tightening of the provisions which protected the international aristocracy. In theory their privileges became even greater than they had been in the League, for on the League Council a permanent member which became a party to a dispute was not permitted to vote on resolutions relating to it. Moreover, in principle the charter adopted at San Francisco subordinated the Assembly to the Security Council in a way that had never been envisaged in the League, reserving wholly to the Security Council the function of maintaining the peace against direct threats.

At the time, this departure from the structure of the League was widely proclaimed by writers and speakers in the leading countries as an advance. It was part of the dominant philosophy in those countries where, in the flush of victory, the future world was envisaged as one in which the Great Powers, more restricted in numbers than they had been after the First World War, would dominate the scene in matters of security, and keep order, by force if necessary, among the medium and small powers.[1]

The assumption that quarrels leading to war were usually started by the smaller powers was a serious distortion of history. Still more unreal was the implicit assumption that the Great Powers would be sufficiently united [2] in outlook to ensure the prompt suppression at the outset of disturbances that might originate among other powers, and to adjudicate impartially on the matters in dispute.

The change from the Council of the League of Nations to the Security Council of the United Nations seem to have been a retrogression rather than an advance, so far as it was designed to give precedence to the exercise of police powers. For these powers were, by design, even less capable of being exercised against a Great Power than they had been under the League Council, and the real aim was the visionary one of policing the small powers by the unanimous agreement of the Great Powers. For the most part this was a utopian aim.[3] It assumed that the Great Powers were more virtuous than the small. It turned a blind eye to fundamental divergencies among the Great Powers. It overlooked the role which the small powers play in the international balance of power. Finally, as it was conceived at the zenith of Great Power influence, so, by the time of its adoption, it already ran directly counter to growing international pressure against domination by a smaller and smaller circle of Great Powers over a larger and larger circle of medium and small powers.

The action of the Security Council when South Korea was invaded was rendered possible only by an error of judgement on the part of Stalin. It was therefore a unique case, never likely to be repeated in principle. As a precedent, it can only be regarded with mixed feelings. It was successful in maintaining South Korea as a separate state. But the excessively large role played by one super-power, the

---

[1] This was the view of President Franklin Roosevelt and, apparently, of Stalin.

[2] Such optimism seems to have originated at " top-levels " where an exaggerated faith in " personal diplomacy " grew up during the War. Those of us who, by the end of the War, had gained much practical experience of working relationships on technical and economic matters on inter-Allied bodies, emerged without illusions as to the prospects of co-operation in peace-time, when the overriding common interests in wartime were no longer present to restrain differences. Although Allied difficulties were not due exclusively to the Russians, it was possible to foresee roughly the lines of divergence between Russia and the West which would occupy the centre of the international stage when the War ended, for political aims always dominated Russian positions on technical and economic matters. The divergencies were perhaps greatest where relations with small powers were concerned. They were concerned more with power than doctrine.

[3] A new version of such an aim is to be found in the proposal that the U.S. and the U.S.S.R. should police the world through monopoly of atomic weapons !

failure to make the military command directly responsible to the United Nations, and the exclusion of China from the United Nations, together with the absence of diplomatic relations between China and the power which controlled the United Nations forces, led to the costly and disastrous involvement of China in the war. Thus, one of the super-powers seems to have started the conflict, and the mis-judgements of the other extended it.[1] The small powers appeared largely as instruments in the hands of the Great Powers.[2]

But these conditions were rapidly modified and complicated in the following years, partly by the growing assertiveness of the medium and small powers and partly by increasing divisions within the com-munist world. The conversion of eastern Europe into satellite com-munist states, largely controlled in the last resort by the Russian army and secret police, was not an unmixed gain to Russia. The subordinate states were politically indigestible. They could not be absorbed into the already unwieldy U.S.S.R. Only a small propor-tion of their peoples favoured communism. The memory of past Russian imperialism and its encroachments on their territories and independence persisted in the border states. Russian economic negotiators after the War drove hard bargains with them. The eastern European empire of the U.S.S.R. could hardly be relied on in an international conflict. Most important of all, Yugoslavia had asserted its independence, and in the nineteen-fifties unrest developed into serious uprisings in eastern Germany and Hungary, and, but for real concessions, would have done so in Poland. The Chinese communists gained power by their own efforts and with their own version of communism.

When insurgents pressed down the Indo-Chinese peninsula from the north, conditions had changed substantially since the Korean War. Russia faced serious problems within the new world of com-munist states which were stirring restlessly under her dominion. Just as the Chinese had made free with communist orthodoxy in their rise to power, so Ho-chi-minh adapted his politics to the art of the possible in seeking the control of Indo-China.

In short, a communist world of separate states had grown up, and, as in the non-communist world, the influence of the super-power and of the Great Powers within it had undergone a comparative decline. Heresies abounded, and, since there were now two great

[1] Since this MSS. was written the important work of David Rees, Korea, *The Limited War*, London, 1964, has appeared and confirms this point. See especially pp. 110–14. This work gives an outstanding account of the war itself but unfor-tunately reflects the conventional " cold war " viewpoint of the nineteen-fifties. It is essentially written from a Great Power point of view and speaks of the com-munist countries as if they were a unity.

[2] The results, however, may have been of value in checking designs against other small powers.

powers in the communist world, heretics [1] could sometimes play off one against the other.

It is against the background of the shifts in the comparative positions of the powers and groupings of powers within both the communist and the non-communist worlds that the roles of the Security Council and the Assembly should be considered. Since each of the Great Powers on the Security Council could block action at will in an emergency, and since issues affecting other powers almost invariably provoked disagreement among them, it is not surprising that in practice the influence and even the functions of the Assembly increased in response to international needs. The deadlock among the Great Powers destroyed the possibility that these needs might be met by the great, and the few selected smaller, powers on the Security Council. The result was that the Great Powers lost exclusive control over the handling of disputes concerning the emerging and reawakening countries. The Assembly stepped in where the Security Council feared, or was too paralysed by differences, to tread.

The partial eclipse of the Security Council through the enlargement of the Assembly and its interventions on certain critical occasions, has raised difficult questions of principle for which no ideal solution exists. The League of Nations and the United Nations, as their titles [2] loosely indicate, were composed of independent states. There are, of course, exceptions in the United Nations, where certain states independent in theory are in practice hampered by various degrees of satellite relationship imposed by a Great Power or superpower. Examples of different degrees of subordination may be found in Bulgaria, the Mongolian People's Republic, and Guatemala. Such exceptions introduce complications which have been discussed in several contexts in the present study, but they can be considered here as partial exceptions only from the general principle that the units of which the international organisations are composed are independent states. This is underlined in the U.N. Charter, which states that, " The organisation is based on the principle of the sovereign equality of all its members " (Art. 2, (1)). As we have seen, the Security Council is not based on the principle of equality of states, either in theory or in practice, and both the super-powers and some of the other Great Powers have several times failed to respect the independence of other members of the United Nations. The

---

[1] There seems to be no adequate reason for replacing this well-established word by the cumbersome " deviationist ", any more than for replacing " doctrinal " by " ideological ".

[2] In these titles the term "Nations" obviously stands for "states", or more precisely " independent states ", since the term " states " is sometimes used to designate an internal subdivision with limited jurisdiction. The general significance of both terms is now hopelessly confused, and each must be examined in its own context.

Assembly, however, does embody the principle of equal voting power for each state, large, medium, and small, and this has come under criticism and challenge from time to time. Hence the following section is given to an analysis of the controversy surrounding the idea of the equality of states.

II

Political Equality and Legal Equality

The widespread disagreement over the equality of states, like that over the equality of men, is due partly to linguistic ambiguities. If we ask, equality in what respects, it must be acknowledged that, ever since states were formed, they have shown marked inequalities in many respects, including all physical characteristics. As to equality, the characteristic on which the widest agreement is found among international lawyers is that of legal equality. All states are treated alike in law as International Persons.[1] Laws and rules cannot be imposed on a minority of states without their consent, nor can the courts in any state legally interfere with the courts in another state. Thus the idea of the equality of states is associated with the idea of the independence of states and in this respect all states, large and small, strong and weak, stand in the same position under international law. Independence is never complete : it applies to those fields of international relations not yet subject to forms of international law and rules that are more than window-dressing.[2]

But within the sphere of international law and rules, and in respect to the recognition of their independence in other spheres, all states stand in the same position in a legal sense.

As to the United Nations, the late Mr. Dag Hammerskold goes further:

> . . . the terms of the Charter are explicit as regards the equal political rights of nations as well as individuals . . . So as to avoid any misunderstanding the Charter directly states that the basic democratic principles are applicable to nations large and small and to individuals without distinction as to race, sex, language, and religion. . . .[3]

[1] See Oppenheim, *International Law, A Treatise*, 7th ed., pp. 238–42 for a standard treatment of the subject. See also Bardevant, " Regles du Droit de la Paix ", in Acad. de Droit International, *Recusie des Cours*, 1936, iv, 587–8.

[2] Underlying my discussion is a rejection of the theories of " auto-limitation " in international law, according to which all obligations on states are self-imposed and absolute " sovereignty " is retained in spite of them.

[3] Introduction to *Annual Report of the Secretary-General on the Work of the Organisation*, 16 June, 1960–15 June, 1961, p. 2.

The structure of the Security Council is inconsistent with this principle. It may, of course, be argued on conventional lines that, at the San Francisco Conference in 1945, it received the consent of the signatories of the Charter. But the comparative ineffectiveness of the Security Council, and the greater success of the Assembly, which is based on the principle of equal rights, appear to demonstrate that the full recognition of the legal equality of all states, and the approach to international disputes and conflicts by recommendations based on majority votes, is more fruitful in practice than any system under which the Great Powers attempt to " police " the small powers is likely to be.[1]

The criticisms of the system of voting in the Assembly are, in effect, criticisms of the principle of the equal rights of states. Let us examine the grounds of objections to the principle of " one state, one vote ".

Most of these objections are based on the idea that a larger state should naturally have a greater voice than a small state in the international community. But the precise significance of mere size is less obvious than it appears to the uninitiated, and the critics are by no means unanimous, either on the grounds of their objections, or on the alternatives which they would substitute for the principle of " one state, one vote ". When they allege that equality in voting violates true equality by giving the same voting power to states which are unequal in significant respects, it is reasonable to expect them to put forward an alternative criterion. Let us consider the possible alternatives.

If the division of mankind into states were no longer the criterion, and the principle of the equality of men were adopted instead, voting would be weighted in accordance with the comparative populations of the countries. China would appear at the top and India second. China and India together would have well over twice as many votes as the two super-powers combined.[2]

If population would be unacceptable as a criterion to Europe and North America, the strength of armaments would be equally unacceptable to other continents, with the possible exception of Australasia. It would hinder [3] disarmament and might even create an incentive to increase armaments.

---

[1] It is true that Mr. Khrushchev has declared that Russia would ignore a vote of all other countries against her in the United Nations. But this would be infinitely more difficult than is assumed in the threat. In practice U.N. activities have led on several occasions to modification of Russian policies or tactics.

[2] One can imagine the expressions on the faces of U.S. senators in response to an announcement of a proposal on these lines !

[3] If it were adopted, the comparative armaments existing at a particular time would have to be used as the basis. But if armaments were subsequently reduced, this basis would lose its *raison d'être*, and the majority of countries would not long tolerate what would appear as the privileged position of those which had come off best when the system was founded.

To adopt national income or wealth as a criterion would be to create a hegemony of the great industrial countries, which would never be accepted by the rest of the world. Nor can any genuine economic criterion be devised which would be likely to gain general acceptance. A property qualification may be tolerable for international financial organisations that disburse funds from a pool to which unequal contributions are made by the member countries. But even in the International Monetary Fund it was only after much controversy that a system of differential voting was accepted.[1] It was based, not upon a single economic measure, but upon a weighted average of a number of economic series. Such hodge-podge measures have no scientific or even rational economic foundation : they are the result of hard bargaining and compromise leading to a form of window dressing that may be passed off on the uninitiated as the product of " expert " knowledge !

But no system of weighted voting, however ingeniously camouflaged to conceal its makeshift basis, could be proposed for the Assembly, which is the body of last resort for the whole membership of the United Nations in respect to fundamental political questions, without infringing on " the equal political rights of nations ", on which as Mr. Hammerskold said, the charter is explicit.

But this does not end the matter. Although the critics of equal voting in the Assembly have not proposed any acceptable alternative the grounds of their objections must be clarified and considered. International law is in the process of growth, and often fails to keep pace with changes in ideas and practice. This is not surprising when observers of the contemporary scene are not themselves agreed on the actual direction of changes, and when some of the central ideas may be variously interpreted. Professor Bourquin has aptly remarked of the idea of " equality of states ", " *Il est peu de notions qui soient plus fertiles en equivoques.*" [2] Even the terms " legal equality ", " equal legal rights ", " political equality ", " equal political rights", have been differently interpreted by different writers.

The interpretation of a term may be influenced by the interpreter's own views on the proper role of Great Powers in the international community. Actually, under international law Great Powers have

---

[1] Some twenty years ago I was present at the first private informal meeting between Lord Keynes and Dr. Harry White to discuss the future international monetary organisation. Lord Keynes suggested as the criterion for determining " quotas " and voting the average values of foreign trade in the last three pre-war years. This would have given the U.K. the highest position. Dr. White countered by proposing comparative national incomes. This would have given the U.S. a long lead. Neither country's proposal stood any chance of acceptance by the other, and the queer combination of criteria that finally came out was a makeshift device to escape a total impasse.

[2] Maurice Bourquin, *L'État souverain et l'Organisation Internationale*, 1959, p. 47

had no superior rights and no legal primacy except that which is implied in the privileged positions which they were given, first in the Council of the League of Nations, and later and far more, in the Security Council of the United Nations, neither of which led to conspicuously successful results. But international lawyers no more escape the spirit of their age than other classes do. Up to and during the First World War the Great Powers of Europe and the United States, and in the later part of the period, Japan, took a dominating part in international affairs. The role of the Great Powers was a self-appointed and not a legal one. Like all vested interests, they desire to cling to it even when the political structure of the world is gradually changing to their disadvantage.

A number of international lawyers have clearly been influenced by the aristocratic view of international society which favours Great Power hegemony, chiefly on the ground that it represents a recognition of what exists in practice even apart from the law, but partly through a distrust of many of the small powers. They interpret the idea even of legal equality in a more restricted sense than others do. Brierly was an eminent example. He would go no further than to say, " The rights of one state, whatever they may be, are as much entitled to be protected by the law as the rights of any other." [1] This not only excludes the idea of equal political rights but also by implication that of equality of legal rights. It is consistent with the idea of the right to equal enforcement of unequal legal rights.[2] In Oppenheim's Treatise a somewhat more liberal view is taken : in defining International Personality, Oppenheim says, " In entering into the Family of Nations a state comes as an equal to equals . . ." [3] On the other hand, he warns that, " legal equality must not be confused with political equality ",[4] and Jenks, in the late nineteen-fifties, summarised the position among international lawyers as follows:

> The concept of the equality of states, while still variously interpreted and widely entertained in its extreme form, continues to evolve towards one of equal protection of the law rather than of an equality of rights and functions.[5]

[1] J. L. Brierly, *The Law of Nations*, p. 124
[2] Brierly wished to substitute the term " independence " for the term " equality " of states. But this, while appropriate so far as it goes, is hardly an adequate substitute. For independence is never absolute (except to the supporters of the " auto-limitation " theory of international law), but is diluted by obligations under international law and by certain forms of inescapable material interdependence. Without the assertion of " equality " the way would be open for reducing unduly the *degree of independence* of the smaller powers. The comparatively primitive state of development of international law accentuates this danger.
[3] Oppenheim, op. cit., p. 236
[4] Ibid., p. 244
[5] C. Wilfred Jenks, *The Common Law of Mankind*, London, 1958, p. 20

As yet the works of the international lawyers have not fully appreciated or reflected the changes, actual and impending, between the Great Powers and the rest of the world. Today, the predominant impression that an independent student of international affairs is likely to derive either from direct experience in the latter, or from a study of the utterances in the United Nations of responsible states-men of the Afro-Asian group and of the more independent of the Latin American countries, is that they have no desire or intention to be drawn into the rivalries and antagonisms among the Great Powers. The Foreign Minister of one of the more powerful, more moderate, and least " anti-western " among them, in discussing two examples in which the small powers successfully resisted the Great Powers in the Assembly, has well expressed this widespread feeling :

> We felt that . . . it was not the time for a cold-war debate in which one Great Power would hurl abuse at the other ; the sooner we had something a little more lukewarm the better . . . the big powers were no longer always having their own way.[1]

The western peoples and the Russians and Chinese are still far from having adjusted themselves to the psychological trends of the age. Like all the peoples who have been in more or less dominating positions in the recent—or, in the case of China the more distant—past, they tend to assume that either they or a related group will retain dominance in the indefinite future or reassert it if they have lost it for the time. Thus we hear such expressions as " America [2] in Britain's Place " : the old-fashioned Briton, as well as many Americans and others, has grossly exaggerated the degree of domin-ance Britain once possessed in the world, and now that he feels it to have passed, or to be passing, he tends to assume that it has been transferred to the United States, with which he supposes Britain to be linked by a " special relationship ". He has not yet understood that, taking all forms of power into account, we are entering an age of wider diffusion of power throughout the world, and that the pro-portions of world populations which European, North American, and Russian populations constitute will long continue to decline. The relation between the size of the population and the power wielded by the state is complicated, and the correspondence is often far from close, but a general and widespread increase which accompanies rapid modernisation may be expected to have far-reaching effects.[3]

---

[1] Jaja Wachuku, " Nigeria's Foreign Policy " in *Africa : The Political Pattern*, Ed. by Millar Maclure and Douglas Anglin, Toronto, 1961, p. 67

[2] Meaning the United States

[3] Japan was an early portent of the shape of things to come.

The supposed [1] role which Britain played in the nineteenth century, when, over the greater part of the world, modernisation was in its infancy, is not one which any single state will be able to play in the future.

Thus there is a considerable gap between the outlook of the more orthodox international lawyers and that of Mr. Hammerskold in his remarkable final report. In his reference to equal political rights the late Secretary-General certainly implied far more than equality in respect to the protection of legal rights under international law. His conception of political equality may be taken to include not only equal legal rights as well as the right to enforcement of laws applicable to the smallest states, but also political equality in a sense that goes beyond mere legal equality. If legal criteria only were taken into account the Great Powers would continue to take advantage of the gaps in international law at the expense of the smaller powers. In his great speech replying to Russian attacks on him Mr. Hammerskold particularly stressed the role of the United Nations as a protector of the rights and interests of small states : the Great Powers can often safeguard their own interests.

The revolution in international relations has raised, and will continue to raise, new issues. It has brought, and will continue to bring, changes in underlying conditions, compelling modifications in day-to-day practices. Ultimately laws and rules may be adopted to take account of some of these changes, but in the meantime improvisations must be made to meet the new needs which arise in new conditions. As Mr. Hammerskold said :

. . . it is one thing to note what the Charter stipulates ; it is an entirely different but ultimately more important question as to what the situation is in practice and what, in fact, is the weight given to decisions of the Organisation when they go beyond the conference pattern of agreement.[2]

---

[1] I say " supposed " because, in view of the sweeping nature of the claim it is surprising how little detailed demonstration has been attempted in support of it. Certainly for a considerable part of the nineteenth century Britain's fleet was an obstacle to adventures overseas by other European powers, but in Europe itself there were a number of developments not in her interests which she could not prevent, and her influence as a land power was very limited. Perhaps it was at its maximum in the period of the Crimean War, when the fruits of her precedence in the industrial revolution and her growing population gave her such reserves of strength that, if necessary, she could have continued the war without France. But in the next decade she failed to check Prussian aggression over Schleswig-Holstein and Austria, and at the beginning of the following decade stood aloof in face of the disaster to her neighbour and then had to accept the unilateral repudiation of the restrictions on Russia's ability to expand to the west which had been the main achievement of the Crimean War.

[2] Introduction to the Annual Report of the Secretary-General, op. cit., p. 7

Later, he added :

> . . . the executive functions and their form have been largely left to practice.[1]

Thus, international practices extend into fields not yet covered by international laws or formal regulations, especially in conditions of emergency, when the member states of the international organisations demand action at all costs, and when, in the absence of action, individual states threaten to act on their own, provoking serious danger of wider conflict.

In these fields the Secretariat has to make its way, often with little or no guidance, facing contingencies almost without precedent, which compel them to improvise quick adaptations to unforeseen circumstances. If, in such conditions, any legal conception could be applied, it would be that of natural law.[2] However, the issues are often concerned with the interpretation and application of principles couched, sometimes deliberately, in general and even vague terms, because of the impossibility of obtaining agreement on more precise terms. When member states are unable to reach agreement, either through diplomatic channels or on international committees, but at the same time shrink from armed conflict because of its unforeseeable consequences, they are sometimes willing, as a last resort, to impose on the Secretariat, under cover of ambiguous resolutions or terms of reference, the task of finding a way out with the least loss of " face " for themselves. In view of the underlying contradictions in this procedure, it is astonishing that, under the late Mr. Hammerskold and Mr. U. Thant, the Secretariat were able to achieve the results they did. Even if this were the only justification of the international organisations that could be found it would be decisive. The consequences of war today would be so disastrous that even such a precarious and internally inconsistent method of keeping the peace should be welcomed and established as firmly as it can be. Recent experience reaffirms the soundness of the view which some of us first adopted through experience in Geneva before the Second World War, that the Secretariat of an international organisation has a role of its own to fulfil, beyond that of merely serving international committees, and that to fulfil it adequately, its members must accept loyalty to the international organisation representing the whole

---

[1] Ibid.

[2] The tide of positivism seems now to be receding, in law as in philosophy and psychology, and natural law will inevitably play an important role in international law, particularly because of the large gaps in a field far less covered, and less provided with sanctions than that of municipal law. For an excellent recent statement of the minimum content of natural law, see H. L. A. Hart, *The Concept of Law*, Ch. IX, section 2. For a more extended philosophical approach see Nathaniel Micklem's address to the Grotius Society, reprinted in his, *The Place of Understanding and other Papers*, London, 1963.

international community, as a higher loyalty than that which they owe to the individual states from which they are recruited.

Groping in the no-man's-lands of international relations, the officials of the international organisations cannot fail to appreciate, nor can they afford to overlook, the growing role and importance of the smaller powers and their unwillingness to submit to the hegemony of the Great Powers. The time has passed when coercive power could be confined mainly to armies and navies, and when the illiterate and semi-literate masses that could not be reached daily through the written and spoken word remained politically quiescent and docile. The threat of armed force may continue to hold certain limited areas to a satellite status in the near future, but it would be impossible for the Great Powers to reduce to and hold in a satellite-status Asia outside Russia and China, and Latin America, and Africa. The satellite yoke sits uneasily on the peoples who bear it now : the movement towards decolonisation will not end when the western countries have granted independence to their last colony. The turn of the East will come, probably long before the twenty-first century opens.

The fortunes of the United Nations have fluctuated from time to time, but the trend is unmistakable. The outstanding fact since 1950 has been the increase in the activities and responsibilities of the Assembly and the comparative ineffectiveness of the Security Council. Practice is turning away from the acceptance by the smaller powers of the hegemony of the Great Powers in the world known to Oppenheim and Brierly when they wrote their main treatises. International lawyers may shake their heads, members of United Nations Associations in the Great Powers may express misgivings over the partial eclipse of the Security Council ; but it would be vain to suppose that the intentions and desires of the original draughtsmen of the Charter, all drawn from the Great Powers, and of the heads of state of the " Big Three " at the time when the Charter was drafted, will ever be realised !

Thus the principle of " one state, one vote " in the Assembly is unlikely to be modified, and it is equally unlikely that the growth in the comparative importance of the Assembly will be reversed. The strength which the system of voting brings to the smaller countries is justified by their greater need of protection, first, against the propensity of the super-powers to use some of them as instruments in their own rivalries and to involve them in the alignments of the " cold war ", and, second, in a more general sense, against the superior powers of coercion which Great Powers can exercise in those fields of international relations not yet brought within the scope of international law and of rules, formal or informal.[1]

[1] It must not be overlooked that the super-powers have also taken liberties with international law without evoking effective protest from other Great Powers.

I conclude that the power of the Assembly, and the influence of the smaller countries, in the United Nations has increased, is increasing, and ought not to be diminished.

III

" Le Tiers Monde " in the United Nations

The increased power of the Asian and African countries in the Assembly of the United Nations has raised important issues for the policies of Britain, France, and other western European countries which maintain special relations with many of the countries concerned. We stand at the parting of the ways. As decolonisation moves into its final stages the lines of a new and, as we hope, more fruitful relationship remain to be established between the former colonial powers and the newly independent states that will command increasing power in the United Nations, and will demand, and ultimately obtain, greater representation on, or a modification of the powers of, the Security Council.

Today Britain and France, and subsequently the multi-national European state into which they are likely to be merged, have the opportunity to establish a new and more fruitful relationship with the rising worlds of Asia, Africa, and Latin America which, in the aggregate, will command increasing power within the United Nations Assembly, and will demand, and ultimately obtain, greater representation on the Security Council. Earlier in this study I have been unsparingly critical of the failure of the Great Powers to recognise, and to adopt their policies adequately to, the changing balance of power in which future international relations will be carried on ; and to accept readily and not reluctantly the new and emerging states on a basis of genuine and not merely legal equality.

But international relations are many-sided, and any analysis would be extraordinarily one-sided which directed its criticisms only to the Great Powers. In the preceding chapters dealing with the emerging countries much has been said of certain tendencies in their domestic development which tend to weaken their internal cohesion, retard their internal development, and destroy the harmony of international relations within the regions concerned. These tendencies must now be considered from a world instead of a national or regional point of view.

Among them, first place should be given to the movements, discussed in Chapters VIII, IX, and X, aiming at unification of emerging states in certain regions, chiefly in the Middle East and Africa.

As we have seen, these movements, in spite of their professed aims, so far appear to have done as much to intensify as to assuage the spirit of disunity. Two consequences, of the greatest importance to international relations, follow.

First, the international influence of the countries concerned is weakened and distorted. It is weakened because outside states obviously give less weight to the positions taken by countries known to be in conflict among themselves than they would give to a unified position known to have been reached on its merits through voluntary agreement. It is distorted because rival aspirants to authoritarian leadership within the region attempt to outdo one another in intransigence over international issues on which bellicose attitudes are popular with the unthinking crowd.

Second, when the disputes lead, as they frequently have done, to attempts on the part of ambitious authoritarian rulers, seeking a monopoly of leadership in the movement for regional unification, to undermine the governments of neighbouring states by radio propaganda, by fostering underground plots to assassinate heads of state and to stir up local riots and disaffection, and by supplying arms through underground channels to conspirators, the Afro-Asian and Latin American countries have in practice violated the fundamental principles of the United Nations Charter and retarded, when they should have helped to extend, the rule of law in international relations. In the Middle East, in particular, the pledges of non-interference in the internal affairs of other members, which all the states which signed the Charters of the United Nations and of the Arab League had given, proved to be worthless. Yet in a world in which the security of these countries depends, in the last resort, on the support which they can muster in the United Nations against violation of their independence by any of the great or intermediate powers which are immeasurably superior to them in arms, it seems ill-advised for Arab or African or Latin American states to undermine, in their relations with one another, the very foundations on which their own protection must rest in the eyes of the world. The intra-regional imperialism of smaller powers which has followed the world imperialism of the Great Powers, is at once a danger to the world and a snare to the countries which engage in it. As we have seen, it is aggravated by the rivalries of the super-powers, each of which sends military and economic supplies to the chief countries practising regional imperialism. Imperialisms dependent on more or less accidental external assistance rest on a precarious basis which may collapse suddenly.

More generally, imperialistic adventures that lead a country into commitments beyond its economic strength cannot be sustained indefinitely, however skilfully they may be served in a political and military sense. The fate of Japan in the Second World War was an outstanding proof of this. Few campaigns based on " combined operations " have been more brilliantly and successfully conducted than that which swiftly gave Japan command of all south-eastern Asia. Yet it was possible to predict, and in certain quarters it was predicted, at the outset, that Japanese economic resources would be inadequate to sustain the vast new empire which had been acquired so swiftly. In armed power Japan was stronger than all the Middle Eastern and African countries combined today, but that availed nothing when its lines of communication and transport were extended beyond the resources at its command to sustain them, and the gratuitous massacres at Hiroshima and Nagasaki were demonstrably unnecessary to effect her surrender.[1] Japan's experience could be studied with profit by all ambitious leaders of intra-regional imperialism.

To recapitulate, the emerging countries, when they co-operate as equals, wield, and will continue to wield, great power in the world. But it consists, and will continue to consist, mainly in other forms of power than armed power. It will be weakened and not strengthened, retarded and not advanced, through ambitious schemes to enlarge the areas of some of the larger Middle Eastern and African states by undermining the governments of neighbouring states on the specious claim that their peoples really want to be absorbed by an authoritarian ruler outside their own territory. Dr. Nkrumah was, no doubt sincere, but he was misguided, in supposing that the sudden proclamation of a single, centralised African state would have given the African peoples increased power in world affairs. The total armed power would have remained negligible. Their votes in the United Nations would have been reduced to one. The former differences would have remained with a change of name from international to inter-regional. If inter-regional disputes have continued within a number of existing states, it seems obvious in a single state of continental dimensions they would have been greatly increased and would have absorbed the main energies of an inadequate civil service, a hastily improvised administrative machine, and a mixed and unevenly recruited army and police force, all of them dependent on a corps of amateur interpreters.

The outcome may be left to the imagination, and at first sight it seems a waste of space even to state a few of the implications of the Nkrumah political recipe, particularly since the other African states rejected it decisively at the conference at Addis Ababa in May, 1963. Unfortunately political slogans do not die easily in the face of rational

---

[1] See, if possible, the excellent report of the U.S. Bombing Survey. This important document seems to have been unknown to many subsequent writers on the subject.

analysis : their appeal to the masses can often be exploited to serve personal or sectional ends. As we have seen,[1] the analogous doctrine of " Arab unity from the Atlantic Ocean to the Persian Gulf ", which in the near future is almost as chimerical as African unity in a single state, has been the most potent and most dangerous force in Middle East politics for several years, and has kept the area in continuous turmoil, serving as a convenient pretext for intra-regional imperialism. Whatever they have thought privately, most politicians have feared even to question openly the verbal inspiration and prompt applicability of the doctrine of Arab nationalism.

The increasing turmoil and intrigue, directed, now towards overturning the government at home, now towards undermining neighbouring governments, all in the name of unity, has created chronic instability, within which rival intra-regional imperialisms have striven for ascendancy. The real aims have been conquest, not voluntary unity, military or party dictatorship exercised from one centre, not representative government and social democracy. The leaders of these movements have honoured freedom with their lips but their hearts have been far from it. They have been responsible for intensifying the widespread violation within the region of the provisions of the Arab League and the United Nations Charters affirming the independence, and prohibiting interference in the internal affairs, of member states.

The danger that the similar provisions in the Charter of the new African organisation set up in Addis Ababa in May, 1963 might meet a similar fate had already receded after the dissolution of the rival Casablanca and Monrovia groupings. The course of events during the conference itself was a further setback to visionary schemes for a single African state. The aim that received the greatest support was that of overturning the Portuguese, the Southern Rhodesian, and the South African régimes. This at least diverted attention from internal differences. As a unifying force, however, it has one weakness. When organisations are formed to encompass the destruction of alien rule by violent means, the instruments of these designs subsequently lose their employment after the passing of the alien rule. When that time comes they are not usually content to retire to the strenuous, but humdrum peaceful labours of healing and reconstruction which are the supreme need of the hour. Sometimes they transfer their talents to revolutionary activities in domestic politics. Sometimes they offer their services in other troubled parts of the world.

With these reservations there are grounds for hoping that Africa south of the Sahara will not follow the Middle East into a condition of regional civil war, if the term may be used, in which the slogan

[1] Pp. 150 and 167

of "unity" is used as a cover for fishing in troubled political waters.

All these sources of conflict between and instability among the emerging countries dissipate the energies and weaken the moral and material power which they are capable of exercising in the United Nations, increase the difficulties in the way of co-operation between them and Europe, and make them a far less effective force than they might be in restraining the doctrinal conflicts of the super-powers and realising the full value and usefulness of neutralism in a divided world.

The movement towards decolonisation which arose out of the spread of political consciousness in Asia and Africa was directed against European countries and the United States, simply because these were the imperial countries from whose sway the emerging peoples desired to be liberated. But imperialism is as old as the political state and had been practised by the ancestors of many of the peoples now seeking liberation from it. Its forms had ranged from annexation and absorption to the enforcement of rights of suzerainty. In modern times it was confronted with rising national consciousness. In a few cases toleration was sufficiently developed to make a multi-national state possible. But more often nationalism had a disintegrating effect upon empires, particularly upon the overseas colonial empires of European countries and the United States.

These historical coincidences created the impression among the emerging peoples that imperialism was peculiar to the western powers. The Russians, for tactical reasons, and later the Chinese, encouraged them in this belief.[1] The extreme nationalist in the emerging country, like the communist in countries governed by communists, though for different reasons, takes it for granted that imperialism is a heinous sin, and that it is peculiar to the West. The very nature of nationalism or communism, he assumes, excludes the possibilities of imperialistic practices.

This belief, which is implied more often than stated, shares the same underlying characteristic as the belief of those western observers who argue that the emerging peoples are not capable of representative government with recognised opposition parties, and that we should not be disturbed if they prefer authoritarian forms of government by their own leaders : there is an underlying assumption of racial or group superiority and inferiority. You assume that your own people hold a monopoly of certain virtues and capacities.

---

[1] On one occasion, when speaking to an audience of Arab students in the Middle East, I referred to "the period of Arab Imperialism" in the later part of the first millenium A.D., and the astonished and at first blank looks of the students brought home to me how novel the idea was to them. Soon, however, the unfailing Arab sense of humour asserted itself and they were all smiling.

In reality, of course, imperialism, as we have seen, appears to be related simply to comparative power and opportunity. There is no reason for believing that the emerging peoples, on the average, are any less self-assertive than the western peoples have been. Experience supports the presumption that " human nature " is, in fundamental respects, similar all over the globe. Future manifestations of imperialism are as likely to show themselves in Asia and Africa as anywhere else, when the emerging countries obtain the power. As we have seen, in the Middle East and south-eastern Asia they have already appeared. So far they have been restricted to attempts at intra-regional imperialism, but that limitation may have been imposed by limitations of power rather than by lack of inclination.

But dreams of revolutionary imperialism, like that of President Nasir, and of opportunist imperialism, like that of President Sukarno, will set back rather than contribute to the common interests of the emerging countries in making the fullest possible use of the United Nations through unified action among themselves to safeguard their independence, to secure economic assistance on conditions neither unduly burdensome nor prejudicial to their autonomy, neither advanced nor withdrawn as political incidents in the rivalries of the super-powers, but based simply on genuine assessments of needs.

The chief hope of the emerging countries lies in the pursuit of these common interests, and, beyond them, in the pursuit of world-wide disarmament and the extension of the rule of law in international affairs. The combined pressure of the emerging and reawakening countries on the super-powers might well prove to be a more effective force than any other, through the international organisations, to break the frequent deadlocks in negotiations on disarmament, for which it is incorrect to put the whole responsibility on the Russians. The competition of the super-powers to gain the support or at least avoid the hostility of *le tiers monde* provides an opportunity.

In these constructive causes bloc voting would become a virtue instead of a vice, and the habits of consultation and co-operation in international affairs would pave the way for closer unity, leading ultimately to confederation, and even, in some areas, to federation.

The emerging countries, however, are as yet far from realising the importance in their own interests of advancing the rule of law in international affairs. For this aim requires that similar actions should be treated similarly, without regard to the identity of those who committed the actions. The world of states is far from having established the rule of law generally, and every time the emerging nations discriminate between countries, by condoning or remaining silent in the face of actions committed by one country which they condemn publicly when it is committed by another, they are setting precedents which may turn to their disadvantage in the future.

But the remedies for this failure on the part of the emerging and reawakening countries to work together for the establishment of the rule of law will take great political and personal courage—that moral courage, as we commonly call it, which, unlike physical courage, is one of the rarest of human qualities.

CHAPTER XIII

EUROPEAN UNITY AND THE BALANCE OF POWER

I

The Temporary Eclipse of Europe

THE revolution in international relations, which originated outside Europe and North America, has been superimposed on far-reaching changes in the balance of power among the great states of the world. A century and a quarter ago, Alexis de Tocqueville had foreseen that Russia and the United States would become the most powerful states of the world in the twentieth century. It is a grim irony of history that the realisation of this forecast was greatly hastened by the forces of fanatical anti-communism, most of all in Germany, which attempted to upset the balance of power at the expense of Russia, and succeeded in upsetting it to the comparative advantage of Russia in the reshuffling of power that followed. By the same act they weakened, at least for a time, the comparative power of Europe, outside Russia, in relation to North America. Thus the subsequent attempt to construct a new balance of power among the long-established countries has been proceeding simultaneously with the emergence of a large number of new countries.

The collapse of Austria-Hungary after the First World War and of Germany after the Second, the reduction of the eastern European countries to the position of satellites of Russia, and the great advances in Russian heavy industry and armed power, created an extraordinary imbalance of armed power in Europe. Not since Napoleon's day had there seemed to be so great a danger that Europe would fall under the domination of one country. The range and destructive power of the new atomic weapons soon made this danger appear as great to North America as to western, central, and southern Europe.

Hence a strong, common interest was forged between the western, southern, and part of central Europe on the one hand, and North America on the other. It is this common interest that lies behind what is loosely called the Atlantic Alliance. "Isolationist" sentiment in the United States—that is, isolationist with regard to Europe [1]—before the War could not recur after it, if only because the

---

[1] This is an essential qualification. The history of United States imperialism is a refutation of the idea that the U.S. was ever isolationist with reference to the world as a whole. See Richard W. van Alstyne, *The Rising American Empire*, Oxford, 1960.

rapid acceleration in the range, and increase in the destructive power, of weapons had greatly increased the vulnerability of the United States. Moreover, in the United States this time a doctrinal bias reinforced considerations of the balance of power. When the external danger came from a country on the far left the response to it was characteristically as forceful as it had been sluggish when it came from the far right in the nineteen-thirties.

But the Atlantic Alliance has had a chequered history, the reasons for which must now be analysed. To a large extent they are to be found in variations in the comparative power of the countries concerned since the end of the Second World War.

At that time continental Europe had only just emerged from a captivity that had stripped it of armed power and crippled its industries, apart from those used to serve the purposes of the conquerors. Britain had only escaped the fate of France by the effects of a geological change that had brought a strip of water between it and the mainland, and by being less unprepared in the air than on land.

The United States, which had been forced into the War after more than two years from its onset, and whose territory had remained immune to attack, emerged with greater armed power and economic resources than ever, although precipitate demobilisation speedily reduced the former. The unnecessary explosion of the atomic bombs on Japan [1] alarmed Russia, which had not yet mastered the secrets of atomic fission and fusion. To gain time, the Russian leaders instructed communist parties abroad to take the offensive. From 1948 to 1952 militant tactics were the order of the day. One aim was to disrupt trade with the Asian tropics, depriving western industries of essential raw materials. Another was to deprive the United States of an outpost in Korea. Neither of these aims was achieved, but each of them was costly to the western allies and drained their military power.

---

[1] No more indefensible act in modern warfare can be found than the bombing of Hiroshima and Nagasaki. It is contrary to all common sense to suppose that, with her navy defeated and merchant fleet destroyed, and her territory open to air attack, a military invasion would have been necessary to induce Japan to give up the fight. No one who knew Japan from the inside could have believed that the sort of resistance made by a small unimpeded force in Okinawa gave any indication of what was to be expected from the mixed population in Japan proper, dependent for its life on a network of communications and transport vulnerable to attack without invasion and needing imported materials to continue the fight. Yet not only American but also a number of British statesmen have continued to defend the atomic bomb attack. It should of course be added that the Anglo-American " terror raids " on Dresden and other cities and the raids on Tokyo and other Japanese cities aimed at deliberate destruction of non-military objectives, were not very far short of the atomic bomb raids in their destructive effects. Taken in their aggregate they represent man's inhumanity to man on the largest scale per unit of time since the world began.

The successful manufacture of the hydrogen bomb in Russia created a second " super-power ", and reduced Russian fears of the United States. But it started a competition in atomic weapons between the super-powers which has constituted a serious danger to the rest of the world, and the end of which is not yet in sight. Britain successfully produced the bomb by its own efforts, but its geographical position and the size of its territory and population precluded its entry into the ranks of the super-powers. France made progress in the same direction. China followed suit and Sweden debated the question whether or not to join in the same quest.

The difficulty in analysing and tracing the frequent shifts in the balance of armed power, and in appraising the prospects for the near future, lies in the rapid technical changes in armaments based on atomic fission and fusion, and in the methods of defence against them. An extensive literature on the subject has appeared, but much of it becomes of only historic interest within a very few years of its appearance. In the present study there is no space to trace the fluctuating course of the recent past, but a few broad issues can be singled out. When the offensive power of the new arms is not offset by an effective defence, a " balance of terror " is said to exist : each side is deterred from taking the offensive, not by the difficulties of penetrating the defence of the other, but by the fear of almost immediate retaliation. Exceptions may occur if the positions of the offensive weapons are known and vulnerable to attack ; the country which strikes first in those conditions might be able to destroy the capacity of the other to retaliate. But as soon as concealment and protection of the offensive weapons is practicable, a sudden over-whelming victory by surprise attack is no longer possible, and stale-mate is reached. It would be well if this were maintained until reduction of armaments were negotiated.

But competition in innovation tends to dominate the military establishments of the Great Powers, and, as innovation takes many forms, it is as likely to upset a stalemate as to create a new one based on different weapons. At this point military establishments become a particularly dangerous vested interest, for, inside governments, their influence will always be exerted on the side of policies aimed at changing the balance of armed power, which can only be achieved by upsetting a stalemate.

Until mankind has reached a level of civilisation at which policies that threaten race suicide will no longer be tolerated, a stalemate in the balance of armed power is the condition most to be desired. The application of atomic energy to armaments, notwithstanding the great evils it has brought to the human race, has perhaps increased the chances of stalemate in armed power. Our first aim should be, therefore, to check further increases in armaments, especially when they are accompanied by qualitative changes. This is the essential basis of a policy of disarmament. The greatest obstacle to the reduction of armaments lies in the difficulty of maintaining stalemate in the balance of armed power at the successive stages of reduction. Within limits such a condition of stalemate is more important than the actual level of armaments.

But disarmament must remain as the goal. In a changing world stalemate is difficult to maintain. If it satisfies the super-powers, which is unlikely, it will not satisfy all the Great Powers. A stable position among the super-powers, if it could be reached, would be disturbed sooner or later by qualitative as well as quantitative changes in the armaments of other powers. Of all the ideas on armaments advanced in the mid-twentieth century, the idea that Russia and the United States could and should combine to prevent other countries, by force if necessary, from developing atomic weapons or from going to war with any weapons, seems the most chimerical. That the many clashes of national interests between them can be set aside ; that the wishes and interests of allies should be ignored or flouted ; that the two powers which were responsible for the threat of nuclear war should and could maintain a permanent monopoly of nuclear weapons by force or threat of force, and that they should, in effect, assume the role of a self-appointed world police, unchallengable in power and influence—these propositions presuppose unbelievably docile attitudes in the world outside the super-powers.

Neither in the communist nor in the non-communist world will the hegemony of a single power be accepted or endured for long. Temporary hegemonies have come and gone over many centuries, and there is no reason to believe that, in the second half of the twentieth century, domination on the part even of the mightiest super-power or super-powers will be established once and for all. With the growth in the number of communist countries, Russian domination weakened, as it was bound to weaken. With the recovery and growth of western, central, and southern Europe, with the rise of Asian and African countries, and the intensification of political consciousness in Latin America, the comparative power and influence of the United States waned, as it was bound to wane. Short-cuts to international peace will not be attained by a narrow monopoly of all technical advances in armaments beyond a given point, and of the weapons based on them. Notwithstanding its immense difficulties and intricacies, the task of disarmament by international agreement must be faced systematically by great, medium, and small powers alike.

Many experts on atomic armaments dismiss, in cavalier fashion, the small and even the medium powers as of no account, and assume that the super-powers, perhaps with the co-operation of the Great Powers, will shape the future world in accordance with the greatest common denominator to be found among their partially conflicting desires. But the spread of atomic weapons, even if it is slow, will be inevitable if the super-powers insist on increasing, or even on merely maintaining, their own armouries and their establishments for research into and development of new and ever deadlier means of human destruction. The chief obstacle to the spread of nuclear weapons has been their great economic cost, the extent of open spaces available for testing them, and the special vulnerability of small, densely populated areas. But the progress of invention and innovation may lead, in nuclear weapons as it often does in peaceful industry, to the replacement of more bulky and costly equipment by cheaper and simpler methods of achieving similar ends.[1] The present relation between the economic cost and the lethal capacity of nuclear armaments is not necessarily a reliable guide to the future.

How then, it may be asked, have the advances in nuclear weapons affected the problem of maintaining a new balance of power on the European continent to replace that which was destroyed by Hitler and his associates ?

In the immediate post-war years, western Europe, apart from Britain, was weak. Time was needed for recovery. Russia under Stalin appeared as a grave threat. In retrospect it seems less clear how far the apparently belligerent tone of Russian leaders, and the aggressive attitude they urged the communist parties in other countries to adopt, were inspired by fears of one-sided possession of the atomic bomb, how far by the temptation to fish in troubled waters in the hope of gaining local advantages, and how far to doctrinal zeal. Since the War had been fought as a patriotic rather than a doctrinal war, it seems unlikely that evangelistic doctrinal zeal could have been relied on to appeal to a war-weary people in a war-scarred land so soon after the cease-fire. Whatever the motive force, the danger seemed real to governments at the time, and, indeed, even if, in the short run, war weariness and reluctance to fight abroad would have stood in the way of aggression, in the longer run the standing danger of an imbalance of power on the European continent had to be met. And in the earlier stages the power of the United States, based on unrivalled natural resources, on assistance from a stream of skilled scientists and technicians escaping from Nazi and Fascist persecution, and on freedom from the direct ravages of

---

[1] This possibility seems to have been in the minds of some of the opponents of the referendum in Switzerland on the proposal for a formal renunciation of nuclear weapons.

war, was much greater than all that western Europe could muster. Hence for some years the post-war Atlantic Alliance was comparatively one-sided, and western Europe, in seeking protection from the super-power to the east, was in danger of becoming a satellite of the super-power to the west.

But in the course of the nineteen-fifties, western, central, and southern Europe gathered strength rapidly. Their economic recovery quickly passed into economic expansion on a scale and at a rate previously unknown in the twentieth century. They entered the nineteen-sixties with a rate of growth, except in Britain, well ahead of that in the United States. On the Continent, the European Common Market and the Coal and Steel Organisation began a process of integration which has come to stay.

These developments naturally predisposed Europeans to demand a greater influence in the North Atlantic Alliance and a greater voice in policies affecting it. At this juncture, however, a new political group took over in Washington. On the road to office it had attacked the previous Administration as wanting in international leadership. President Eisenhower, whatever his shortcomings, had been remarkably tactful in his dealings with Allied personnel, both military and civilian. His advice that there should be less talk of " leadership " and more of co-operation was both wise and timely. But his successor swung in practice towards the opposite view, partly out of temperament and partly under the influence of his advisers.[1] At the outset, some British writers and politicians hailed the change of attitude with approval, and commended the " Kennedy touch " to their own political leaders.

As so often happens in public discussion of international affairs, the underlying issues were obscured by surface controversies, in

[1] Much was made by British writers of the introduction of *young* men into the new government : it was commended in many circles as a model for other countries, and disparaging remarks were made concerning the ages of European statesmen. But the results, especially over Cuba, were not altogether happy, and perhaps the most successful individual was the more experienced Mr. Averell Harriman, over seventy years of age. However, the conclusion would seem to be merely that age in itself is of only secondary importance, being related simply to experience, and that the elusive qualities that characterise the best ministers, officials, and advisers in international affairs are related to temperament, judgement, capacity, and psychological insight as well as experience. To harp on age *per se* may serve the ends of domestic political struggles for power but it diverts the public mind away from an appreciation of the true criteria. Again, some British writers laid great stress on the early period of the Kennedy administration on the " brilliant young intellectuals " gathered around him. But in international affairs brilliance is less important than patience, tenacity, and at times, restraint. Actually the members of Harvard University and the members of the American Historical Association, who issued critical statements on the Cuba affair in 1961, showed a much better grasp of international affairs than President Kennedy's " brilliant " advisers did.

which rival political spokesmen used international affairs as an instrument of domestic policies and ambitions. The fundamental issue was the fact and significance of the rapid expansion of Europe's strength and influence, and its approach towards a position of equality with North America. In continental Europe the spirit of defeatism had gone. A new generation was rising in conditions of greater prosperity than the older Europe, for all its distinction, had ever enjoyed. The jeremiads of certain writers who, during and just after the Second World War, in mournful and admonitory accents had written off Europe as decadent and European power, influence, and achievement as belonging only to past civilisation, now eclipsed by the rising New World overseas, appeared within little more than a decade as mere curiosities in the history of thought.

The reassertion of European influence compelled the United States as well as the European countries to re-examine the position of the North Atlantic Alliance, in which the United States had played a dominating role, so far at least as armaments were concerned. It was inevitable that the European members would demand equality. For a time these objections could be met by pointing to the larger material contributions made by the United States. An increasing awareness of the growing strength of its partners then led U.S. Government spokesmen to speak of the future equality of Europe with the United States. But the coincidence of this development with the establishment of President Kennedy and Mr. Macnamara in the key positions underlined the inconsistency, if not contradiction, between the abstract principles enunciated and the actual practices followed. Moreover, after the Cuban crisis President Kennedy, gaining self-confidence and reacting to the U.S. public's approval of " a tough line ", let it be known that one of his chief aims was to assert strongly the role of the U.S. as the " leader of the free world ", and to act unilaterally in the affairs of various parts of the world where crises or difficulties arose and agreement with allies was difficult to attain.

Looking at the manifestations of United States policy from outside, it appeared as if its authors were attempting to make the best of both worlds, in deeds following the one, and in words paying tribute to the other. In the Far East and Latin America, in the Congo and in New Guinea, the U.S. followed wholly independent lines, some of which led in radically different directions from those followed by European powers. In armaments, the basis of previous policies was overturned in the light of technical advances. But the United States urged that Britain should enter the European Common Market, partly to strengthen Europe and bring it to the position of an equal partner with the United States in the North Atlantic Alliance.

As Professor Kissinger has put it :

We (the U.S.) have consistently recognised that a strong and united Europe would be of benefit to freedom everywhere. . . . Having made this wise choice, however, we have recoiled before one of the necessary implications. It was inevitable that countries with the historical traditions of our European allies would not be content forever to depend entirely on the protection of our nuclear power. Even if we believe the Europeans are wrong in their technical arguments, we must allow that their desire to play a greater role in matters affecting their survival is a healthy sign of restored vigour.[1]

Or, as a judicious British writer puts it :

It is surely an illusion for Americans to suppose that they can have all the advantages of alliance with an equal, while retaining the privileges which go with superior power.[2]

II

The Reassertion of Europe's Position

But if both the government and the people of the United States found it difficult to adjust themselves to changed external conditions, and to reconcile themselves to what might appear to many as a less exalted role, so, in a somewhat different way, did many British people. Old-fashioned imperialism among the few, and traditional insularity among the many, closed their vision to the changes which had made Britain, like the United States, a smaller part of the whole, though a weightier and more prosperous part than ever before. They failed to see that opportunities for future development would be greater if closer links were established with rapidly advancing neighbours creating a united power as great [3] and influential as any in the world.

To excuse this insularity of outlook it has been frequently argued that Commonwealth ties and a " special relationship " with the United States offer better prospects than closer relations with Europe do. Let us consider each of these suggested alternatives.

The openings for closer relations within the Commonwealth are

---

[1] H. Kissinger, " Strains on the Alliance ", in *Foreign Affairs*, New York, January, 1963, p. 273

[2] Kenneth Younger, " The Consequences for External Policy ", in *Political Quarterly*, January-March, 1963, p. 10

[3] Except perhaps in extent of territory. While denser population reduces costs of movement it involves greater hazards in modern warfare.

different in kind from, and therefore no substitute for, the openings for closer relations with Europe. On the economic [1] side, a Commonwealth *zollverein* is so obviously out of the question that space need not be taken to argue the matter. Other special economic arrangements discriminating against outside countries would be damaging to, and would create ill-will among, many countries scattered over the world. Forms of unification among scattered and far-flung territories are on a different plane from those among contiguous territories. On the political side, it may be said that differences in economic interests are carried over into political relations, and other political differences among far-flung territories and among territories of radically different traditions and in radically different stages of political development are added to them.

The Commonwealth is an institution of great and unique value, but it serves, and can only serve, different purposes and functions from those that would be served by a unified European *communuté* joined by Britain. Even the interests of its different groups of peoples—those who are a part of " Europe overseas " and those of indigenous Asian, African, and Central American ancestry—differ in important respects. The interests of the first are the interests of states already modernised and enjoying high standards of living ; those of the second are the interests chiefly of states in the process of modernisation. The first, in the main, occupied their territories as colonisers dominating the indigenous peoples there before them. The second have memories of a state of dependency under Britain from which they have emerged only in the mid-twentieth century. The first look on Britain as the source from which their recent ancestors derived their social heritage ; the second, while recognising important elements derived from Britain, look beyond these to other and older social heritages.

The mingling of these " two worlds " in the Commonwealth, with Britain as the focal centre and linchpin, makes it a unique bridge between Europe and the " Dominions " on the one hand, and between both of them and a large and leading part of *le tiers monde* on the other. Since one of the main views pressed in the present study is that British policy should be directed towards closer and closer understanding between Britain and the emerging countries, the importance of the Commonwealth hardly needs to be stressed further. But it lies in a different plane, and serves different functions, from those of association with Europe.

The idea of a " special relationship " of Britain to the United

---

[1] In international affairs economics without politics is an abstraction without a real counterpart. It can only be used in a rough, provisional sense in analysis to divide inter-related issues into parts that can be handled more conveniently in a first approach.

States has given rise to much misunderstanding. Its practical application was seen to its fullest extent in 1941 to 1945, when the submergence of the continental Allies and the aloofness of Russia led to a close co-operation, and in some fields partial integration, between the war efforts of the U.K. and the U.S. This collapsed immediately after the end of the war with Japan, when Lend Lease ceased without a substitute, when the U.S. Senate repudiated the agreement which President Roosevelt had made on the development of atomic energy, and hard terms and impracticable conditions were attached to the post-war loan made to Britain. Co-operation returned with the Marshall Plan, but this time in company with all western Europe.[1] However, beyond this direct co-operation between governments there is a similar, though not identical, language, and there are legal and political heritages derived from centuries of earlier history. It was largely owing to the political experience derived from Britain that the original founders of the United States were able quickly to make a " going concern " of the new state,[2] and avoid some of the troubles of the emerging states of the twentieth century. All these things are matters of fact and not of conjecture or mere sentiment.

But it does not follow that such special relationships of the past imply any necessarily closer association or relationship today than that which exists between other western states, at least beyond the continuance, possibly, of habits of consultation which began with the Second World War on a larger scale than those between most Great Powers.[3]

Britain and the United States are two separate, independent states whose interests do not always coincide. The elements of British heritage in the United States have been largely overshadowed in many parts of the country by the much greater immigration from other areas in the last eighty years. The British visitor and short-period resident is apt to frequent higher educational and other circles in which British reputation is high : he often leaves the country with little or no direct experience of the masses whose votes count and whose sentiments circumscribe the international scope of action of the executive branch of the government. In most of these circles Britain counts for no more—in some of them it counts for less—than some of the other countries. For them the idea of " special relationship " to Britain has no meaning. Thus while in the country as a whole, including some of its influential people and important institutions, the special cultural relationship will persist, it should not be counted on in inter-

[1] It would quite properly have been in company with all eastern Europe also, if Stalin had not blocked it.

[2] See Louis J. Halle, *The Nature of Power*, for an enlargement of this point.

[3] I think this is probable, but it cannot be proved or disproved for some time to come.

national negotiations and international arrangements, which will be
of the same general character of those between other independent
states. No special favours should be sought, nor should Britain aspire
to be chief satellite of the United States. Britain should have its own
policies, providing for co-operation with the United States in matters
of common interest, but actively opposing the dangerous aspects of
her policies in the Far East and Latin America, and occasionally
elsewhere.

All countries have " special relationships " with their neighbours,
sometimes marked by co-operation, sometimes dominated by suspicion. A larger neighbour may inspire fear, a smaller one, cupidity.
Britain and France are neighbours comparable in political and
economic strength and development. Twice in the present century
they have fought together against a powerful common enemy. Thus
their common interests are great and their destinies in the modern
world inseparable. Yet Britain has tended to look too exclusively
outside, France inside, Europe. British insularity and French self-
centredness have hindered and are still hindering co-operation.

III

Britain and Atomic Weapons

No single objective is more important to Britain than that of
establishing, first, closer co-operation and, later, unity between the
international policies of Britain and France. If the main thesis of the
present study is valid, the most disturbing feature of the controversy
early in 1962 over Britain's application to join the Common Market
was not President de Gaulle's faults of strategy and tactics but
British failure to recognise the valid elements underlying his international outlook. Whatever President de Gaulle's shortcomings as
a statesman may be, it is absurd to suppose that the springs of his
opposition to Britain arose from a sentimental " anti-Americanism "
or a desire to take a petty revenge for the petty slights which he
received from Allied heads of state during the War. On the contrary, the President correctly perceived, what his British critics overlooked, that if Britain, France, and the other European countries
were to count as equals and make their voices effective in the determination of western international policy, they must concert their
efforts in Europe to build up a unit or association, independent of
the United States, with a single voice in international policy. In the
stage reached in 1962, however, he suspected that if Britain entered
the E.C.M. she would still aim at retaining a "special relationship "
with the United States, she would not be whole-heartedly European,

devoted first to European interests, but would tend to concert with the United States the policies she adopted in the European community, and thus hinder the creation of an independent Europe, equal in strength to the United States, and able to demand an equal voice in the policies affecting them both.

A strong case could be made for this point of view. In the controversies in Britain during the negotiations, many utterances in part of the Conservative and most of the Labour Party seemed to bear such an interpretation. Certainly the danger envisaged by President de Gaulle was real : it was disturbing to find so little appreciation of it in Britain, where an insular outlook respecting our European neighbours is combined with a naïveté regarding the political structure of the United States and the realities of its political life.

But when all allowance has been made for British limitations, President de Gaulle, it seems to me, for all the fine sweep of his vision, ranging beyond " cold war " banalities and the passing moods of the hour, glimpsing the changing future structure and distribution of world power and wealth and the passing of present doctrinal fanaticisms, nevertheless fell a little short of greatness as an international statesman. His means were not well adapted to the ends he had in view. The international statesman with a far-seeing vision must be capable of impressing it on his contemporaries at home and abroad. President de Gaulle was too aloof, too withdrawn from contemporary statesmen in his own and other countries. At home he compensated for this by direct touch with the French people. He it was, the overwhelming majority of them felt, who had rescued France from the long nightmare of the Algerian War, and peacefully achieved the decolonisation of French Africa to the south. Thus by using the referendum he could set aside the politicians, and dominate the machinery of government, as no other executive power had been able to do since Napoleon III. But abroad he had no such court of appeal. Even where the statutes of the Rome Treaty, and the circumstances of European politics, enabled him to block Britain's entry into Europe, he could only force his European partners reluctantly to acquiesce in a step to which they were opposed and which in the future they would strive to undo. More than that, he failed not only to convince them of the sound element in his position but even to expound it adequately. Thus he could be plausibly represented as acting out of petty motives, or stubborn prejudices, or nationalist pride and vainglory. With his fine command of language it might at least have been expected that he could clarify in detail to his European associates the grounds for his actions and the purposes they were designed to serve.

But his faults of strategy and tactics went much further. It is one thing to accept his view that if Europe is to obtain an effective voice in the policy of an Atlantic Alliance it must independently combine its resources to establish a power equal to that of the United States. It is another to contend that the exclusion of Britain from Europe would help to achieve this aim. Britain had indeed been slow to realise the extent to which its interests were bound up with those of continental Europe. It had naïvely cherished the illusion that a relationship with the United States established during the exigencies of world conflict by war-time personalities no longer in political life, could continue in peace-time and serve as a substitute for closer relations with Europe. But the tide had turned. The Prime Minister had seen the light. In Mr. Heath he had found a tireless and imperturbable negotiator. Behind Mr. Heath sat two of the ablest civil servants in Whitehall, Sir Eric Roll and Sir Herbert Andrew. A great majority of the Conservative Party had been carried along in the tide. The rising Liberal Party had adopted European unity as a leading item in its policies. Only the Labour Party, which had drifted far from its internationalism of the twenties, when MacDonald had transformed the whole European outlook in a few months in one of the most brilliant diplomatic accomplishments in the century, were still wedded to older patterns of thought. Apart from France, all the countries in the Common Market were convinced that Britain was genuinely ready to accept the political as well as the economic clauses of the Rome Treaty. All were prepared, and some were eager, to admit her as a full member. The majority of public men in France who had been associated with the movement for European union seem to have shared this view.

It appeared, therefore, that it was only a matter of time before Britain joined in the new Europe, and that the effect of General de Gaulle's tactics would be to delay rather than to advance the movement not merely towards union, which he himself did not desire, but also towards the development of a concerted European international policy, which was his foremost aim. Moreover, the suspicion that he was really seeking French or French-West German hegemony in " Europe des patries " tended to retard the co-operation of Italy and Benelux.

The alternative strategy open to the President in late 1962 was to encourage the adhesion of Britain to the Common Market and aim at convincing her statesmen of the wisdom of giving priority to building up a unity of view within Europe on international policy, and then confronting the United States with a negotiating strength, resting on a prosperous and growing Europe, equal to her own. The chances of accomplishing this were favourable. The Prime Minister and his colleagues had already undegrone a swift and notable conversion to a European point of view, and converts are often prepared

ultimately to go further in a course than those who had already
adhered to it in a more conventional and less ardent form. To work
on a larger scale in a wider setting would have raised the level of
statecraft and presented broader political issues to overshadow the
conventional domestic political themes that had lost much of their
older relevance and appeal in the changing Britain of the mid-
twentieth century. The new vision thus created would have per-
colated through from politicians and administrators to the public—
already dissatisfied with the sterility and artificiality of much of the
content of party politics.

Thus it would seem that the President would have been well
advised to have ignored the admittedly clumsy and ill-timed Nassau
agreement and other psychological blunders of Britain's Cabinet and
some of her ministerial spokesmen, and to have pursued his aims
through the new and closer direct contacts of the Common Market
and associated bodies. To advance boldly into closer relations with
Britain bore greater promise of success than to rebuff her, curtail
existing relations with her, and offend France's partners.

This is not to acquit British statesmen and the British people of
considerable responsibility for the failure. Mr. Heath and his team
did all that could be reasonably expected of them but the aftermath
confirms some at least of the misgivings regarding the attitude of
many British people towards Europe. To the student of international relations the most disquieting feature was the continued
absence of widespread feeling of the dangers to Britain of a divided
Europe facing not only the policies of Russia but also those of the
United States. Great Power psychology still seemed to dominate the
sentiments of the majority. The Cuban crisis for a time accentuated
it. President Kennedy's spectacular handling of the final crisis commended itself to many British people to an extent which overshadowed and diverted attention away from the original causes of
the crisis.

Whatever hypothetical or potential dangers seem in the abstract to
threaten mankind with a war fought with atomic weapons, the fact
remains that the actual occasions on which the dangers came, as it
were, above the horizon during the nineteen-fifties and early sixties
were all concerned with the policies of the United States in eastern
and south-eastern Asia and in the Caribbean and Central America.
Since the Second World War the United States has become, on a
much larger scale than ever before, a leading imperialist power,
intervening unilaterally in various parts of the globe in pursuance of
policies of spheres of influence and balance of power. By comparison, British imperialism in the last quarter of the nineteenth century appears to have been milder and on a smaller scale. We
Europeans have an area of common interest with the United States

in the scheme of shifting balance of power ; but common interests are sometimes set aside arbitrarily when the United States acts unilaterally in continents in which European powers also have interests, particularly when such actions create the risk of a more general war in which Europe, because of its position in the North Atlantic Treaty Organisation, would be exposed to mass destruction in a dispute in which she had no voice and for a cause in which she did not believe. This is what might have happened over Cuba and what may yet happen over the Far East or Latin America.

Faced with revolutionary changes in the weapons of warfare and the international distribution of armed power, the political parties, the public, and many professional students of international affairs have tended to lose sight of the main issues and the most serious dangers in the relations among states, and to concentrate their attention exclusively on the problems of nuclear armaments and alliances based on nuclear power. In Britain and in some parts of continental Europe certain sections of opinion appear willing that Europe shall be a satellite of the United States, out of fear that to show signs of independence would provoke withdrawal of the United States from the Atlantic Alliance, leaving Europe alone to face possible threats from Russian nuclear power. Likewise Australia under the Menzies Government refused to follow the British Government in recognising China, and instead followed the United States in its Far Eastern policy, perhaps more from a fear of China than of Russia, and of " conventional " arms in overwhelming quantities than of atomic arms.

But these fears are based largely on misconception. It should not be supposed that the United States would co-operate in the defence of western Europe or Australia unless it were in her own national interests to do so. Only through naïve misconceptions of " special relationships " could it ever have been imagined that the United States was acting philanthropically in entering an " entangling alliance ". Nor can it be supposed that she would cease to co-operate as long as it was in her own interests to continue. Considering the immense stakes of super-power politics it seems incredible that the United States would act against its own interests out of pique at the refusal of Allies to follow her in policies which they believed to be contrary to their interests and to endanger their existence.

Such considerations do not exclude future changes which will lessen the comparative contribution of the United States to the defence of Europe, and transfer the main or the whole responsibility to the European powers themselves. The role of military bases abroad diminished as the range of " guided missiles " increased. Even when forward launching sites were still necessary they could be placed on the ocean, either in submarines or in ships, with the advantage of mobility.

But this placed Europe in a position to provide its own defences and emerge from dependence on the United States for its capacity to deter would-be aggressors. There might still be good reasons for maintaining an alliance with the United States to serve common interests but it would be an alliance of equals, and no longer an alliance between an imperialist super-power and a group of half-satellites.

But this presupposes either the reduction and eventual elimination of nuclear weapons by the super-powers, or the development in Europe of nuclear weapons adequate to deter an attacker. We must continue to work and hope for the reduction of all armaments and the elimination of nuclear weapons, but in the meantime a decision has to be made on the policy of Britain and the rest of Europe during the period before significant steps have been taken towards disarmament. On this, doubts, hesitation, confusion, and sharp conflicts of opinion arose and increased during the fifties and early sixties. The divergencies ranged from the groups which urged unilateral repudiation of nuclear weapons to those which desired national or regional entry into the ranks of the super-powers, with many uneasy and shifting compromises within.

The " nuclear disarmers " in Britain were a modified counterpart to the pacifist " no more war " groups of the inter-war period. But they included many who were not pacifists, whose aim was simply to prevent the further spread of nuclear weapons, and who believed that an example from Britain would influence countries that were hesitating whether or not to enter the ranks of the nuclear powers.

The suggestion that she should concentrate wholly on " conventional weapons " ignores the fact that her total contribution in that direction would be ineffective in a continental war where her army would be outnumbered many times. Her inferiority in numbers, so far as it can offset at all, can only be offset by quality of weapons. The suggestion that she could help to " police the world " by maintaining garrisons at critical points overseas shows a failure to realise that the days of imperialist " policing " are numbered, and such garrisons as remain, though they may be temporarily needed, are an embarrassment to be removed as soon as circumstances permit, not an asset to be cherished and enlarged. They hinder the completion of that accord with *le tiers monde* which Britain has gone far to establish and which should be a foremost element in her future policy.

The alternative course would be to retreat into a position of " neutralism " or " non-alignment " resembling that of Switzerland and Sweden, and to abandon all alliances and commitments on defence. Then Britain's defence would ultimately depend, as that of Switzerland and Sweden depends, on the rivalries among the super-powers and the Great Powers, which create fears among potential aggressors that action against non-aligned countries might disturb the balance of power to their disadvantage, and perhaps provoke wider conflicts that would end in nuclear warfare. The mobilisation of sentiment in the United Nations against aggression may be expected gradually to strengthen these restraining influences.

Abstention from armed alliances suits the interests of Sweden and Switzerland. At one time there seems to have been a possibility soon after the War that the whole group of Scandinavian countries, sooner or later including Finland, might have joined in a close regional alliance standing outside the western and eastern groupings and interposing a nonaligned buffer group of states that would have collectively exercised a tempering influence on the doctrinal antagonisms between states to the east of them and states to the west of them.

But Britain is in a radically different position. In the company of France she has played a vitally important role in the present century in frustrating two colossal efforts to establish an autocratic control over Europe and subsequently over the world. She has wide, if now largely informal, responsibilities scattered around the globe. Her society stands as an example, unexcelled and only equalled in a few cases, of assured and sustained personal freedom and liberty in an increasingly authoritarian world. The values which she cherishes, and for which, since 1914, millions of British and French citizens have died, may again be exposed to external attack in the years to come, and power, material as well as moral, may be needed to defend them. If, therefore, alone or in concert with others, she can establish, or contribute to the establishment of, a defensive power calculated to give pause to any potential assailant, she is under an obligation to do so and cannot justifiably evade that responsibility by taking the chance that her security will be assured as a mere by-product of stalemate among contending powers in a world in which the rule of law is as yet in an early if not primitive state.[1]

Yet, if the alternative of standing alone as a " neutralist " or " non-aligned " power, withdrawn from all alliances, is unsatis-factory, it seems to me preferable, on the whole, to a policy of abandoning nuclear weapons while remaining outside Europe and allied to the United States, relying on the nuclear arms of the United States for protection, and opposing the development of nuclear arms in Europe. This, as far as can be seen at the time of writing this chapter, appears to have been the policy most favoured within the

[1] Nothing in this paragraph is intended to imply any criticism of Sweden and Switzerland, whose circumstances are quite different from Britain's.

British Labour Party.[1]   It is a measure of the insularity of that party in the mid-twentieth century, and of its departure from the international outlook which characterised it in the nineteen-twenties. For such a policy places Britain in the position of a satellite of the United States, a small and weak unit in an alliance overshadowed and dominated by one of the two super-powers which possess a monopoly of the most effective modern weapons.   It exposes Britain to the danger of becoming involved in conflicts initiated by actions which the United States takes to maintain her position in her spheres of influence in various parts of the world, notably in the Far East and Latin America.   Though these actions have been taken unilaterally and without consultation with Britain and other European countries, they have exposed the latter to an ever-present risk of becoming involved in a world conflict through their alliance with the United States, and the facilities which they give to, as well as the co-ordination of their own forces with, the U.S. forces in Europe. And this might happen even though the European members of the Alliance had no part in, and disapproved of, the U.S. policies and actions that initiated the chain of events leading from peace to war. It might have happened over Cuba in 1962.[2]

Some sections of opinion, not only in Britain but also on the European continent, have been all too ready to drift into complacent acceptance of a U.S. " umbrella " to protect them from the dangers of easterly storms.   This, up to a point, may have been necessary in the earlier years of the post-war period, when there were fears of Russian encroachments.

As we have seen (p. 60) a new balance of power had to be constructed after the War.   The former Allies were slow to recognise it before the Korean War.   Thereafter, however, and notably from the time when Russia began to produce atomic bombs, Britain and the other European countries fell into a position of increasing dependence : public opinion tended to relapse into a fatalistic attitude which accepted this dependence as inevitable.

To challenge this assumption was President de Gaulle's most constructive and important contribution at the time of the negotiations in 1962 on Britain's entry into the Common Market.   British, American, and Australasian reactions to this challenge exposed the

---

[1] A minority of members have not wished Britain to remain outside Europe, but even most of these seem to have been ready to give the United States a monopoly of nuclear arms, and have been opposed to European efforts to produce nuclear weapons.

[2] Curiously, Labour leaders seem to have been just as prone as those of other parties to allow the origins of the conflict over Cuba to be obscured by the circumstances of the final crisis to which it led, and which was marked by President Kennedy's determination to assert a " sphere of influence " policy even at the risk of nuclear war.

" insular " outlook, not only of Britain but of the English-speaking peoples generally.[1] The Labour and Liberal parties espoused policies leading to increased dependence on the United States and thus to a diminished power to assert European interests when they clashed with United States policies in other continents. The Conservative Party strongly asserted the demand for an " independent deterrent ". But here, like President de Gaulle's in a different context, their means were not well adapted to the end which they sought. The " independent " weapons they aimed to produce was dependent in important respects on U.S. contributions. In addition, the hastily improvised Nassau agreement was reached in disregard of French sentiment. Once again, Britain had neglected its next-door neighbour to keep in step with a more distant country.

But the Conservative Party, and with it considerable sections of British opinion, was advancing, though President de Gaulle did not appear to realise it. The Cabinet's application in 1962 to join the Common Market was a genuine application, which carried with it acceptance of the political as well as the economic clauses of the Treaty of Rome, and the compromises requested were designed only to meet obligations to outside countries and agriculturalists during a short transitional period. If the application had been accepted, Britain would have been drawn into the midst of the stream of European advance and her destiny would have been merged decisively with that of the rest of Europe. It would have been a great historical achievement for the leaders of the Conservative Party.

And this, I suggest, is where the future lies for Britain. If, as I hold, neither the unilateral repudiation of all nuclear weapons on principle, as the Committee for Nuclear Disarmament have advocated, nor the abandonment of them and the substitution of U.S. nuclear protection, as the Labour and Liberal Parties have recommended, are compatible with fulfilment of Britain's European responsibilities, but would place her irrevocably in the position of a U.S. satellite, then it is above all necessary to turn to Europe. Western, central, and southern Europe, strengthened by the accession of Britain, can form a centre of power hardly inferior to the United States, possessing the equipment of modern industry in its most advanced forms, freed from the strains and tensions of governing overseas peoples no longer willing to accept external rule, fashioning in their place constructive relationships with overseas areas whose initiation into the modern world had begun through the ancestors of the present British, French, Dutch, and Belgian peoples. In a world in which political autocracy in various forms is widespread, it

[1] There were a few individual exceptions, notably that of Professor Kissinger, a refreshingly independent thinker.

is more important than ever that the balance of power should be maintained at a level and in a setting that will protect existing political liberties and provide hopes of their gradual extension to other areas.

It would be all the better if this development could take place in a world free from the nightmare of nuclear weapons. But realities must be faced, however ugly they appear in a moral and physical sense. As long as the super-powers fail to begin disarmament, or even to halt the increase of nuclear arms, the hope of preventing the spread of nuclear armaments is vain—all the more so in a world of continuously advancing technology.

If Britain alone, or the whole of Europe, renounced nuclear weapons, other countries would not follow suit, and the only result would be to weaken them still further and make them dependent on U.S. protection not only against Russia but in the future against China or perhaps even Egypt and other overseas countries which, with the aid of more simplified methods invented in the future, may well develop atomic weapons, perhaps inferior to the most deadly possessed by the super-powers, but sufficiently devastating to place at their mercy those countries which have renounced nuclear weapons. We Europeans should surely retain enough spirit to refuse to allow ourselves to be placed in such a humiliating position.

Moreover, in the absence of any measures of disarmament, the renunciation of nuclear weapons by Britain, or all of Europe, would certainly not be in the interests of overseas countries in the Commonwealth and in former French colonies, and, at least in the longer run, it would not, in reality, appear to be in the interests of the United States, for, with the spread of future nuclear weapons outside Europe and North America the western countries would be failing to use perhaps one-half of their industrial resources in the production of up-to-date armaments.

Europe cannot afford to remain in a permanently subordinate position. To withdraw from the production of nuclear arms can only leave Britain either as a satellite of the United States, or as an ineffective neutral on the sidelines. It is strange that so many members of the British Labour Party are either willing to see Britain in the first of these roles, or so ill-informed on international affairs that they do not even grasp the consequences of the policies they support.

If, as I hope, such policies are rejected, and if Britain is to remain a nuclear power, she must choose between three possible lines of development. The first is to continue atomic development in isolation, except for exchange of information with the U.S.[1] This, I

---

[1] In spite of the important help given by British scientists in the construction of the atomic bomb during the war, the U.S. subsequently shut off all information from Britain, until the latter produced the bomb independently. If Britain had

believe, is preferable to an abandonment of atomic weapons. Since future technical developments are unpredictable, it is at least prudent to maintain the capacity to take advantage of them if they turn to the comparative advantage of countries in positions like Britain's. Beyond this, however, an " independent deterrent " is useful so long as it has the chance of surviving the first assault of an enemy. For, however contemptuously controversialists, influenced by a variety of motives, may speak of the sort of nuclear weapon that Britain, and, later, France, may be able to produce, it is clear that Russia or any other potential assailant would have to consider carefully the far from negligible losses to them which would follow an attack on these two countries. The Russians themselves are under no illusions on the matter : their attacks on the idea of the spread of nuclear weapons in Europe show that they take the effectiveness of such weapons seriously.

But the most that can be said for Britain's proceeding alone and independently in the development of nuclear weapons is that, in the absence of moves towards disarmament among the super-powers, it is certainly better than renouncing nuclear weapons.

Having discussed this alternative let us return to the European solution. Here again we are faced with two possible methods of approach. The first, though it is not purely European, requires agreement and co-operation among the European powers to create a force manning nuclear weapons in Europe, to be composed either of separate national contingents or of intermingled contingents from the countries of the North American Treaty Organisations.

These proposals, however, appeared in closer examination to be little more than window dressing. In both cases the ultimate decisions regarding the atomic weapons were to be made by the President of the United States. The European representation in the forces concerned, far from being a means of genuinely sharing power, was little more than a façade to screen United States hegemony and Europe's satellite status.

In any case, however, a fatal flaw existed in all these schemes. They were unacceptable to France. No mixed force without France could be adequately representative of Europe. An attempt to by-pass France is an attempt to divide Europe, and could only increase Europe's dependence on the United States at a time when its growing strength and capacity were fast restoring it to a position of equality.

At critical points in the discussion of these questions in the late nineteen-fifties and early nineteen-sixties this central issue tended to be overlain with a mass of technicalities and with a variety of other

---

followed the policies recommended by the Labour and Liberal Parties no information on U.S. developments would ever have been obtained.

issues, some of them only of passing importance. The position of the United States fluctuated with bewildering rapidity, and on the important issue of the relation between nuclear and non-nuclear forces was completely reversed. Nothing illustrates more clearly the inevitable friction in relationships between a dominant power and its allies than the spectacle of the former putting pressure on the latter to follow it in reversing a policy which, a short time earlier, it was vigorously urging them to adopt. In an alliance of equals, important issues are the subject of negotiation before a policy is changed. In this particular case the wisdom of the change was doubtful. It is unlikely that, if a conflict broke out in the nineteen-sixties, the Russians would accept the U.S. strategy of attempting first to con- fine it to non-nuclear weapons, and then, if nuclear war started, would be willing to confine their targets to military establishments and spare cities.[1] Assuming that they were weaker in nuclear arma- ments it would hardly appear in their interests to do so. If they were stronger, it is doubtful whether it would be in the interests of the U.S. to maintain this strategy. The scepticism of the British and French authorities was justified.[2]

The proposals for a " multilateral " or " multi-national nuclear

[1] Mr. Emanuel de Kadt, in his *British Defence Policy and Nuclear War* (London, 1964), effectively disposes of the dangerous contention of some American writers that, after a nuclear war, a country " . . . can and will return . . . to much the same pattern of living as before " (p. 121). Chapters IV–VIII are an excellent contribution to the subject. But in two preliminary chapters and in a " Conclu- sion ", Mr. de Kadt ranges far outside the scope of his own special contribution, to support contentions that by no means follow from the latter but are merely a restatement of a familiar argument that Britain should disarm so far as nuclear weapons are concerned but still remain in the Atlantic Alliance. In the text I have argued that this is to get the worst of both worlds, and that neutralism is the logical and sensible outcome of the position which Mr. de Kadt is supporting. By contrast, Miss Coral Bell, in *The Debateable Alliance* (London, 1964), effectively disposes of the idea that Britain's nuclear arms have not added to her international influence in great power circles (pp. 94–103). The excellent judgement shown in the greater part of that study makes it all the more surprising that Miss Bell should later so misconceive the temper of *le tiers monde* as to imagine that the Common- wealth could be turned into a security alliance, that she fails to appreciate that Britain's interests are bound up with Western Europe and that she subscribes to John Strachey's dream of world government through U.S.-Russian domination.

[2] For a searching critique of the scheme produced by the Rand Corporation and accepted by Mr. Macnamara when he became Secretary of Defence, see Professor Kissinger's article, " N.A.T.O.'s Nuclear Dilemma ", Reporter, 28 March, 1963, pp. 22–37.

Since this chapter was written Brigadier S. F. Giffin in an article, " Untangling the Alliance," *Orbis*, Philadelphia, Vol. VII, No. 3, expresses approval of a situation in which " Western Europe will move towards a political union so close that a regional nuclear deterrent could come under centralised West European control ". Regarding the effectiveness of such a " deterrent " he adds later, " The addition of British nuclear weapons to a European nuclear arsenal would provide a short- cut towards a real deterrent capability ".

deterrent " were by no means designed to produce a truly European means of nuclear defence, or equality between Europe and the U.S.A. Whether the forces were organised in separate or inter-mingled national contingents they would constitute an instrument under U.S. control—a means of perpetuating U.S. hegemony.

Thus the three approaches so far examined would lead Britain and other European countries either to a neutral position or to the posi-tion of a satellite of the United States.

The fourth and final course of action open to Britain is, in one direction, more nearly continuous with earlier developments than two of those already considered are, but in another direction it makes a radical departure from all of them. It would maintain the pro-duction of atomic weapons in Britain but no longer in isolation from Europe. Britain, I suggest, should offer to pool her resources with those of France in both civil and military research and production in the field of nuclear power. This step would immediately open the way for her entry into the Common Market and the Coal and Steel Community.

The Rome Treaty, together with integration of British and French work on nuclear arms, would only represent the beginning of a series of moves to unite Europe in many other political and economic fields. The common interests of European countries are wide and deep. Overshadowed in the past by internal cleavages, they have never yet received adequate expression in international affairs.

To some continental observers, indeed, Britain has often appeared in the past as a divisive force, concerned above all to maintain a balance of power that would prevent the unification of the continent.

A formal case can be made for this view, but it does not necessarily follow that, in the pursuit of a balance of continental power, Britain was damaging the interests of European peoples in the long run. All depends on the nature of the unity that might have been achieved in the absence of British intervention, and the means by which it would have been achieved. Surely, not even the sternest French critic would have wished Britain to allow Hitler to unify Europe. Nor, with all the knowledge now avilable, could a modern critic seriously contend that Bonapartism would have served the European peoples, and the world beyond them, better than the development of con-stitutional government in the nineteenth century. Britain may indeed be criticised adversely for its lack of zeal and initiative in advancing the cause of unity by agreement, but hardly for setting

---

Similar views have been expressed by Professor Kissinger, ibid ; by Robert C. Wesson, *The American Problem* ; *The Cold War in Perspective* (London, 1963), Ch. IX ; and by Ronald Steel, *The End of Alliance, America and the Future of Europe* (London, 1964), Chs III and IV.

back the cause of unification through conquest, followed by dictatorial rule, or even for using its influence to prevent any single country from gaining an overwhelming predominance in armed power.

This issue, indeed, is related to that which has already been discussed earlier in respect to the Middle East and Africa. The pursuit of unification may be a blessing or a curse according to circumstances. Behind it lies an all-important consideration—whether the liberties of the individual in society are advanced or set back by it.[1]

IV

The Problem of West Germany

One of the chief difficulties in establishing European unity lies in the position of West Germany. The haste with which she was rearmed on U.S. insistence confirmed the suspicions and fears of Russia, which had been aroused by the U.S. monopoly of the atomic bomb in the early post-war years. In the eyes of the public in Western countries the real nature of the problem of Germany has been confused by doctrinal trappings. Actually it is a problem, not of communism, but of balance of power. It has to do, not so much with the balance of armed power at the moment as with the anticipated effects on it of the future development of German arms, in particular the possibility that atomic weapons might be added to them. A rearmed and reunified Germany within an Atlantic Alliance would appear to Russians as a formidable threat on their borders. It is vain to expect that they will agree to it, and an attempt to coerce them would bring war. This is the penalty which Hitler's fanatical anti-communism has brought on Germany, and West Germany's allies of to-day, though they sympathise with her desire for reunion, will not risk a suicidal war in an attempt to achieve it. In the near future there is no prospect that the *de facto* partition of Germany can be undone. There stands against it the strongest of all forces in international relations—that which is concerned with the preservation of a balance of power, which, in Russia's case, has already been upset twice in the twentieth century, at an immeasurable cost in human life and suffering.

Under partition, West Germany has made extraordinary advances ever since the retarding influence of the " Morgenthau Plan " was eliminated. It will have an assured future in a unified Europe of the Common Market countries and Britain. Unfortunately a substantial section of the population remains unreconciled to a continuation

[1] See pp. 155–60.

of partition in the near future, and political leaders, who can hardly be blind to the international realities, have not yet gone far to educate the public to appreciate them. West Germany has been an obstacle to the well-advised attempts of the U.S. Government, especially under President Kennedy, to reduce tension between Russia and the West. Thus a dangerous issue remains, hindering the cause of co-existence, and exposing the United States, Britain, and France to the risk of conflict, and the certainty of continued friction in support of aims which are unrealisable in the near future. And this issue is aggravated by the refusal of West Germany to recognise the Oder-Neisse line. Both these issues strengthen the relations between Russia and her Eastern European satellites, and both are concerned with classical balance of power considerations, not with political doctrines.

The wisdom and skill of Dr. Adenauer were drawing West Germany into closer and closer relations with the Western European countries. It is in this direction that the best hope of the future, and probably the only solution, lies. The rapprochement between Adenauer and De Gaulle was therefore an important step in the right direction and superficial British critics of it showed little political insight. Dr. Erhard seems less European and more " Atlantic ". Like many British politicians and writers he shrinks from the the choice between being a satellite of the United States and being a part of a unified Europe. Dr. Adenauer seems to have made the choice, although domestic political considerations have made his utterances cautious. His influence in retirement is likely to remain in a European direction.

Thus the entry of Britain into Europe, and the rapid development of political union would be the most hopeful means, if not of completely solving the German problem, at least of drawing the West German people into such close and fruitful relations with their western neighbours that they will identify themselves inescapably with a new European state and permanently turn their backs on all aims that risk new conflicts to the east of them. That will represent a necessary adjustment to the new and dangerous world in which their new associations have developed.

CHAPTER XIV

POLICIES OF THE NEW EUROPE

I

The Multi-National State : Contrasts in Europe and " Le Tiers Monde "

EUROPE today is no longer in imminent danger of forced unification by conquest from within. Only Russia, which is not an exclusively European country, has the power to overwhelm the rest of the continent, and, if she had the desire to do so, she could indulge it only at the imminent risk of war with another country even more powerfully equipped with nuclear weapons [1] than she is. Moreover, it is doubtful whether Russia, if she could subdue, would wish to unify the rest of Europe. She has opposed the unification of neighbouring states, even when they were satellites under her dominion. In Europe outside Russia, since the partition of Germany, no single power has had the desire or the ability to overrun the continent. Unification, if it comes, must come by agreement.

When it comes, it must come also in the form of a multi-national state. National sentiments are deeply rooted in the European peoples. There can be no single European nationalism in the strict sense, at least for some time to come. That is not a sign of weakness. Britain is stronger and not weaker for being a multi-national state. Europe organised as a unitary state would be weakened by discontented regional groups. I am aware of the view among some French and other members of the resistance movements during the war that a new sense of brotherhood was felt in the stress of danger when members of resistance movements in different European countries worked together, and that this supplies the model for European unification and implies a single European nationalism. It is, undoubtedly, necessary that a sentiment of European kinship should be strengthened, but to require repudiation of present national sentiments seems neither necessary nor practicable as the condition of developing a feeling for Europe. To bring pressure to bear on the individual to drop local attachments altogether for wider ones is the way to provoke a reaction against the quite proper attempt to broaden his out-

---

[1] Even apart from this it is doubtful, as we have seen, whether she would wish to engage more scarce resources in holding down satellites.

look. Either it will destroy the unity it professes to seek or, if it succeeds, it will destroy cultural variety to no purpose.

It is just because there is no single overwhelmingly dominant power in the group of European states in question that the time is ripe for steady advance towards unity by agreement. The remarkable renaissance of France in the post-war period has set back the fear of German domination of continental Europe, and the addition of Britain would remove it still further. Europe is thus in the fortunate position that unity can only come by persuasion and negotiated agreement.

Superficially, there might appear to be an inconsistency between the earlier chapters pointing out the dangers of some of the movements aimed at unification in parts of the Middle East and Africa, and the present chapter arguing for integration in Europe. But this would be a misreading of the central thesis in my treatment of the problems of the integration and disintegration of states. The size of the state is of primary importance only when a state is too small to afford the apparatus of a modern government, having regard to the natural resources with which it is endowed ;[1] or too large, at the existing level of technology and organisation, for the control of the whole area by a single government.[2]

In other cases the size of the state, according to the premises of this study, should be a secondary consideration. The existing size, and proposals to change it, should be judged by their probable effects on political liberties and cultural variety as well as on economic efficiency, and, in some cases, notably Europe, on the problems of defence. The first of these criteria is outstanding, but at times there may appear to be a clash between political liberties and the prerequisites for defence. The extent of the divergence is commonly exaggerated. The morale of the people is a leading factor in the efficacy of measures of defence, and the substitution of authoritarian for representative government creates a divergence between the government and important sections of the people that weakens the sense of unity in the state. As we have seen, premature attempts to unify by conquest, or by intrigue and conspiracy, in Asia, Africa, and Latin America, do not create really strong states. Schisms within are a double menace, creating a constant danger of unrest, plots, and risings at home, as well as aggressive excursions abroad by authori-

---

[1] Obviously this is not definable in terms of area. A very small state, Kuwait, for example, may be embarrassingly rich if oil resources are found on it. If it is argued that it is immoral in some sense to permit such small states to remain independent when neighbouring states without oil remain in poverty, the answer is that the benefits may be spread through trade, migration, and, still more, through investment, without destroying the independence of the small state.

[2] This seems to have been a leading factor in the downfall of some of the empires of the ancient world.

tarian rulers who seek to divert attention from domestic difficulties and divisions.

The new independent states created by decolonisation need time to consolidate their foundations before combining into larger structures. In the early stages of their establishment and development they have not yet the resources which are available to the older European states. Their statesmen have first to extend their experience, their civil services are not yet sufficiently developed, education has to be established in greater depth as well as breadth, and, above all, the electorates in some of the countries, as well as many of the leading politicians, have to learn the necessity, on the one hand, of tolerating opposition, and on the other, of conducting it with reasonable self-restraint and with responsibility. To undertake ambitious schemes of union before these resources have been built up on an adequate scale is to weaken and not strengthen the collective power and influence of the emerging countries in the counsels of the world. As the Middle East shows, premature drives towards fusion tend to fall into the hands of militarist dictators and narrow doctrinaire politicians, who try to perpetuate themselves in office, destroy the political liberties of all but a narrow section of the people, and arrest at its outset the political education obtainable only in the free political activity without which an emerging society sinks into a rigid class division between rulers and ruled, while modernisation of the material basis of society is accompanied by an atavistic lapse into the ways of ancient tyrannies dominating the political basis of society.

If these dangers still existed in Europe, it would be better to halt, or at least to reduce greatly, the speed of the movement towards early European integration. But after the tragic lessons of the past, we need no longer fear their return in the European countries concerned. Since no single country can dominate the movement towards a greater degree of unity, the entire process must necessarily be conducted through representative forms of organisation and government. There will be no proscribed classes or parties either on the right or on the left, and all groups will be able to make their contribution to the laborious but rewarding task of forging a larger unity. There are obstacles to be overcome, obstacles arising out of provincialisms of outlook and from the practical difficulties of co-ordination in economic matters. But none of them is insurmountable, or even supremely difficult to overcome, in an area where toleration and freedom of speech are now deeply rooted, and where education, technical training, and administrative experience are at the highest levels to be found in the world today.

II

Equality or a Satellite Position

The intensification of the move towards European unification in the late nineteen-fifties and in the early sixties came opportunely at a time when dependence on the United States, which began earlier through the temporary weakening of Europe as a result of war and occupation, was in danger of becoming a habit, and of sapping the vigour, initiative, and self-confidence of Europeans, insular and continental alike. This drift into dependence was accentuated by the provincialism of many in the younger generation of the intelligentsia, notably those in the Labour Party,[1] and by a wave of national self-criticism during the period which, while healthy in principle, was carried to morbid extremes in some circles, and tended to become a mere instrument in domestic controversies. Conditions [2] abroad were exalted and sometimes idealised in order to disparage conditions at home, for which, of course, the domestic opponents of the critics were alleged to be responsible. These insincere uses of international comparisons distorted the true comparative picture : many institutions and practices abroad were held up as examples to copy in Britain when, in reality, they had been under severe criticism for some time, and were in process of modification, in their countries of origin ! But the realities were not widely appreciated in Britain, and short visits to show-pieces abroad did not disclose them. The net effect was to reduce confidence, and favour acquiescence in transatlantic dependence, by default if not consciously.

Notwithstanding his defects of method and strategy, it remains, then, to the great credit of President de Gaulle, on this issue, to have risen above domestic clamour and firmly reasserted the role of France and the prospect of an independent Europe. For Europe to deprive itself of the right and opportunity to produce the new weapons, with no assurance either that the powers already possessing them would begin to disarm or even cease to produce more of them, or that other powers would not produce them in future, would be an abdication of responsibilities for securing its defences and recovering its independence. Nor, as many critics have pointed out, is there any assurance that the country on which Britain is asked to rely for its

[1] This stood in strong contrast to the earlier history of the Labour Party. Unfortunately the leaders were not alone. The anti-European attitude of the late Mr. Gaitskell and of Mr. Harold Wilson was popular with the rank and file.
[2] The rest of Europe, however, was left outside the comparisons, even though, in most fields, it had more to offer than North America, Russia, or other areas.

" nuclear " defence will always be ready to extend it on acceptable conditions.

Likewise it was to the credit of Mr. Macmillan and his Cabinet that, in the face of attacks from the other parties and from a number of influential writers and spokesmen, as well as a less responsible agitation from the ill-regulated movement behind the Committee for Nuclear Disarmament, they rejected the idea of unilateral abandonment by Britain of nuclear weapons. Their opponents belittled the efficacy of any British nuclear weapons, or at least the means of delivering them. But even a second-rate nuclear weapon, known to be supported by effective means of delivery, will inevitably make a would-be aggressor pause ; for no country can afford to leave out of its reckoning the damage to the centres of its key cities which a few hydrogen bombs can inflict.

But Mr. Macmillan unfortunately stopped short of the most effective course open to him. The limited possibilities available to Britain when developing her weapons alone, and the serious political difficulties which France faces in respect to testing grounds in Africa, could have been partially remedied at a single stroke by pooling British and French resources. The gains in defensive power, in political influence, and in prospects of economic development, would have been immense. Here was a genuine community of interest and a genuine " special relationship " among neighbours, forged in the two most terrible wars in history. What could be more appropriate than the pooling of British and French nuclear development and the establishment of a common policy on nuclear defence in the future ? Looked at in a longer perspective it seems astonishing that this opportunity should not even have been considered in Britain during 1962. What more effective contribution could Britain have offered, when applying to join the Common Market, towards the extension of the political liaison to which the Rome Treaty committed its members ? An imaginative stroke such as this would have made all the difference. In 1963 Britain would have been firmly in the Common Market and the Coal and Steel Community, and Britain and France would have been negotiating with the United States in N.A.T.O. from a much stronger position.

In the event of Anglo-French collaboration, it would be open to other signatories to the Rome Treaty, if they desired, to make their contributions to the development of an independent European nuclear weapon of which the foundations would have been laid by Britain and France. With this opportunity before them, there would be no incentive, in view of their limited individual resources, to proceed alone. For a time West Germany would be well-advised, for diplomatic reasons, to remain outside these activities. Later, as European integration advanced, it would become obvious that the

German element in the new Europe could never reach a dominating position over the whole, and the old fears associated with the appalling course of German history from 1933 to 1945 would pass away.

Given this foundation, the common interests of the new Europe would draw the countries step by step into greater unity. The precise stages could not be foreseen and would be determined by future circumstances, and opportunities. The formation of a common international policy, and the establishment of an integrated economy in a form and by means outside the scope of this study, would have to be taken up from the start. The countries would begin with the immense advantage of possessing the best civil services to be found in the world today, and with a wealth of experience of the working of representative institutions. There, indeed, lie the conditions of success. Never were they presented in such measure before. Individual freedom, freedom of opposition parties, representative government, all these terms retain their reality in these European countries, free from the inversions and perversions that have corrupted language and destroyed true political life and community, or strangled it at birth, over large areas of the world.[1] To the tradition of political liberty there is added the tradition of the public services which provide the capacity for organisation and administration without which the stability of government and of society would be endangered in modern societies based on highly specialised activities. If western Europe is compared in these respects with the areas of Asia and Africa in which schemes of unification are advocated or attempted, further justification of the case for expediting unity in Europe and proceeding more cautiously in the Middle East and Africa will be unnecessary. This does not imply any general superiority of Europeans over Asians and Africans : it is a matter of experience, tradition, and resources at a particular time in history. It may be hoped that the necessary political experience will be acquired in Asia and Africa at less cost than Europe has incurred, and in less time than Europe has taken to acquire them.

It remains to consider the relations of the new Europe, thus conceived, with the United States and the Commonwealth. The popular currency of vague and superficial slogans has spread many misconceptions on the idea of a united, independent Europe.

Of these, none has led to more confusion than the idea of a " Third Force ". Taken at its face value the phrase is applicable

---

[1] I do not refer only to communist areas but equally to the extensive non-communist, including " anti-communist " authoritarian régimes. To those with experience of authoritarian régimes and sham " representative " government, as well as of intolerant democracies, it seems astonishing how little western European peoples (insular as well as continental) appreciate the liberties and security they enjoy in comparison with the greater part of the world.

to the future Europe here conceived, which would constitute a power comparable with the United States and the Soviet Union. Unfortunately the term " Third Force " has been used controversially to imply much more than this, even though there is nothing in the words to convey such additional meanings. It is commonly taken to denote a third super-power standing in a wholly neutral relation to the two other super-powers and mediating between them.

The term, when used with these accretions, cannot be applied to the conception of the future Europe which is outlined in the present study. For reasons which have already been stated, the new Europe, with Britain in it, would still find, for some time, that its interests would require co-operation with the United States in some form, with the object of maintaining the balance of power in Europe and North America. The United States would have an even stronger interest in co-operating than it has now, simply because Europe would be stronger than it is now.

However, this conception of Europe's future role has not so far gained support in Washington during the early nineteen-sixties. President Kennedy and his advisors for a time seem to have entertained an ambitious and even an imperial view of the proper international aims and policies of the United States. He conceived himself, and his entourage conceived him still more, as a man of action, determined to break what he regarded as the inertia of his predecessor, and above all to assert the " leadership " of the United States in the " free world ".[1]

For some time previously, as we have seen, under different régimes, the United States had urged both Britain and the western European countries to unite. It was supposed that economic recovery and advance would be more rapid in a single state than in a group of separate states. Loose analogies were drawn with the United States in support of this view, which exerted a wide appeal during the early post-war years of difficulty for Europe. But later the continental European states, having completed their recovery, grew faster than the United States, even without benefit of union. Finally, United States Governments believed strongly that a unified western and southern Europe would constitute a more effective " bulwark against communism " and partner in " the cold war " than a Europe of separate states. This seems to have carried the greatest weight in the United States, which has always been more influenced by the fear of left-wing movements than Europe has.

As we have seen, recovery, rapid growth, and a trend towards unification reduce Europe's willingness to accept a satellite role. Yet

---

[1] Apparently his successor wishes to follow him in this role, with the difference that, although equally liberal at home, he is a more conservative imperialist abroad, if we may judge from his attitude to the militarist coup in Brazil.

governments in Washington are subject to immense pressures, coming partly through senators and representatives, and partly through closely organised and lavishly financed " pressure groups ", in the direction of extreme nationalism and imperialism. The circumstances of the Second World War unexpectedly placed the United States and the Soviet Union in dominating positions at the end of the War, and their peoples tended to assume that these were permanent positions. Just as the Russians have been faced with the necessity of adjusting their position to new and rising communist countries, so the United States, in different ways, has to adjust itself to the restoration of older as well as the rise of newer countries which will not accept the supremacy of any single power. In the early nineteen-sixties it was said over and over again that British people must adjust themselves to the loss of empire and the overshadowing of Britain by larger countries. But it is absurd to single out Britain in isolation. With the rise of new countries and the restoration of older countries which had been temporarily weakened, and with the rapid increase in the world's population, all countries except the new [1] ones must undergo a similar readjustment to the changes in the distribution of power. As in the United States, so in a number of other countries, the statesmen and the best educated few are the first to appreciate this, and only after a long interval, and after serious difficulties and dangers, can the unthinking masses be brought, if not to an understanding, at least to a resigned acceptance, of the new forces in a changing world.

In these changing conditions the true interests of the United States will be best served by fully recognising the growing desire for independence of the new Europe in respect to armaments as well as in other fields, and by accepting a genuine, not merely a verbal, equality in a limited Atlantic Alliance. It would be easy to misinterpret the significance of the anti-European attitude of the leaders of the British Labour Party [2] in the early nineteen-sixties. The statement of Mr. Wilson in Washington, summarised neatly in *Le Monde* to the effect that " *les États-Unis sont les gardiens au nom de l'Occident de la force dissuasion nucleaire* ", reveals a politician more at home in domestic than international affairs. Apparently Mr. Wilson did not realise that the realities behind this verbal dressing are, as already shown, that of a satellite relationship of separate European countries to the United States. At first sight this seemed to suit Washington's idea of an alliance where the equality remains purely formal. But no party in Europe could assume the responsibilities of office without

[1] The new countries have adjustments of their own to make to unfamiliar surroundings, but they are different in kind.

[2] Fortunately the Trade Union Congress was much more cautious and intelligent on the subject. It is curious that the anti-European and particularly the anti-French strain in the Labour Party came mainly from the middle-class " intellectuals " rather than the workers' leaders.

18

soon becoming aware that the relationship was one of dependence and not equality. It would be realised also that Britain's renunciation of nuclear development would have no effect on France, China, and other countries, and that Britain would become more dependent than ever before on the United States, whose policy she could not hope to control or influence at critical points. When the party and the sections of public opinion which had followed it learned the facts of international life, they would either turn to neutralism or return to nuclear development.

On the other hand, frank acceptance of a strong and integrated Europe on a basis of genuine and not merely verbal equality would reduce the earlier strains and tensions and the widespread dissatisfaction on both sides of the Atlantic with the actual workings of the unequal alliance. To stop short of this acceptance would be to fight a long rearguard action designed to hold back a restored Europe from resuming its proper place in the world's counsels. There is no future in such a policy.

III

Europe, the United States and " Le Tiers Monde '

The implications of European equality have to be considered from the points of view of armaments and international policies. On the least favourable assumption that disarmament makes no progress, the new Europe that began with the Rome Treaty could be extended by the admission of Britain and the pooling of Anglo-French nuclear armaments and their development, and would become an independent nuclear power co-operating with the United States as far as appeared advantageous to both sides. Certain forms of U.S. assistance might be given to Anglo-French nuclear development and future European experience and technical advances disclosed to the U.S. The nuclear forces, and the final control of their disposition and, if the worst came, to their use, would remain in separate U.S. and European hands. Any other solution, such as those proposed under the misleading titles of " multilateral " and " multi-national " forces, has meant that, if the worst came, the President of the United States would in effect decide alone the fate of Europe. In the politically lethargic moods of British public opinion on international affairs from the late nineteen-fifties some circles hardly appeared averse to evading national responsibilities in this way, but it is hardly conceivable that the majority will be content to do so in the future.

The case for handing over to the United States European responsi-

bilities for nuclear armaments and European decisions for their disposition and use can only be based on the idea that European statesmen are more likely than those of the United States to endanger the
world. This supposition is without foundation. Europe risks more
complete destruction than North America in the event of war.
European public opinion, from long and painful experience, is now
more restrained than U.S. public opinion, when questions involving
communism arise. The form of government in the United States
enables greater pressures to be exercised on the executive powers,
particularly in times of excitement. Fanatical anti-communism has
remained strong in the United States. As a British observer wrote of
the Cuban crisis :

> At the height of the tension over Cuba, last October, Wash-
> ington was a frightening place. Its streets prickled with the
> fearful conviction of three-quarters of a million people that an
> atomic warhead would come whistling down on them at any
> moment from the south—and, worse, with the grim belligerence
> shown by almost everyone, Republican and Democrat alike, in
> support of " strong-arm " tactics at any cost. In buses, in shops,
> strangers asked : " Did you hear the President's speech ? "—
> and followed it, like one burly, unsmiling man, with an out-
> raged wrath : " We should show Khrushchev we mean what
> we say, go down and drop bombs on all those damn bases.
> Show them we're tough ".[1]

In an atmosphere like this, the executive arm of the government
works under a continuous handicap, with a narrowing room for
manoeuvre. It is not new in the United States ; it is at its worst when
Latin American and Far Eastern issues are concerned. In Europe
the public often shows ignorance over international issues, but the
ignorant elements are commonly willing to leave it to the government in external matters. They are conscious of their ignorance.
In the United States the corresponding classes confidently hasten to
tell the government what it ought to do : the " tough line " towards
anything resembling communism abroad as well as at home is popular. In the
first half of the nineteen-fifties a single demagogue, with the enthusiastic backing of these political elements, was able to cow opposition
and largely dominate the machinery of government, greatly intensifying fanatical anti-communism and destroying for an indefinite
period the possibility of a rational United States policy towards
China. Disreputable demagogues come and go : in themselves they
have been unimportant, and no monopoly of any one country.

---

[1] Susan Cooper, " The Ingrown Americans ", *Sunday Times, Weekly Review,*
11 April, 1963, p. 21.

But the reactions of U.S. public opinion to them were alarming, and the Cuban crisis showed that fanatical elements of the right remain as an influential force in respect to foreign policy for an indefinite period to come.[1]

Thus there is no ground for supposing that a new Europe, initially based on the Rome Treaty and including Britain, in which the Anglo-French nuclear arms and research were pooled, would be less likely than the United States to act with due sense of the vast responsibilities resting on those who would command the power in the twinkling of an eye to bring death to millions of fellow-creatures and total devastation to the land on which they dwell, and who would also be aware that, within the hour, reprisals would bring a similar fate on them. The widespread recognition of this fact is of the greatest importance if, as I have argued, the demand for a more independent Europe grows.

The role of armaments and the role of international policies in the Atlantic Alliance, as in any other alliance, cannot be wholly separated. If the weapons at the disposal of the new Europe were qualitatively similar, even though quantitatively inferior, to those at the disposal of the United States, the importance of Europe in relation to the balance of power with respect to Russia and China would be so great that it could no longer be ignored in Washington, as it has so often been in the past.[2] Armaments are not an end in themselves ; they are no more than an instrument. The fundamental difficulty in the Atlantic Alliance has been that of serious divergencies in policies. It was inevitable that some divergencies would arise out of differences in the interests of the parties to the alliance in more distant areas of the world. But the actual divergencies have gone far beyond these points. The most far-reaching and the most dangerous of them have arisen out of the radical divergencies, already discussed, between the tempers of the public in the United States and Europe respectively, and in the systems of democratic government, which offer different opportunities for intransigent elements to block necessary adjustments in policy. The exclusion of China from the United Nations and the economic boycott of Cuba were not actions in the genuine interests of the United States itself : the first, at least, would have been abandoned before the end of the nineteen-fifties if those who held the executive responsibilities of government had been able to follow their best judgement. But the facts of political life in the

---

[1] There are signs that this force is increasing rather than diminishing.

[2] The view held in some Labour Party circles that British concentration on pre-nuclear forces would be a major role ignores the point that the Labour Party would be no more ready than other parties to restore conscription and that in any case British forces would be small compared with those of the U.S. and the rest of Europe.

United States must be recognised : they are unlikely to change in the forseeable future.

When Europe reaches equality with the United States, its influence on the policy of a more limited Alliance will obviously be greater, and even the United States public will realise that it will be in its interests at the very least to compromise on differences of policy. But differences will remain, partly because of real differences in interests and partly because of continuing radical differences in U.S. public opinion even after the necessity of some compromise with a more powerful Europe is realised. In particular, the exaggerated fears of communism are likely to continue, even if in slightly modified form. The interests built up around anti-communism are too strong to be dislodged for some time to come.

Hence, the question will always be present, how far should the alliance extend ? In the past a dependent Europe has usually given way to the United States when differences in policies to be pursued in specific areas have arisen.[1] But this cannot be expected to continue in the new Europe. The primary purpose of the alliance was, and must still be, to establish and maintain the balance of power in Europe, replacing that which the two World Wars destroyed. The united armed power of the alliance has to be adequate to offset that of Russia. This aim is independent of the nature of the ruling régime in Russia. The alliance is not and must not be an alliance " to contain communism ". Our interests in Europe are to eschew doctrinal conflicts in international affairs, and resolutely resist any attempts from outside to draw Europe into them. The only hope of international peace is to establish the general principle that each country will determine the nature of its internal régime. This principle, like all general principles, is not absolute but subject to practical limits at the extremes : slavery and the grosser forms of discrimination will inevitably incite pressures from abroad. But even these pressures have to be applied with care: group prejudices within a state cannot be removed overnight by legislation, and the external pressure can only be directed usefully to securing that the legal basis of discriminations, where they exist, should be removed, and that measures should be taken to overcome the mass prejudices that lie behind them. The emerging countries, in particular, have a strong interest, which some of them do not always recognise, in the principle of non-interference, for new countries with untried or inexperienced governments stand particularly in danger of external interference.

Now a great difficulty within the Atlantic Alliance has been that the United States has looked on Latin American, Asian, and African

[1] One great British newspaper, which opposed nuclear weapons for Europe, though it was unusually well-informed on the United States, resigned itself to the conclusion that the United States would always get its way in the end.

countries mainly from the point of view of the " cold war ". As previous chapters have shown, its obsession with communism has dominated its policies. In some parts of the world it has bolstered up dictatorial régimes because of their anti-communist zeal, and in others, simultaneously, it has denounced dictatorship and proclaimed the virtues of democracy. In some cases these contradictions have been illustrated from time to time in respect to the same country. Whatever defects may be found in the policies of Britain and France towards *le tiers monde* they are not a result of doctrinal obsessions. In the United States public opinion would have made it impossible for any government to act towards any territory in an analogous way to that in which Britain has acted towards British Guiana under Dr. Jagan's premiership.

Such issues as these are not subject to satisfactory or even workable compromises. Britain's responsibilities to the Commonwealth will continue, even when she is inside the new Europe, which itself will collectively acquire important relationships to the former colonial territories of Britain, France, and Belgium. It is essential that both Britain and the rest of the new Europe to come should always treat these new countries and the Latin American countries as ends in themselves and not as instruments that may be subordinated to doctrinal rivalries of the super-powers.

Thus the Atlantic alliance seems best regarded, in effect, as chiefly designed to sustain a balance of power directly between Europe and North America on the one hand, and Russia on the other, but within the Alliance a change towards equality between Europe and North America is necessary.[1] As to the policies of Britain and in future of the new Europe, and those of the United States, towards other parts of the world, there will remain fruitful areas of co-operation in some regions and on some subjects, but on others the divergencies are too great to be reconciled in the near future, and the position adopted by the Macmillan Government in the early nineteen-sixties in respect to trade with China and Cuba, and the admission of China into the United Nations pointed the way to future policy when such differences arise. British policy and the policy of the new Europe towards the countries of Asia, Africa, and Latin America will have to be pursued consistently as an end in itself without contradictory deviations resulting from U.S. pressure.

[1] See, however, the discussion in the next chapter (p. 263) of the question whether the Alliance will be needed when a sufficiently close approximation to equality is reached.

IV

Economic Aid and Intra-Regional Balance of Power

A difficult problem remains concerning the relations between the Western countries and the emerging countries. Britain, France, the United States, Canada, and Belguim have given economic assistance on a substantial scale to these countries. Often such assistance indirectly affected the distribution of political power in the receiving countries. The supplying countries are firmly attached to genuine representative government, and would not consciously wish to advance authoritarian forms of government at the expense of more representative forms. Britain correctly opposes interference in the domestic affairs of independent countries, even when they change to more authoritarian government. It is generally ill-advised to give assistance on a discriminatory basis according to the nature of the political régimes in a group of countries. Among the emerging and reawakening countries it exposes the governments of the most favoured receiving countries to attacks on the ground that they are "lackeys of imperialism". It accentuates intraregional antagonisms. And when an authoritarian displaces a comparatively democratic régime by *coup d'état* or revolution, a supplying country which cuts off assistance opens itself to the charge that it is interfering in domestic affairs : sometimes even opponents of the new régime resent what they regard as encroachments on their country's independence. The attempt of the United States to embody discriminations of this type in the "Alliance for Progress" was unsuccessful.

The difficulty remains. Western peoples who are true to their heritage would desire, if they could find a way, to help the cause of representative government and of individual liberty in the emerging and reawakening countries. But, in the long run, as I hold, this is only possible in so far as the methods chosen do not encroach on the independence of the countries concerned. The growth of liberty and representative government must originate within a community ; it cannot be imposed from without. Hence, in supplying economic assistance, the ideal is neutrality between different areas and régimes. But, whatever the intentions of the supplying country may be, the practical difficulties of distributing assistance without affecting the comparative positions of countries under different political régimes, and the comparative positions of contending political groups within countries, appear to be insuperable. All that can be done is to make every effort to convince the peoples concerned that the supplying countries will respect the independence of the receiving countries, whatever the nature of their régimes.

The fine example of Secretary Marshall in his initial approach to economic aid for Europe, which was perhaps as close to the ideal as it is possible to get, has not since been followed in large schemes of United States assistance. The most effective, if not the only effective, appeal of government spokesmen to the Congress whose votes are needed to sanction the expenditures has often been an appeal based on the argument that the funds are necessary to assuage economic discontent that might open the way to communism. Economic aid to the emerging countries by both super-powers has been widely regarded as incidental to the " cold war ", and designed primarily to serve doctrinal ends concerned with communism.

The analysis in the present study leads to the rejection of this view. The idea that the emerging and reawakening countries will be an easy prey to communism, Russian or Chinese, unless the western countries intervene actively to stave it off, either by political or by economic means or by both, is likely to be regarded by historians of the future as more important in the history of ideas than in the history of actual events.

But it does not follow that economic conditions have no effect on the nature of political régimes. In much of Latin America and in the Middle East societies in the process of modernisation are struggling to shed the pre-modern elements in their culture. But the resistance in the present generation is strong, and in the short run, the rate of change desired by the younger revolutionaries can only be attained, if at all, by authoritarian methods. Hence the temptation to substitute coercion for persuasion, and dictatorship based on military force for representative government.

But all this is associated with, and in fact is an offshoot of, an intense passion for national independence. It is utterly at variance with the fundamental principles of Russian communism and Chinese communism. Soviet Governments have been willing from time to time to permit communist collaboration with " the national bourgeoisie "[1] during the rise of nationalism in the emerging and the remaining colonial countries : from near the middle of the nineteen-fifties it became a more or less standard doctrine, though, of course, it would be changed if, in future conditions, it no longer suited Russian national interests. But there are limits to the possibilities of accommodating Russian or Chinese communism to the nationalism of the emerging countries : as soon as divergencies arise between the

---

[1] See especially the frequent confirmation of this in *The World Marxist Review*, an orthodox Russian communist journal.

interests of the latter and that of Russia, communist parties which maintain external links with Russia appear to fervent nationalists to be violating the most sacred article in the nationalist creed.

At the same time the emerging countries have been reluctant to impair their relations with the Soviet Union. They have aimed, correctly, at maintaining diplomatic relations with both East and West, and refraining from political commitments to any of the contending super-powers and Great Powers. Some of them have simultaneously treated communists at home savagely, and communist governments abroad courteously.

The Soviet Union, on her part, for political reasons has sometimes cut off economic aid to other communist countries for long periods of time. But in spite of political disagreements she has not extended the same treatment to the emerging nations, and has continued to give both economic and military assistance to countries whose ruthless treatment of communists within their borders is denounced in Russian international broadcasts and at the annual meetings of communist parties in Moscow.

The United States, under Secretary Dulles, had abruptly gone back on its earlier engagement to assist in financing the construction of the Aswan Dam in Egypt apparently on the ground that Egypt had accepted arms from Russia. Later she reversed this decision, and began to follow in some areas, though not in Latin America, a policy similar to that of Russia, and from similar motives concerned with the balance of power.

These fluctuations and inconsistencies illustrate political dilemmas that confront Great Powers in the distribution of economic assistance. Since 1952 Egypt has been a *Societé militaire*,[1] under which political activity is stilled. The United States and the Soviet Union disapprove of the Egyptian régime, though for different reasons. Similar considerations apply to Indonesia, except that President Sukarno is an opportunist ruler rather than a military dictator, and political parties, though ineffective, remain. The economic and military assistance to the Egyptian and Indonesian Governments certainly strengthen the régimes and help to perpetuate the rulers in office : its effects are not neutral with respect to the internal political development of the countries.

But the effects of economic and military assistance are not confined to domestic politics. In Egypt and Indonesia they extend particularly to international relations within the respective regions. Both President Nasir and President Sukarno have used external successes to support their internal positions. But external adventures

---

[1] To borrow from the title of the able analysis by Anouar Abdul-Malek, *Egypte, Société Militaire*, Paris, 1962.

are costly, in economic terms as well as in the use of skilled personnel.   Egyptian expenditures on an elaborate system of propaganda
through a monolithic press and powerful radio transmitters, and
secret activities through agents abroad, have undoubtedly been high,
though their exact amount cannot be determined.   This machine
was set in motion from the mid-fifties against every régime in the
Middle East that was unwilling to accept Nasir's leadership in the
area.[1]   Without U.S. and Russian economic and military assistance
external adventures would necessarily have been on a smaller scale
and available resources would have had to be concentrated on
economic survival in the face of acute population pressure.   Admittedly, Cairo's propaganda falls on many receptive ears through the
Middle East.   Most subversive movements have some local roots.
But, at the margin, Egyptian propaganda and underground activities
have played a considerable role in the overturn of governments and
in the general instability of society in the Middle East.   Particularly,
they helped to undermine the imperfect and incomplete elements of
representative government which existed in Iraq and Syria before
1958 and in Syria between 1961 and 1963.

In so far, then, as the extensive Russian and United States economic aid to Egypt has set free Egyptian resources for external
adventures, it has assisted a movement towards totalitarian and
militarist forms of government which, if successful, would extinguish
the last flickering lights of political liberty in the Middle East.

Yet this result can hardly be desired, either by the United States
or by the Soviet Union.   Such paradoxes again illustrate the power
exerted by countries in *le tiers monde*, even when their armaments are
negligible in comparison with those of the Great Powers.   So important does it appear to the United States that Egypt should not fall
into the Russian camp, and to the Soviet Union that she should not
fall into the western camp, that each super-power is prepared to
make sacrifices to frustrate the other.   I do not believe that the fears
of either are well grounded.   The strength of the communist movement in the Middle East has been grossly exaggerated : in crises the
communists have exposed their weakness and lack of solid political
roots in the region.   In the early nineteen-sixties their influence was
receding everywhere.   Nor, on the other side, could any Middle
Eastern country, regardless of the political complexion of its government, afford to enter the western alliance in face of the unanimous
disapproval of the other countries of the region.   There is no serious
danger of either communist or western domination in the Middle
East.   The dangers come mainly from totalitarian tendencies of

---

[1] Plots against the lives of President Bourgibua, King Hussein, and Premier
Qasim, one of which caused the death of the whole Jordanian Cabinet, were either
instigated or assisted by Egypt.

domestic origin and growth, associated with militarist forms of Arab nationalism, endeavouring to impose unification instead of seeking voluntary coalescence of equals. This is not in the interests of the western countries or of Russia. It keeps the area in a constant state of unrest and tension.

Since the malaise in the Arab countries of the Middle East in the early sixties is of domestic origin, the remedies have to come from within. Ill-advised interferences in the past by the West and, very recently, the East, have contributed to present difficulties and the only reasonable course today is to respect the independence of the countries concerned. But, as we have seen, this is only a partial solution of the problem of how to render assistance without tilting the internal political balance in the wrong direction. Perhaps the best among a series of imperfect methods would be a collective scheme of assistance under which the total amount for the region would be fixed, and the receiving countries themselves would set up a committee to determine how it should be distributed within the region. Preferably the whole operation should pass through the machinery of the United Nations. But difficulties would remain, until some of the emerging countries developed a greater sense of international responsibility.

Space will not permit the extension of these illustrations to other parts of Asia, Africa, and Latin America. But enough has been said to show the dangers of using international economic assistance primarily as an instrument in the struggles and rivalries of the Great Powers.

The Atlantic Alliance cannot be extended beyond its specific functions relating to the balance of power around the North Atlantic, into the problems of the emerging world of Asia, Africa, and Latin America. Obviously the wider the scope of agreement between Europe and the United States on the emerging world the better, so long and only so long as the countries in that world are treated as ends in themselves and as independent states in the same sense as the countries of the old world are.

But it is illusory to suppose that the vast majority of the people of the United States, who, through the power of the purse, set limits, and often narrow limits, on what U.S. Governments can do, will suddenly change their activities in the near future ; that they will regard the Caribbean in a less proprietary sense than in the past ; that they will not continue to regard as the chief purpose of economic assistance the prevention of " communist subversion and take-over " in the receiving countries ; and that the pursuit of that purpose will not lead to a strengthening of non-communist authoritarian régimes in some of the emerging countries. The example of the United States should be emulated in respect to the scale on which, but not to the manner in which, nor to the aims for which, economic aid has been disbursed since UNRRA and the Marshall Plan ended. The new Europe should establish its own relations of economic assistance with the emerging world in full respect for the independence of the countries concerned, and divorced from doctrinal aims.

CHAPTER XV

THE SUMMING UP

I

New Elements in the Balance of Power

SINCE the middle of the twentieth century the struggle for group freedom has been spreading to all the corners of the earth, animating with a new or intensified political consciousness peoples who had hitherto lain dormant under rule which rested ultimately on external sources of power. Freedom in this sense means freedom of the group from what is felt to be alien rule. At first the most spectacular manifestation of this wide-sweeping movement was the movement for decolonisation, or liberation of groups living in a dependent status in areas generally distant from the country where the ultimate seat of power lay. But other stirrings have been heard, in Asia and Africa in nineteenth-century European fashion, from groups submerged within surrounding peoples from whom they feel distinct. Finally, the peoples of countries reduced to a satellite relationship to Great Powers have become increasingly restless, and serious political eruptions have occurred among them from time to time.

Unfortunately, movements for group freedom do not necessarily make for the extension of individual freedom. When the former has been attained, new obstacles to the latter often arise, through the ambitions of political leaders, the difficulty of establishing a deep-rooted sense of legitimacy in respect to the new political institutions and governments, and the intractable problems of modernisation and economic development.

But the political liberties of the individual must be won from within a community : an attempt to impose them from outside would violate group freedom and the spirit of nationalism which is the main current of the age among the emerging peoples, and would appear as a return to colonialism.

The strength of the demand for group freedom leaves open no other approach to international peace except that which is based on mutual recognition of the independence of states, small as well as great, within the framework of a growing body of international law and understandings, and sustained by the international organisations. In the foreseeable future this is also the only practicable approach to the spread of individual freedom. As long as fundamental divergencies exist among states over the relation of the individual to society, over the scope of individual freedom under the law, and over the forms of political constitutions and the right to choose and change governments, freedom itself would be set back by the merging of democratic and authoritarian societies under compromise forms of government. The highest achievements of freedom in society would be lost. Consequently respect for the independence of small states as well as great must be a cornerstone of the international order.

New forces have appeared in international relations which, if wisely guided, can bring a great accession of strength to small states, and stronger support for their independence than has yet existed. In the aftermath of decolonisation the membership of the United Nations has been greatly increased, giving numerical preponderance to Asian, African, and Latin American states in the United Nations Assembly.

This opens a great opportunity. Whether or not it will be taken depends on the quality of statesmanship in the new countries. Political leaders with unruly followers, and ambitious, authoritarian rulers, are beset with temptations to engage in aggressive external policies calculated to divert attention from the causes of internal dissatisfaction. The opportunities to fish in troubled regional waters have been greatly extended by the divergencies between the geographical distribution of nationalist groups and the geographical distribution of the independence movements which preceded decolonisation. These divergencies created pressure towards integration in some areas and disintegration in others. The confusion increased with the growth of sentiments wider but also vaguer than nationalism, which proclaim the doctrine of unity over vast areas. The ideas of Arab nationalism and African nationalism, though they correspond to real feelings of kinship, have so far done more to retard than to advance the cause of unity, and the best prospect in the near future is to seek closer relationships in regions within regions, such as East Africa and the Maghreb. But neither the approaches towards the closer relations needed in some areas, not those towards the decentralisation and local autonomy needed in others, can be expected to succeed under authoritarian rule. The growth of genuine representative government is a necessary, though it may not be a sufficient, condition for the settlement of the problems of political integration and disintegration.

In its absence, the attempts to form sub-regional unions, which are the only practicable form of unification by consent in the near future, are facing opposition from ambitious political leaders with wider aims of their own, who are bent on suppressing all traces of competition, however limited. Presidents Sukarno and Nasir are obvious examples, and President Nkrumah has recently shown signs of opposition to East African Federation.   In 1964, President Nasir, with Iraq temporarily a satellite, with a large army of occupation in the Yemen, and helped by substantial economic and military materials from Russia and the United States, appears to be aiming at Egyptian domination of the Fertile Crescent and Arabia in the guise of Arab unity, putting an end to the hopes of a sub-regional federation in the south which would embody increasing elements of representative government and leave freedom of association to the workers of Aden.   The gulf between rulers and ruled, always wide in the Middle East, is becoming still wider, with dangerous consequences for the future.

Just at the time when communist autocracy in Russia and Eastern Europe is being tempered through the hard experiences of the older and the influence of a newer generation, and is beginning the long, slow trek towards genuine individual freedom and representative government, many parts of the Afro-Asian world are moving rapidly in the opposite direction, particularly but not exclusively those in which revolutions have occurred.   Today, more than ever, revolutions produce aspiring Napoleons among young officers or other young revolutionaries allied to them.   Then the new governments prove to be more autocratic and much harder to remove than those overthrown by revolution had been.   To many of the original revolutionaries the disillusionment is complete.   It can only be repeated : this is an age of the extension of group rather than individual freedom, of the removal of foreign and the establishment of native rulers, rather than the removal of autocratic and the establishment of democratic government.   The rise of intra-regional imperialism modifies even this conclusion ; for example, all—apart from a few of the urban dwellers—in the Yemen regard Eygptians as foreigners, and many of the Papuans in West New Guinea would have preferred to remain under the new liberal Dutch rule rather than be placed under Indonesian authoritarian rule.

In some of the areas concerned the new regimes resting on military domination are characterised by the youthfulness of the men controlling the governments.   The " young officer " group, at once radical and authoritarian, which was checked after a sharp struggle in Japan in the nineteen-thirties and recently in Turkey, has triumphed throughout the greater part of the Middle East and in some parts of south-eastern Asia.   Many of these areas are characterised by economic confusion at home and chronic hostility to most of the outside—especially the Western-world.[1]   When the outcome of the " struggle

[1] It seems possible that one factor in the remarkably successful modern development of Japan and India in contrast to much of the rest of Asia may be the proper blending of age and youth, experience and energy, moderation and drive, in the direction of affairs.

between the generations " is government by youth movements the consequences are even more dangerous for international than for domestic relations. The older and more experienced leaders of the middle class usually have considerable knowledge and understanding of the outside world, while the young politically conscious classes, knowing it, if at all, only through academic studies, tend to interpret it in fashionable doctrinal generalities which are not drawn from actual contemporary conditions. Certainly there are many exceptions, but not enough to correct the imbalance which occurs when governments are composed entirely of very young men.

It should not be supposed, however, that until *le tiers monde* acquires wiser leadership in international affairs it will not be a powerful force in international relations. The present state of the world demonstrates the contrary. Both Western and Eastern policies will have to reckon increasingly with the Afro-Asian-Latin American countries as a major force in a world which has finally disposed of the idea, so dear to the hearts of such opposite types of statesmen as Franklin Roosevelt and Stalin, that the Great Powers should and would be able to run the world authoritatively and use force to impose their wills when they think it necessary to control the smaller powers. Such days are gone. Oddly enough those two war-time leaders, by seeking to further the decolonisation of other countries than their own, contributed to this end without perceiving the contradiction in their aims. As in labour relations, so in international relations, conciliation and arbitration accomplish more than coercion. When they both fail temporarily, restraints which include coercive means must come through the combined authority of the great and the smaller powers if wider and more dangerous and long drawn out conflicts are not to be provoked in the longer run.

But although *le tiers monde* will be an increasingly powerful force to be reckoned with even in its present turbulent condition and internal disunity, its power will not be used to serve its long-run interests until it recognises as its chief aim the extension of the rule of law in international relations. Since its armed power is comparatively limited and, except for the power to wage guerilla warfare, much inferior to that of the rest of the world, its interests will obviously be best served by making the most of the other forms of power. Among the wide variety of these forms, the moral force of respect for law and equal treatment before the law is bound to play a growing part in the long run if the human race has the will to survive. But at present the methods used to pursue intra-regional imperialism in western and south-eastern Asia, and the embryonic forms of it beginning to show themselves in Africa, are a grave setback to the growth of international law.

For the present the emerging countries would do well to throw

their main energies on the one hand to the task of domestic development, and on the other to strengthening their influence in the world
by working through the United Nations to uphold political independence, non-intervention—either under or above ground—in the
domestic affairs of other states, and the advancement of the rule of
law in international affairs. In support of these aims " bloc voting "
is all to the good, and there is much scope for the Afro-Asian and
Latin American countries to work together more effectively than
they have in the past. But discriminatory bloc voting which con-
demns an action in one country and upholds or condones a similar
action in another, retards the growth of the rule of law in international affairs, which the emerging countries have the greatest
interest in upholding for their own protection. Discriminatory voting in this sense is a form of political tribalism, and sometimes nepot-
ism, favouring countries with whom there is alleged to be a " special
relationship ", perhaps of kinship. The growth of a real international community is set back by such actions, whether they are
committed by the Afro-Asian group or by the Great Powers.

The nation-state is still the best instrument through which individual freedom can be realised in most parts of the world, and
denunciations of nationalism, in the abstract as distinct from particular excesses of particular nationalisms, are misplaced. In some
areas, where genuine representative government is firmly established, a number of nation-states can merge into multi-national
states without undue risk of prejudice to individual freedom. Some
European countries have reached this stage, and Britain, already a
multi-national state, will find its greatest future role in the world by
joining such an enlarged multi-national state.

But nationalism in itself is not enough to create an international
community. Internally it does not guarantee individual freedom ;
it merely provides the least unfavourable framework for securing and
maintaining it. Externally, it does not guarantee international
peace ; it merely, when realised, may reduce the sources of conflict
by removing the need to struggle for group freedom.

Consequently the international organisations are indispensable in
a world of separate states. The development of the United Nations
into an increasingly effective instrument is a condition of the survival
of humanity. The international organisations are instruments
through which the forms of power other than armed power can be
brought to bear on international issues with maximum effect, and
around which the rule of law in international matters can be
strengthened and extended.

Paradoxically, the rapidly growing deadliness of armaments, dat-
ing roughly from the last quarter of the nineteenth century, which
was an outcome of the advancing industrial revolution and reached
19

its climax with the mastery of atomic fission and fusion, has indirectly given additional importance in international relations to the forms of power other than armed power. For the countries which possess atomic weapons can only use them at the imminent risk of mutual destruction, and those which do not possess them can only use their modern weapons at the risk of drawing the super-powers into the war.

II

Disarmament, European Union and Atlantic Alliance

But it does not follow that the level and distribution of armed power in the nineteen-sixties can be permitted to continue without grave risk of general and irreparable ruin. The Cuba crisis illustrated this clearly. Acts of aggression contrary to international law were committed by a super-power against a small neighbouirng power. The second super-power attempted to take advantage of the opportunity, created by the appeal of the small power for protective arms, to reduce slightly its inferior position with respect to nuclear striking power. The first super-power then showed itself ready to unloose nuclear war unless the *status quo* were restored. At the critical moment the world was saved by the statesmanlike action of the head of state of the second super-power, who was prepared to discount that primitive psychological consideration known as " loss of face ". During the whole period Britain was in imminent danger of obliteration through her alliance with the first super-power on terms which gave her no restraining influence over the latter's actions and policies elsewhere in the world.

Consequently, although the stalemate in armed power to which the rivalry of the super-powers has led will give other forms of power an increasing role in international affairs, which will be reinforced by the accession to the international community of many new Asian and African states, it does not follow that a stable balance of power has yet been reached in the world, or that existing armaments can be left where they are, let alone increased, without imminent danger of world catastrophe. The adjectival part of the term " super-power " is related only to armed power, and the total comparative power of the super-powers, as well as that of the other Great Powers, will continue to decline as the revolution in international relations advances. But the rivalries and differences among the Great Powers remain, and competitive striving to maintain prestige before the rest of the world might yet touch off a nuclear war. In one sense, the competitive growth of armaments is a symptom of underlying sources of friction, but in another sense it is a source of friction in itself. The hope of disarmament is slender unless other sources of friction are allayed, but a halt in the growth, followed by preliminary reductions, of armaments will make a direct contribution to allaying friction. Thus disarmament is not an issue to be pursued in isolation, as the experience of the League of Nations after the rise of the Nazis showed. But today a frontal attack on the level of armaments must be resolutely pursued simultaneously with redoubled efforts to reduce substantive sources of friction.

Unfortunately mankind—particularly idealists in a hurry—when faced with inherently complicated issues like general disarmament, tends to seek refuge in the pursuit of panaceas taking the form of simple, negative political aims such as that of the " ban the bomb " movement. Who is to ban it ? Presumably the British Government. But the British Government could only ban the bomb in Britain. What contribution, then, could British renunciation make to world peace ? Clearly it would please the Russians on the one hand, and those American politicians who desire a U.S. monopoly of nuclear weapons in the N.A.T.O. But the significant question is whether it would bring either disarmament or peace any nearer.

The case for the renunciation of nuclear weapons by Britain, and, it may be added, France, rests upon the assumptions that it would set an example that would be voluntarily followed by other countries, and that it would reduce the chances of the spread and the irresponsible use of atomic weapons. As we have seen, there is no foundation for either of these assumptions.

Proposals for one-sided disarmament have long been a familiar part of the pacifist's creed. But proposals for the one-sided renunciation only of the latest and most effective weapons are more novel. They have strangely attracted a peculiar collection of adherents united in little else. Paradoxically, some of these argue that at least part of the funds saved from nuclear arms should go to increasing non-nuclear arms—particularly ground troops and bomber aeroplanes. Now the destructiveness of different weapons is a matter of degree.[1] Pacifists are at least consistent, but the humanitarian sentiments of the non-pacifist elements opposed to European possession of nuclear weapons seem a little confused. Those who, like Mr. Harold Wilson, conceive of the United States as the " trustee " of nuclear weapons on behalf of an Atlantic Alliance, and hint that there should be a collective control over all decisions concerning them, have been living imaginatively—so far as this issue is concerned—in a strange

[1] Estimated casualties at Hiroshima were 71,379, in the bombing of Dresden by " conventional " bombs 135,000, of Tokyo 83,793. Hydrogen bombs are, of course, immensely more destructive. But pre-atomic weapons have also become steadily more destructive.
Estimates cited in David Irving, *The Destruction of Dresden*, London, 1963, p. 210.

world, in which the U.S. Senate has relinquished its power over policy, and the masses of the American people have undergone the most memorable conversion since St. Paul first saw the light. If the United States bears the cost and monopolises the supply of nuclear weapons it will itself make the critical decisions concerning their possible use. It will also continue to determine its own policies in what it conceives to be its own interests, and its judgement on this will continue to depend in the last resort on those elements—not necessarily the most enlightened—which control the cumbersome political machinery of the country.

Britain is a part of Europe. The onset of every great international crisis in the twentieth century, and the primary impact of two World Wars, have shown that her most important special relationship is, and will continue to be, with France. But isolationist tendencies, linguistic indolence, and prejudices on both sides have hindered the *rapprochement* between the peoples and between their governments which is in the interests of both of them, and which the circumstances of the future will impose on them.

Already, considerable progress has been made in the nineteen-sixties. Among Conservative Party leaders a striking change took place from the late nineteen-fifties. Led by Mr. Macmillan, they were converted to a European outlook with respect to the Common Market countries, embracing the political as well as the economic aspects of the Treaty of Rome, and they were able to carry their party with them. Some Labour Party leaders, weary of exclusion from office, looking for popular issues on which to discredit the government, thought they had discerned one in the Common Market. But the party was divided on the issue and even the perverse parochialism of its " intellectuals " seemed unlikely to prevail long, particularly since the Trade Union Congress refused to commit itself.

Unfortunately, Mr. Macmillan's conversion to a European outlook did not extend to the problems of armaments and defence. By striving to perpetuate in peace-time the temporary " special relationship " of Britain to the United States which was appropriate to war-time emergencies, and by insisting on a British instead of a European " nuclear deterrent ", he prolonged, psychologically as well as materially, the dependence of Britain on the United States which was temporarily unavoidable during the period of post-war reconstruction. By his unneighbourly refusal to share British advances in nuclear techniques with France, when the interests of both countries demanded a joint effort, he alienated President de Gaulle and blocked his own aims with respect to the Common Market. By conniving at the omission instead of seeking the inclusion of France in meetings with the United States he confirmed the suspicion that Britain was not yet genuinely European in outlook.

Yet the estrangement cannot last. The forces making for European unity are based on common interests too strong to be stemmed indefinitely by prejudices and misconceptions. The sounder elements within " Gaullism " will survive President de Gaulle : they were not concocted solely by, nor were they ever the exclusive property of, any single individual. Objectively considered, they reflect the common international political interests of western and southern Europe,[1] of which Britain is an integral part. The most important criticism of Gaullism is, not that it goes too far in this direction, but that it does not go far enough.[2] Indeed, in those memorable later months of 1962, a momentum was gathering which, but for the intervention of President de Gaulle, would have committed Britain to a position in the van of those countries that would soon have been pressing far beyond the conception of *Europe des patries*,[3] towards a European state that would play a leading role of moderation in the world, standing for freedom at home and coexistence abroad, reconciled to the revolution in international relations, and forming new links with Asia, Africa, and Latin America, based on the unreserved recognition of political equality.

Leading journalists, and Labour Party leaders, including Mr. Harold Wilson, who have argued for Britain's withdrawal from, and against any European development of, the production of nuclear weapons, on the ground that relations with Russia would be improved and a source of provocation avoided, have misconceived the real issue. Naturally the Russians, like the Americans, would like to enjoy a monopoly of nuclear weapons. All monopolists believe in monopoly—for themselves. But all monopolists delude themselves when they imagine that the rest of the world will accept their monopolies indefinitely. The immediate threat of world disaster comes, not from the spread of nuclear weapons, which would be slow in any case, but from clashes between the super-powers, which already possess and are adding to them, and neither of which can be trusted with them any more, or even as much, as western Europe, which is freer of doctrinal obsessions and political fanaticism than either of them.

It is hard to imagine a greater disservice to the cause of international peace than a defeatist attitude towards disarmament,

[1] The Iberian Peninsula has temporarily excluded itself from this group, but it cannot indefinitely resist the representative forms of government which are the foremost political characteristic of the area, or stem the tide of decolonisation in which the area has led the world.

[2] The collapse of the drive for a European Defence Community in 1954 was due to French hesitations as well as to Britain's international myopia.

[3] That is, in the meaning which President de Gaulle gives to the term. On the other hand I would accept the term in a more limited sense in which it could be taken to signify a multi-national state.

20

shown even by some outstanding writers who, on this point, it seems to me, mistakenly credit themselves with "realism". The result is to deflect energies into the pursuit of panaceas such as unilateral nuclear disarmament, "preventing the spread of nuclear weapons", policing of the world by the super-powers, and so on. Such proposals all suffer from the fatal flaw that they would place the great majority of the human race at the mercy of a few self-appointed monopolists of armed power. Mankind will not and cannot accept such a position. The quest for freedom, the spirit of resistance to domination from without will never die. Disarmament is difficult, but since it has become a condition of survival it is not utopian.[1] If the time and energy directed towards panaceas had been given to disarmament, greater progress would have been made towards finding acceptable methods of disarming by stages without unduly disturbing the balance of armed power in the process. There is no time to be lost : if the huge military establishments of Russia and the United States persist in their competition in innovations the precarious balance of armed power may suddenly be upset. Let no-one be deceived by the dream of "preventing the spread of nuclear weapons" while leaving intact the supplies of those powers which already have them in quantities sufficient to make the earth uninhabitable.

The most urgent need of the hour is disarmament, and the prospect, in its absence, of a unified Europe with its own nuclear weapons, and of powers in other continents following suit in time, is the most effective means of putting pressure on the super-powers to take disarmament more seriously than either of them has yet been prepared to do. It is regrettable to find so many otherwise able British students of international affairs who still reflect a habit of dependence on the United States acquired just after the war under special but temporary conditions. The world has changed since then. It is time for Europe to shake off the dependence forced on it in its early period of reconstruction, and to reassert its equality with the United States. The form and scope of the Atlantic Alliance cannot remain as it was in the early nineteen-sixties.

The common interest of western and southern Europe and the United States in face of the greatly augmented power of Russia since the removal of the German and Austro-Hungarian counterweights which existed in the early years of the century remains as an essential feature of the world balance of power in the nineteen-sixties. But a reconstructed Europe is now capable of assuming greater responsibility for its own defence, and its position as a satellite of the United States is no longer tolerable. For the decisions which the United

---

[1] For an important recent study by a diplomat with practical experience of the subject, see Sir Michael Wright, *Disarm and Verify*, London, 1964.

States makes with respect to its nuclear weapons are partially concerned with other issues than those arising out of the common European-North American interest, sometimes with issues on which we Europeans have no common interest, and are not in accord, with the United States.

It can, indeed, be argued that when a united Europe approaches equality with the United States, the *raison d'être* of the alliance disappears. The rise of atomic weapons and of flexible, mobile, and concealed methods of propelling them to their targets, renders classical military alliances obsolete.[1] The conditions in which members of an alliance support each other in long drawn-out military campaigns have obviously disappeared with the Second World War. Not only the outcome of a war but the fate of the human race may be decided in a few minutes. To a large extent this view appears correct and when Europe returns to its normal practice of building its own defences with the weapons of the day NATO will no longer be needed, at least in anything like its present form.

Although I am acutely conscious of this radical and permanent change in the foundations of war and strategy, and although it plays a leading if underlying role in the present study, I have provisionally retained the idea of an Atlantic Alliance in a limited sense concerned with the balance of power in Europe—in its widest sense—and North America in the near future. The unification of Britain and the Common Market countries and the pooling and development of British and French nuclear resources, leading to the establishment of independent means of defence with the advanced weapons of the day, will take time, and in the intervening period it will be in the interests of Britain, the Common Market countries and the United States alike to maintain some association as a safeguard against possible " adventurism " from elsewhere. In the study of international change it is easy to overlook the element of time and the problems of transition from one state to another. We cannot afford to neglect interim periods and their special if temporary dangers. That is why, in the mainly radical approach to contemporary international relations in the present study, conservative elements are retained at certain points.

As long as the super-powers fail to disarm, there is no case for the renunciation of nuclear weapons by Britain and France, or by the new Europe, when it is established. On the contrary they will have no alternative but to develop their own up-to-date nuclear weapons, and to control them without veto power from the United States.

---

[1] On this subject see General Pierre M. Gallois, " La logique de l'ère nucléaire et ses incidences ", in *L'Avenir de l'Alliance Atlantique*, Paris, 1961. The theme also runs through Ronald Steel's, *The End of Alliance*, London, 1964.

They are more and not less likely to exercise the fullest restraint and sense of responsibility than the super-powers are. They cannot afford to be drawn helplessly along, as they were over the Cuba crisis, to share unwillingly in the consequences of the lag in the psychological decolonisation of the United States with respect to tropical Latin America, or to remain perpetually dependent on the United States against the possibility of " adventurism " on the part of the other super-power. They cannot afford to be drawn, as they were for several years in the nineteen-fifties, into partial association with an attempt to isolate one-quarter of the world's inhabitants from normal diplomatic and economic intercourse and from membership in the international organisations. For their future international role in the world requires them to co-operate with the constructive elements in the reawakening countries, in order to direct the new sources of power other than armaments into the advancement of the rule of law within a balance of power not confined to the Great Powers of Europe and North America but now including the many new powers of Asia, Africa, and Latin America, comparatively weak individually but strong collectively and no longer to be ignored or taken for granted.

III

Britain's Area of Choice

Although the British record on decolonisation is one of the most outstanding features of international relations in the post-war world, the more old-fashioned elements in British public opinion, and large sections of public opinion in other countries, have failed to see that it represented the culmination of policies of long standing, the final stages of which, owing to the effect of the war in heightening political self-consciousness throughout the world, had to be completed more rapidly than had been anticipated. It is absurd to suppose that intelligent British observers seriously believed that colonial peoples would remain in a dependent status in perpetuity. Even so imperial a thinker and administrator as Sir Harry Johnston at the beginning of the century could foresee the coming of independence within a century.[1] The child-like romanticism of the " Empire Loyalists " has had no place among serious students ; it has merely provided light entertainment and material for cartoonists. The same may be said of " anti-British " elements in other countries who proclaim that Britain never granted independence except in response to physical force.

[1] Sir Harry Johnston, *Common Sense in Foreign Policy*, London, 1913, p. vi.

Consequently, the idea that after the war Britain suddenly "lost an empire" and has fumbled uncertainly in the quest for a new vocation in the world to replace that which she occupied, or was supposed to have occupied, before the war, is grossly misleading. The transformation of Empire into Commonwealth had begun much earlier : the final stages were changes in tempo, not in direction nor in the ultimate goal. Britain has a greater, not a diminished, role in meeting the needs of the Commonwealth than she had in meeting the needs of the Empire. To suppose that Britain's problem is to find a substitute for Empire is to misconceive the changing structure of international relations. The shift from Empire to Commonwealth has actually created an important bridge between Britain and the now independent Afro-Asian world. Decolonisation in the former French Empire has performed a similar service on a smaller scale for France, especially since the Algerian war ended. In these respects Britain and France have been able to adjust to one of the main features of the revolution in international relations more readily than a number of other countries, including the United States, which is fighting a rearguard action against Latin America's drive to assert its *de facto* independence.

The problem of Britain's future role in the world is of a quite different character and would have been substantially the same, though probably more difficult, if the transformation of Empire into Commonwealth had gone more slowly. It is concerned with great power relations following the revolution in armaments, the establishment of the new category of super-power, and the recovery and growth of Europe. Britain has three choices and, from the point of view of the present study, only three. The first is to be a satellite of the United States, the second to retreat into a neutralist position resembling Sweden's, and the third to join the Western European countries and Italy in a single multi-national federal state. What might appear at first sight to be variations on these three positions turn out on closer examination to be approximations to one or other of them.

So far, Britain has tended to drift into the first of these positions. But it has been saved from complete commitment by the initial decision of the Labour Government of 1945–51, firmly maintained by Mr. Macmillan's Government in spite of U.S. opposition, to develop and retain nuclear weapons. The Labour Party's declared policy in the reverse direction would complete the slide to an unwanted satellitism, which in turn might well lead to a reaction that would end in neutralism. Some of the more conservative elements in public opinion, lamenting the largely mythical glories of past empire, see in the United States a successor to the British Empire, and, playing on the supposed "special relationship", are content with a satellite role, applauding " strong " action to control *le tiers monde* !

But association with " strong action " in *le tiers monde* is just the way to offset one of the chief assets of Britain and France in a decolonising world.   It is already a handicap to Britain that, owing to the intra-regional imperialism of Presidents Nasir and Sukarno, limited participation in local military conflicts, including the use of the Aden and Singapore bases, is temporarily necessary.   But all military bases in *le tiers monde* are a dangerous liability, to be shed as soon as inescapable responsibilities to countries in *le tiers monde* can be finally discharged.   Declarations by Western countries that the bases at Aden, Cyprus, and Guantanamo will be held indefinitely are unwise : they embarras the more friendly and deepen the antagonism of the less friendly countries in *le tiers monde*.

The dream of those on both sides of the Atlantic who see the English-speaking peoples as an " elite " which, in the last resort, has a mission to run the world, will fade.   The English-speaking peoples constitute only a small minority of the world's population : in the twenty-first century it will be still smaller.   The same may be said of the English- and Russian-speaking peoples taken together.   The extraordinary notion that permanent peace will come from a world domination exercised by these peoples will, I venture to predict, go the way of other dreams, based on wishful thinking, of short cuts to international peace.   The quest for peace can never be separated from the quest for freedom, and a world order based on freedom cannot be established through the hegemony of a self-appointed group.

Although I have argued that neutralism is to be preferred to satellitism, it is not the appropriate role for Britain, whose interests are inseparably bound up with the continent of Europe, and first of all with France, Belgium, and the Netherlands.   In the middle sixties British relations with France are in the doldrums, through error and deficiencies on both sides.   It is astonishing that, though our two countries are separated only by a narrow strip of water, and London is nearer to Paris than to the north of England and to Scotland, our political relations are so absurdly distant.[1]

Just forty years ago relations between the two countries had reached an equally low point when the first Labour Government took office.   M. Poincaré was even more at odds with Britain than

---

[1] In some fields of learning this sense of separation has also persisted for a number of years, notably in philosophy.   But attempts are being made to end it.   M. Pierre Dubois, reporting on a philosophical conference in Britain, speaks of " le désir de jeter un pont entre nos deux mondes philosophiques qui continuent allègrement à s'ignorer l'un l'autre ".   *Revue Philosophique*, Janvier–Mars, 1964, p. 131   This is the spirit in which political relations should be approached.

President de Gaulle is today. French troops occupied the Ruhr. The reparations question had created general economic confusion. Mr. Ramsey MacDonald at once started his remarkable exchange of personal letters which influenced even the inflexible Poincaré, and when Herriot succeeded the latter, the whole European scene was transformed in a short time by the combined action of the British and French Premiers.[1]

The popular notion of a supposed choice between a European and an " Atlantic " approach to international affairs is a confusion of ideas. European union, as far as the Common Market countries and Britain are concerned, is a concrete, practicable measure that would serve the interests of all parties concerned. It means a merger by stages into a single federal state. But an analagous " Atlantic Union ", or " Atlantic Community ", is a dream incapable of being transformed into concrete reality in the foreseeable future. There is not the least sign that the people of the United States would give up their independence to be merged with other countries some five thousand kilometres from its nearest and ten thousand from its farthest border. The two ideas are not competitive. A large area for trans-Atlantic co-operation will always remain. The magnificent achievement of the United States in maintaining representative government over an area the size of Europe, unbroken except for *de facto* racial restrictions now fast crumbling under a determined effort, is a guarantee of fruitful relations with a future European union. The cloud on the horizon at present lies in the absence of signs of psychological decolonisation in respect to Latin America and in intransigeance towards China, as well as the ever-present danger from the forces of which Goldwater is a symbol.

IV

Independence, Interdependence, and the Rule of Law

The idea of independence has not lost its relevance in the second half of the twentieth century. In many respects interdependence has grown : it is inescapable, and to ignore it would bring disaster. But interdependence exists within a framework of independent states, and the area in which independence remains relevant is as significant as it ever was. The growth of individual freedom still depends upon it. Nationalism must not be judged merely by its excesses, and by

---

[1] How one could wish today for something analogous to the spectacle of the great, cheering crowds lining the route when the British Premier visited Paris, and shouting, " Vive MacDonald ! Vive la paix ! A bas la guerre ! "

the excrescences which have adhered to it. For a long time to come
world government could only mean tyranny.

In the last resort international peace, like internal peace, can only
come through the growth of the rule of law. The conception of law
merely as orders backed by threats and forcible sanctions is as misleading in the consideration of international law as it is of municipal
law, although it is often used to discredit existing international law.
Laws, to be effective, must be associated with the conceptions of duty
and obligation, and the growth of the rule of law is associated with
the growth of this moral sense. It is on this that world peace
ultimately depends, and the international organisations will play a
leading and indispensable role in fostering it.

But if the international bodies are to fulfil their role, their membership must be universal. No countries need the international
organisations more, or even so much, as the Asian, African, and
Latin American countries do. Yet these countries have given only
scrappy, half-hearted support to Britain in her recent advocacy of
the admission of China to the United Nations. In the contrary
sense, they embarked, after the Addis Ababa Conference, on a concerted drive to secure the expulsion of two countries from the international organisations because of their internal or colonial policies.
South Africa and Portugal were already suffering from intellectual
isolation : in politics they still lived in the seventeenth century.
No useful end could be achieved by cutting them off still further
from the rest of the world. Outlawry never advances, and usually
sets back, the growth of the rule of law. The emerging countries
have yet to learn how to use their rising power in the international
organisations to their own long-run advantage. When they throw
their support only behind their " chosen peoples ", and direct their
attacks only against peoples outside the fold, opposing practices and
policies in the latter while condoning them in the former, they run
the risk of turning international relations into glorified inter-tribal
relations, in which actions are judged, not by their intrinsic nature
but according to the identity of the doer.

There are no simple, single causes of, or simple single remedies for,
international disputes and conflicts. The pursuit of balance of power
is essential, but, as we have seen, it is not enough. The international
organisations are indispensable, but their value depends on the
extent to which they are used to advance the rule of law rather than
as instruments for short-run sectional advantage. There is no substitute for disarmament, but progress towards disarmament must be
linked with progress towards the removal of the sources of international friction. Whatever weapons men have, they will not fight
on an international scale without cause ; and however defective
their weapons may be, they will not keep the peace regardless of pro-

vocation. The pursuit of freedom will not fail, however strong dominant groups may be at the moment. While armaments continue, mankind will not long permit a monopoly of the most modern and most deadly weapons in the hands of one or two countries : indefinite continuance of the present distribution of armed power would gradually lead to a tacit alliance of the rest of the world against the monopoly position of the few powers which possess the weapons.

The integration and disintegration of states will continue in the foreseeable future. If integration is to exceed disintegration, it must advance by consent and not by imperialism. Integration is not an end in itself : when it reduces individual freedom the seeds of subsequent disintegrating tendencies are sown, and the harvest will be reaped by future generations in one of many possible ways. European integration will not endanger individual freedom within, and will strengthen it elsewhere by creating a more powerful group which will be a living example of the possibilities of combining freedom and order without political fanaticism. But individual freedom must be won from within the independent groups into which the world is divided : attempts to impose it from without would set precedents leading to clashes that would bring unimaginable disaster to an over-armed world. The passion for group freedom is the central feature of the revolution in international relations in our age, and in the emerging countries as yet it appears to exceed the passion for individual liberty and toleration which is the foundation and glory of British society.

The scope and the observance of the rule of law in international affairs cannot grow in a world divided into two opposing camps led by two super-powers which, by competitive coercion and bribery, endeavour to gain the support and avert the opposition of the medium and small powers, pressing them to take sides in the quarrels of the mighty. Few conceptions of international relations have done more harm than that associated most prominently with the name of the late John Foster Dulles,[1] but which was shared by many others in various countries in the nineteen-fifties. No balance of power would be more fragile, and none would bring greater disasters when it broke down, than that which was purely bilateral, untempered and unrestrained by intermediate groups and single powers without commitment to any side. The tensions and the breaks in the unity of such hypothetical " camps ", which often evoke lamentations among the powers trying to form them, are commonly a healthy sign of independence, a protection against the dangers of doctrinal conformity and fanaticism, and a convincing proof of the long-run supremacy of

---

[1] It is unfortunate that Mr. Dulles's name does not lend itself to the coining of an analogous term to " de-Stalinisation ", which would conveniently epitomise one of the foremost needs in western international policies.

nationalist over doctrinal lines of cleavage in human affairs. For a clash of national interests is more susceptible to compromise than a clash of fanatically held doctrines can ever be. A world of independent states permits different peoples to live according to different customs and doctrines so long as independence is respected. The acceptance of coexistence—one of the few respectable words which the language of international relations has invented—must be a leading aim of our generation.

Great modifications have taken place in Russian doctrinal attitudes since Stalin's death, although some of them may have begun earlier. This does not change the considerations of balance of power with respect to Russia which the western countries must maintain as a common interest. But it does reduce the danger that conflicts of interest will be aggravated by fanaticism.

Unfortunately, the welcome signs of reduction of tension between the super-powers at the time of the Test Ban Treaty were clouded over by signs of a tendency to transfer the " Cold War " to a different alignment, in which China would take the place of Russia. Fortunately, President de Gaulle's decision to recognise China has modified this tendency.

It would be difficult to imagine a more ill-advised policy for the later twentieth century. Attempts to maintain a boycott against China would set back the rule of law and undo the efforts of Britain and other western European countries. The wise policy would be in the opposite direction, aiming without delay at bringing China within the comity of nations. To isolate a country and treat it as an outlaw is the most appropriate way to encourage it to act as an outlaw. China has justifiable grievances over its exclusion from the international organisations for many years. The British and French interest is to work for their removal without delay and for extending normal trade and diplomatic relations with China. The decline of tension over Russia should be followed by steps to begin a similar easing of tensions over China. More generally, the spirit behind " cold war " psychology resembles the spirit behind a number of other emotional and doctrinal complications of international relations. It is based on what Professor Butterfield has described as a pagan form of morality. Its keynote is in effect Voltaire's famous slogan, " *Écrasez l'infame !* " Human ills of the present time, it is held, are due first of all to villainy and wickedness, especially that which is associated with the wrong doctrines. It is the spirit of old religious conflicts transferred to secular life. The fanatical anti-communist's hatred of communists, the Ba'athist's and Nasirite's hatred of opponents of " Arab nationalism ", the vague but passionate denunciations of " the imperialists " in some of the emerging countries, all share the assumption that what is wrong with the world is the result of plotting by malevolent enemies of the good and the true.

But if these conceptions of morality are among the most dangerous elements in international affairs ; if there is no greater danger to peace than the self-righteous attitude of the doctrinaire, wedded with fanatical zeal to his doctrine, believing in it wholly and convinced that a frontal show-down must come in which his doctrine will triumph over competing doctrines or he will perish in the attempt, it still remains true that morality is as important as knowledge and understanding in international affairs. The aims and methods of Machiavelli's Prince do not lead towards the ends cherished in Machiavelli's *Discourses*. The objections to the self-righteous moral ideas of the doctrinaire and the fanatic are themselves moral as well as practical objections. Values cannot be abstracted from the study and practice of international relations. In the last resort it is on the growth of the moral sense and the development of moral responsibility as much as on the growth of knowledge and understanding that the chances of international peace will depend.

INDEX

Abdu, Mohammed, as philosopher of liberal Egyptian nationalism, 85

Abdul-Malek, Anonar, 259

Acheson, Secretary Dean, 37

Addis Ababa, conference at, 36, 214, 278

Aden base, 276

Adenauer, Dr., European outlook of, 243

Africa, xi, 54, 57, 60, 63, 70, 71, 72-3, 75, y8, 83, 87-90, 91-2, 103, 105, 125, 129, 131, 135-6, 150-1, 170, 171-3, 187, 211-14, 245, 249 255-6, 261, 263, 267, 271, 274
  countries of, and United Nations, ch XI, section III

Africanists, International Conference of, Co-operation in, between French- and English-speaking scholars, 172

Albania, assertion of independence of, 14

Albertini, Luigi, classic on origins of First World War, 182n

Alexandria, bombardment of, 79, 86

Algeria, 42, 92

Alva, Duke of, failure of, to reduce Holland, 152n

Anglo-French nuclear development, 252, 273

Arab imperialism, 61, 167, 216

Arab League, 167, 168, 213

Arab nationalism, 80, ch. IX, 215

Arab trading interests, 61

Arabi Pasha, 31, 82-5, 86

Arbenz, President, U.S. underground plot against, 43, 113

Arevola, Señor, military coup against, in Guatemala, 113

Asia, xi, 5, 39, 54, 57, 60-3, 65, 66, 71, 72, 73, 75, 78, 82, 87-90, 91-2, 105, 110, 125, 129, 131, 135, 141-2, 187, 211-14, 245, 255-6, 261, 263-7, 274-6
  countries of, and United Nations, ch. XI, section III
  south-east, 25, 63, 115, 174, 266, 271

Atlantic Alliance, 219-20, 224, 255-6, 261, ch. XV, section II, 277, divergencies in policies, 223-6

Atomic weapons, ch. XV, sections II and III attempts to monopolise, effects if Britain renounced use of, 238, indefensible dropping of, on Japan 220n, independent European, 238-9
  Russian development of, 221

Australia, 64, 233-4
  refusal to recognise China, 36, 191, 194

Austria-Hungary, 10
  collapse of 219, 272
  successors to, 33

Avon, Lord, formerly Sir Anthony Eden
  and rôle of doctrines and balance of power at Suez, 45
  at Geneva conference in 1954, 42
  lapse of judgement of, in 1956, 42-3
  resignation of, in protest against appeasement, 52

Ayub, General, 166

Ba'ath Movement, 31, 120n

Baldwin, Stanley, 32

Baldwin II., and Kingdom of Jerusalem, 11

Bardevant, Professor J, 204

Baron, Hans, on imperialism of Duchy of Milan, 132

Baring, Sir Evelyn, later Lord Cromer, 82, 83, 85
  elements in common with present Arab nationalists, 86

Barthou, untimely assassination of, 34

Bassett, Professor Reginald, 6

Batista, President, 113

Belgium, 100, 132, 257, 276

Bell, Coral, 240n

Benelux, 173

Blunt, Wilfred Scawen, his understanding of Egyptian nationalism, 84-5

Bolivar, Simon, and disunity in Latin America, 168

Borodin, Michael, 20, 109

Bourgiba, President, 260n

Bourquin, Maurice, 206n

Brierly, Professor J. L., and equality of states, 207, 211,